CHIEFS WITHOUT INDIANS

Don M. Cregier
University of Prince Edward Island

UNIVERSITY
PRESS OF
AMERICA

Copyright © 1982 by

University Press of America, Inc.

P.O. Box 19101, Washington, D.C. 20036

Library of Congress Cataloging in Publication Data

Cregier, Don M., 1930-
   Chiefs without Indians.

   Includes index.
   1. Great Britain--Politics and government--1910-
1936--Addresses, essays, lectures. 2. Asquith, H. H.
(Herbert Henry), 1852-1928--Addresses, essays, lectures.
3. Lloyd George, David, 1863-1945--Addresses, essays,
lectures. 4. Liberal Party (Great Britain)--History--
20th century--Addresses, essays, lectures. I. Title.
DA576.C73 1982   841.083'092'2   82-17546
ISBN 0-8191-2806-6
ISBN 0-8191-2807-4 (pbk.)

This book is dedicated to Mary Bradley and J. Reilly Osborne, teachers who introduced me to the pleasures, perils, and responsibilities of historical study.

iii

ACKNOWLEDGMENTS

I wish to acknowledge with thanks the permission of the First Beaverbrook Foundation, Washington State University, the Duquesne University Press, and the Society for History Education to use copyrighted material. The cartoons are reproduced by permission of the Mansell Collection of London.

CONTENTS

PREFACE

This short book traces the author's intellectual odyssey. It started with his choice of a dissertation topic over twenty years ago. What began as a study of the British Liberal party's decline in the twentieth century progressively came to focus upon the career of David Lloyd George--whom many Liberals, and others, have blamed for that decline.

At first I admired Lloyd George almost without reservation. I was captivated by the Welshman's courage and perseverance in the face of English elitism, snobbery, and standpattism. But as I dug deeper, and my own research was enriched by that of others, I became convinced that Lloyd George's rivals, enemies, and critics frequently had a case. They deserved, if not always r.spect or esteem, at least understanding and sympathy. The reader may suspect that disenchantment--arising from two decades of research into a single theme--has had some influence on my outlook.

The thesis on the Liberal party never was published. I restructured several chapters into journal articles. Other sections, much revised, were integrated into Bounder from Wales, my study of Lloyd George's early life. Additional plunder from the manuscript, altered almost beyond recognition by my subsequent research and my reaction to that of fellow Lloyd George-ologists, eventually will become part of two projected volumes on the Welshman's premiership and his final years.

Chiefs Without Indians brings together seven of my previously published essays on the faltering Liberal party and its leaders between the world wars. It is intended, especially for undergraduates and general readers, as an introduction to the research and literature on Asquith, Lloyd George, and the lesser Liberal chieftains--and their contemporaries in other parties--implicated in the collapse of an historic political institutio. Each essay except the first has been revised .o take account of the work of other scholars published since the article first appeared. Nevertheless, the reader should be warned that the collection has the obvious weakness of parts written at different times and affected by the author's changing viewpoint.

xi

There is, also, an Epilogue reviewing Arther Cyr's authoritative study of today's Liberal party.

                                        Don M. Cregier

"Old Acres"
Arlington, Vermont
August 1982

PART ONE

The Decline of the Liberal Party:
A Chronology, 1885-1935

1885, July.	The Gladstone government's Franchise and Redistribution Acts of 1884-5 enfranchise many thousands of urban and rural workingmen, and establish the "one man, one vote" principle of roughly equal parliamentary constituencies represented by a single M.P. The political power of the great Whig/Liberal aristocratic families, little damaged by the previous electoral reforms of 1832 and 1867, is dealt a heavy blow.
1885, August.	Joseph Chamberlain, Liberal minister and founder of the National Liberal Federation, issues an Unauthorized Program advocating many radical and democratic reforms aimed at the newly enfranchised electors. The program irritates William E. Gladstone, the Liberal party leader, and many other Whiggish and moderate Liberals, but draws many of the new voters to the party in the December general election.
1885, December.	Gladstone, again prime minister, launches the "Hawarden kite" announcing his conversion to Irish home rule. Home rule becomes the dominant, almost exclusive, theme of the remainder of his political career, and perforce of the Liberals during this period (1886-94).
1886, May.	Some 90 Whiggish, moderate, and radical (Chamberlainite) Liberal M.P.'s cross the aisle of the House of Commons in opposition to Gladstone's Irish Home Rule Bill. Most of them, and their followers in the constituencies, become associated as Liberal Unionists with the Conservative party, eventually merging with the latter in the early twentieth century. Except in 1892-5, the Conservative-Liberal Unionist alliance is in power until 1905.
1886-92.	With many Whiggish and right wing Lib-

erals now sitting as Unionists, the Liberal party moves slightly leftward. Several "Lib.-Lab." candidates are adopted in predominantly working class constituencies, and social reforms advantageous to workingmen are endorsed. But middle class Liberals, disproportionately Nonconformist and from the Celtic Fringes (Scotland and Wales), control the National Liberal Federation and the whips' office.

1891, October. The National Liberal Federation adopts the Newcastle Program, a hodgepodge of radical, democratic, social--but mostly "faddist" (especially temperance)--reforms supposed to attract a wide spectrum of voters. It has little interest for working class electors.

1893, January. The Independent Labour party is founded by Keir Hardie--elected to the Commons as an Independent Labour member in 1892--and other socialists and trade unionists irritated by the tepid social program of the Liberals and their preoccupation with home rule.

1893-1927. Robert (later Sir Robert) Hudson is secretary of the Liberal Central Association, the whips' office.

1894-9. Following Gladstone's retirement the Liberal party is shaken by a leadership struggle between Lord Rosebery, Sir William Harcourt, and John Morley. The veto by the Conservative-dominated House of Lords of home rule and much "faddist" legislation introduced by the 1892-5 Liberal government demoralizes the party's middle class rank and file. Workingmen accustomed to voting Liberal are disgusted by the party's unwillingness to promote social legislation more vigorously.

1899-1902. The Liberal party is split between "Liberal imperialists" who approve of the South African War (except for details) and "pro-Boers" who oppose

4

it. The party leader, Sir Henry Camp-bell-Bannermann--elected in 1899--increasingly leans toward the latter position. A semi-schismatic Liberal Imperialist Council, including such prominent party men as Lord Rosebery, H. H. Asquith, Sir Edward Grey, and R. B. Haldane, is active between 1900 and 1902.

1900, February. The Labour Representation Committee (L.R.C.) is formed to support the election of Labour M.P.'s unaffiliated with either major party. It is a federation of various labor and socialist bodies, including the Trades Union Congress and the Independent Labour party.

1902-3. The conservative government's Education Act abolishing the nondenominational board schools infuriates Nonconformist Liberals and revives rank and file enthusiasm.

1903, March. An electoral pact is arranged between Liberal Chief Whip Herbert Gladstone and Ramsay MacDonald of the Labour Representation Committee, to avoid contests that would benefit the Conservatives.

1903, May. The inauguration of Joseph Chamberlain's tariff reform (protectionist) campaign divides the Conservative party and rallies Liberals behind free trade. Early in 1904 a small group of free trade Conservative M.P.'s, including Winston Churchill, cross the floor and become Liberals.

1905, December. Sir Henry Campbell-Bannerman forms the first Liberal government in a decade. It and its successors will be in office nearly ten years as the last Liberal governments.

1906, January-February. In a Liberal parliamentary landslide, the party elects 400 out of 670 M.P.'s and obtains 52.6 percent of the contested vote. A considerable number of the new Liberal M.P.'s are lower middle class Nonconformists. 29 canddidates of the L.R.C. are also elected, most with the aid of the Liberal-Labour electoral pact. After the election the L.R.C. renames itself the Labour party.

1907.

The House of Lords rejects several major and many minor Liberal bills alleged by the Conservatives to be "faddist" and not in the public interest. Labor and social legislation is allowed to pass. There is frustration and discontent in the Liberal ranks.

1908, April.

Herbert Henry Asquith replaces the dying Campbell-Bannerman as prime minister and Liberal party leader. David Lloyd George becomes chancellor of the exchequer.

1908-10.

Numerous pieces of social legislation are enacted by Asquith's government, some of them proposed by the Labour party.

1909-10.

Lloyd George's People's Budget of 1909, with its controversial land taxes directed at the landlord class, infuriates the Conservative leaders. They decide that the House of Lords will reject it in order to force a general election. The Liberal cabinet decides to come to grips with the issue of ending the Lords' veto.

1910, January and December.

In the two general elections fought on the veto issue, the Liberals and Conservatives elect almost the same number of M.P.'s, but the Labour and Irish Nationalist members give the Liberal government a majority in the House of Commons. The cabinet, in order to retain essential Irish support, agrees to promote a home rule bill once the veto is ended.

1911, July.

The Parliament Act enables government

6

to enact legislation over the objection of the Lords, but it must be approved during three successive sessions of the same Parliament. With its mandate due to expire in 1915, the Liberal government presses forward with home rule and other partisan bills.

1911-4.   The "death of liberal England" is portended by sharpening labor unrest, feminist violence, the growth of extremism in Ireland, and intense hostility between Liberal and Conservative politicians.

1912-3.   The Liberal party is shaken by the Marconi Scandal, in which Lloyd George and other ministers are alleged to have used official information for private gain. Although they are cleared after an investigation, doubts about their probity remain and contribute to declining intraparty morale and mounting interparty bitterness.

1912-4.   Searching for a new and winning issue for the Liberal party to fight on in the next general election, Lloyd George initiates a land reform campaign, beginning with an elaborate policy study by a committee of experts.

1913-4.   As the passage of a home rule bill becomes more certain, Protestant Unionists in northern Ireland, supported by the Conservative party and officers in the British army, take steps to resist. The possibility looms of a civil war in Ireland, and an army mutiny. There is disillusionment among radical Liberals at the government's passivity. A Lloyd George scheme, to allow those Irish counties with Protestant majorities to opt out of home rule, fails to satisfy the disputants.

1914, August.   The outbreak of the First World War

superficially unites the opposing parties and compels them to put aside divisive domestic issues, especially Ireland. (The Irish Home Rule Bill is enacted but implementation is postponed for the duration of the war.) But antagonism takes new channels, such as the struggles over conscription of manpower and wartime civil rights. Ordinary Liberals are greatly disillusioned by the failure to avoid war and the harsh demands of total war. The more hawkish Liberals form ranks behind Lloyd George, who becomes the spokesman for patriotism, regimentation, and an all-out war effort, as against the business as usual attitude of Asquith and his friends. A small section of Liberal M.P.'s, and a larger number of Labourites, follow Ramsay MacDonald into outright opposition to the war, organizing a pressure group called the Union of Democratic Control. Many Liberals belonging to the U.D.C. defect to the Labour party after the war.

1915, May.　　　　Asquith jettisons the Liberal government and becomes head of a coalition ministry in which Liberals still occupy the best places. Lloyd George, as munitions minister, becomes a veritable industrial dictator, ruthlessly subordinating peacetime production to military needs.

1915, September.　Adoption of the McKenna Duties on luxury goods brings an end to unrestricted free trade and infuriates rank and file Liberals.

1915, December–
1916, January.　　A crisis over military conscription in the cabinet and Parliament is resolved by the victory of the Liberal and Conservative compulsionists. Many Liberals retreat into sullen and passive opposition to government policies.

1916, January.　　A Liberal War Committee is formed by backbenchers demanding a more forceful

8

prosecution of the war in accordance with the wishes of Lloyd George.

1916, April - June.

Republican extremists stage an abortive rising in Dublin, following which the British military authorities execute the leaders. The Irish public reaction to the executions begins the erosion of the Irish Nationalist party, one of the most reliable sections of Prime Minister Asquith's political following. The collapse of the Nationalists speeds up after the failure of Lloyd George's negotiations to bring home rule into limited operation during the war.

1916, November.

Circulation by Lord Lansdowne, a Conservative cabinet minister, of a memorandum suggesting a negotiated peace brings to a head the quarrel between hawks and doves in the government and Parliament. The former are animated by fear that Asquith and his friends may be leaning toward peace.

1916, December.

Lloyd George assumes the premiership after a coup against Asquith. He is supported by about half the Liberal members of the House of Commons (especially the War Committee group), as well as most Conservatives and some Labour M.P.'s. Lloyd George installs a small, dictatorial war cabinet, and imposes a regime of war socialism upon the national economy which has general public support. The Asquithian Liberal ex-ministers fail to project their leadership upon the dispirited anti-compulsion Liberal M.P.'s or the radicals who opposed entering the war. The Liberal party machinery remains in Asquithian hands, but--with a political truce in effect since August 1914--it has deteriorated badly and continues to do so.

1917-8.

The split between Asquithian and Lloyd Georgian (Coalition) Liberals widens over such issues as treatment of conscientious objectors, Irish conscription, and conduct of the war. The climax is the confidence vote of May 9, 1918, over the truth of official statements about British military reserves in France. The subsequent granting of Coalition "coupons" to selected Liberal candidates in the December 1918 general election is to be conditioned largely by how M.P.'s voted in this division.

1918, February.

The Representation of the People Bill extends the franchise to almost all men as well as to married, and some single, women over thirty. There is also a major redistribution of seats and redrawing of constituency boundaries. The greatly increased electorate and the restructuring of constituencies favors the growth of the Labour party, which soon after adopts a new socialist and mass membership constitution so that it can appeal to the wider electorate.

1918, December.

In the so-called "coupon election" (from the endorsement given to candidates sponsored by Lloyd George's government), 127 Coalition Liberals are returned but only 36 Asquithian Liberals. Asquith loses his own seat. Labour, with 60 M.P.'s, becomes the official opposition. The Conservatives, most of whom support the Coalition, have an overall majority in the House of Commons.

1919-35.

There is a steady decline of Liberal strength in elected local government bodies as the Liberal vote is eroded from left and right. (There is some evidence that this decline at the local level began before the war.) Nationally, there is a secession of radical Liberals to the Labour party, many defecting in protest against the prewar Liberal foreign policy and the party's surrender of priniciples during the war; others because the party seems to be faltering after 1918; still others in disgust at Lloyd George's behavior or policies. Right wing Liberals, many of whom approved of the "anti-socialist" Coalition, pass into the Conservative party after its fall.

1919-22.   Liberal intellectuals disturbed by the torpor of the Asquithian party leaders organize a "think tank," the Liberal Summer School. During the twenties the Summer School makes a significant input to Lloyd George's various policy studies. Between 1919-22 Lloyd George makes desultory moves to create a Center party of his Liberal and Conservative followers, but nothing comes of them. Strongest resistance, at least until 1921, is by the Coalition Liberals, upset about creeping protectionism and Conservative vetoes of proposed social reforms.

1920, February.   The Asquithian Liberal fortunes show a slight upturn as Asquith regains a seat (Paisley, Scotland) in the House, but most of the steady Coalition by-election losses are to Labourites.

1920, May.   Coalition Liberal speakers are shouted down at the Leamington conference of the National Liberal Federation, extinguishing halfhearted feelers for party reunion. Lloyd George thereafter establishes a separate Coalition (later National) Liberal organization, but it has weak roots in the constituencies.

1920-1.   An ill-defined scheme to unite anti-Lloyd George Conservatives and Liberals under the command of an independent Tory, Lord Robert Cecil, is aborted by Asquith's refusal to relinquish his party leadership.

1922, October.   The Lloyd George Coalition falls after a revolt of Conservative back-bench M.P.'s and peers. The Conservatives

11

have been disturbed for months by the Coalition's adventurist foreign policy (especially a near war with Turkey), Lloyd George's misuse of honors, the Lloyd George Fund derived from the sale of honors, and the rise of the Labour party--which the Coalition with Lloyd George was supposed to avert. In the subsequent general election, the Asquithian and Lloyd Georgian Liberal parties return about 60 M.P.'s each, the Conservatives win a majority, and Labour--much strengthened--remains the official opposition.

1923, January-March.
Reunion of the two Liberal factions is promoted by rank and file members of both sections but discouraged by the coolness of the leaders, Asquith especially.

1923, November.
The Liberal party is reunited--officially--following Prime Minister Stanley Baldwin's call for a general election over the protection issue. The low-key squabbling between the two factions recedes but does not end. Differences over money become acute when Lloyd George refuses to surrender the capital of his Fund to Liberal headquarters.

1923, December.
The Liberals elect 158 M.P.'s in the "protection election," putting them a strong third after Labour's 191. In spite of intrigues to prevent Labour, the official opposition, from forming a government, Asquith (still the party leader) and Lloyd George agree--although with different motives--to back a Labour ministry.

1924, January-October.
During the minority Labour government, the Liberal party is in an invidious position. It supports with its votes a cabinet in which it has little confidence, whose prime minister--Ramsey MacDonald--does his best to weaken the Liberals so that Labour can capture their seats and become a majority

party. The Liberals also are torn by internal feuds over money, policies, and personalities.

1924, October. A demoralized and impoverished Liberal party, after bringing down the Labour government in a no-confidence vote, in the ensuing general election is reduced to only 40 M.P.'s as the pendulum swings against it from both right and left. As Asquith has been defeated in his constituency, the chairmanship of the Liberal M.P.'s devolves upon Lloyd George, but several Asquithians reject his lead and form an independent Radical Group.

1925, January. A special Liberal convention launches the Million Fund, an effort to raise a million pounds from loyal and wealthy Liberals before the next general election. Although staunchly pressed by Asquithians hoping to free themselves from dependence on the Lloyd George Fund, the campaign fails badly.

1925-6. The Asquith and Lloyd George Liberals pursue a now muted, now clamorous struggle for supremacy in the party. One point of contention is Land and the Nation (the Green Book), the radical report--published in October 1925--of a Land Inquiry Committee sponsored by Lloyd George. Although Asquith (now known as Lord Oxford) tries to restrain the hostility of his followers toward Lloyd George, probably only the attraction of the latter's Fund saves him from being read out of the party.

1926, February. A Liberal Land Conference endorses the Green Book, after some modification, but several prominent right wing Liberals defect to the Conservatives.

1926, May-June. Lord Oxford splits conclusively with Lloyd George over the Liberal party's official stand toward the General Strike. An open power struggle between the two leaders ends abruptly when Oxford is incapacitated by a stroke.

1926-7.   After Lord Oxford resigns the leadership in October 1926, Lloyd George becomes the de facto--but not the official--head of the party. He takes command of the headquarters machinery, dismissing the Asquithian office holders including the veteran Sir Robert Hudson. The Lloyd George Fund is put at the disposal of new party officials chaired by Sir Herbert Samuel. Intransigent Asquithians reject Lloyd George's ascendancy and establish the dissident Liberal Council, under Lord Grey of Fallodon's presidency.

1928, February. Britain's Industrial Future--the Yellow Book--is published by Lloyd George's Liberal Industrial Inquiry. It is approved in principle by an Industrial Conference of the party in March.

1929, March.   Another of Lloyd George's policy studies, We Can Conquer Unemployment--the Orange Book--is published. Its program becomes the central theme of the party's campaign in the 1929 general election.

1929, May.   The general election is a disappointment to the Liberals. In spite of its clear-cut platform, vigorous campaigning by Lloyd George's machine, and expenditure of huge sums for electioneering, the party elects only 59 M.P.'s.

1929-31.   Lloyd George and the Liberal M.P.'s support a second minority Labour government. They try to persuade it to promote an imaginative economic policy and enact an electoral reform bill that would help the Liberals to win more seats.

1931, March-   Sir John Simon and other Liberal
June.   M.P.'s reject Lloyd George's leader-

14

ship when he continues to exhort them to vote with the faltering Labour government. Simon and his allies also indicate their disenchantment with free trade.

1931, August–October.
With Lloyd George seriously ill and hospitalized, Sir Herbert Samuel as acting head of the parliamentary Liberal party leads it into the National government presided over by former Labour Prime Minister MacDonald. For the first time in almost a decade Liberals obtain ministerial posts. Over Lloyd George's objections, Samuel agrees to a general election in which the Liberals will fight under the National rubric.

1931, October.
In the election 74 Liberals are returned, all but four of whom (the Lloyd George "family party") back the National government. The government's adherents include about equal number of "official" (Samuelite) and "National" (Simonite) Liberals. Representatives of both groups are given ministerial jobs. Lloyd George stands down from the chairmanship of the Liberal M.P.'s.

1932, March.
The cabinet, in an unusual "agreement to differ," allows the Samuelite Liberal ministers to oppose the Import Duties Bill establishing protectionism.

1932, July.
The Samuelite-Simonite split becomes official with the creation of a separate protectionist Liberal National organization, loosely associated with the Conservatives.

1932, September.
The Samuelite ministers resign in protest against the Ottawa Agreements confirming protectionism.

1933, November.
Most of the 30-odd Samuelite M.P.'s cross the floor of the House of Commons into opposition.

15

1935, January.	Lloyd George, ignoring the Samuelite Liberals, launches a "new deal" campaign aimed at either converting the National government to his reconstruction schemes or electing enough "progressive" M.P.'s to put a government into office willing to do so.
1935, June.	Having failed to convert the National cabinet, Lloyd George set up a nonpartisan Council of Action to endorse candidates in the forthcoming general election.
1935, November.	In the general election, both the Samuelite Liberal and the Council of Action go down to defeat. Only 21 official Liberals and 67 candidates approved by the Council are returned. (33 Liberal Nationals are successful.) Unable to form or influence a government, and with Samuel out of the House of Commons, Lloyd George rejoins the official Liberals but continues to take an independent course. Sir Archibald Sinclair becomes leader of a party generally seen as no longer a "party of government."

PART TWO

THE LIBERAL ROUT: As Cartoonists Saw It

By early April 1915 the lines were becoming clearly drawn within the Liberal government between those viewing the European war as an instrument of foreign policy which--however important--should not obscure other issues and principles, and those committed to fighting for total victory over the Central Powers.

David Lloyd George, acknowledged leader of the Liberal hawks, a minority within the cabinet, had demanded and (on April 8) been given the chairmanship of a ministerial committee to mobilize the nation's human and industrial resources for production of war munitions.

In this cartoon Raven Hill depicts a martially outfitted Lloyd George guiding a munitions wagon toward the battle front, while striving vigorously to keep his balky team--"Capital" and "Labour"--in unison. The cartoon's theme recalls the Welshman's description of himself as an "ambulance driver" during the debate over the National Insurance Bill in 1911.

A month later, following establishment of the first Coalition government, Lloyd George obtained his own ministry of munitions and soon had arrogated almost dictatorial power over industry and manpower.

DELIVERING THE GOODS.

THE NEW CONDUCTOR

Lloyd George's accession to the premiership was undeniably irregular. Prime Minister Asquith was the duly chosen head of a Coalition government, commanded a substantial majority in the House of Commons, and was the leader of the Liberal party. Yet this plurality of roles failed to protect Asquith from a complex backstairs intrigue which, if not actually plotted by Lloyd George, was brilliantly exploited by him. For the first time since the eighteenth century a British prime minister was brought down by skulduggery.

For reasons partly patriotic, partly personal, the victim of the camarilla chose not to make a fight of it on the floor of the Commons, as he could have done and was advised to do by some of his friends.

Although rumors of the conspiracy against Asquith circulated freely, there was considerable public relief that Lloyd George was at last in complete charge of the war. He had consistently been the most dynamic minister in the war governments. Now he was free to orchestrate grand strategy as he had for so long wanted to do. It is as the masterful new conductor that Raven Hill portrays him in this cartoon. But he was not masterful enough to bring victory in 1917 as the cartoonist evidently hoped.

THE NEW CONDUCTOR.

OPENING OF THE 1917 OVERTURE.

A FORLORN APPEAL

Former Prime Minister Asquith did not relinquish the Liberal party leadership when he left No. 10 Downing Street. The elaborate machinery of a major party remained at his disposal through the war and after the Armistice of November 11, 1918. Only those constituency organizations represented by M.P.'s favorable to Lloyd George could be said to be outside Asquith's dominion, and even many of them still acknowledged the latter as the party's head. Although personal relationships between the factional chiefs and their colleagues were tense and at times hostile, a postwar reunion of the party was seen as possible as late as the spring of 1918. Alternatively, if the Lloyd George government were discredited during the war, its Liberal adherents could either be ejected from the party or readmitted on terms.

The Asquithian leaders took the risk of trying--unsuccessfully--to bring down Lloyd George in the "Maurice debate" of May 9, 1918, over the truth of an official statement about troop reserves in France. This incident proved to be decisive in splitting the party. From this point on, Lloyd George took steps to forge an electoral alliance with the Conservatives, which eventuated in the issuance of letters of approval--derisively called "coupons" by Asquith--to both Liberal and Conservative candidates prepared to support an indefinite continuation of the Coalition into peacetime. Some 150 Liberal candidates, mostly incumbents, were awarded this document, dated November 20, 1918. Raven Hill's cartoon offers the impression of a ragged, decrepit Asquith begging to be received into the warmth of Coalition Lodge or, if not that, at least permitted to repossess his property, the Liberal name. Lloyd George denied both pleas.

A FORLORN APPEAL.

Mr. Asquith. "COALITION, ERE WE PART, GIVE, O GIVE ME BACK MY—ER—PARTY!"

THE BABES IN THE WOOD

The meaning of the 1918 election still eludes historians. While the Conservatives, "couponed" and "uncouponed" together, won a substantial majority of Commons seats, it is not at all certain they would have done so well without the votes of Liberals hoping the Coalition would continue. One can only speculate upon the results had there been the traditional straight fight between Liberals and Conservatives, a larger turnout of the new, greatly enlarged electorate; or intervention by fewer hopeless Labour candidates.

It was a bad election for Liberals of all stripes. The Asquithians--including their leaders satirized here in Partridge's cartoon--were devastated, returning fewer than one-fifth of their candidates. Nor were the 127 Coalition Liberals very secure. With many of their seats in urban constituencies threatened by Labour, they were hostages to the goodwill of their Tory partners in the Coalition. The words that Partridge puts in the mouths of the Liberal leaders smothered by Coalition votes prophesied the fate of the "Coalies" in the next election, when they were not only abandoned but repudiated by their Conservative guardians.

Partridge's allusion is to the old English folk tale of the trustful children left in the wood to die by their evil guardian and buried by autumn leaves. From left to right the "babes" are Walter Runciman, Herbert Samuel, H. H. Asquith, Sir John Simon, and Reginald McKenna. McKenna, Runciman, and Simon finished at the bottom of three-cornered polls.

THE BABES IN THE WOOD.

The Old Liberal Nursery (*moribund but sanguine*). "NO MATTER—A TIME WILL COME!"

A WOMAN OF SOME IMPORTANCE

Although deprived of his Commons seat, Asquith was still the official Liberal leader. From outside the House he engineered the selection of a Liberal sessional chairman (Sir Donald Maclean) and a chief whip (George R. Thorne). Neither was a former minister or senior party chieftain. Moreover Thorne--and to a degree Asquith--had to accept the ignominy of an eccentric radical, James M. Hogge, being imposed upon them as joint whip by the anti-Lloyd George Liberal M.P.'s who proudly called themselves the Wee Frees.

The Wee Frees under Maclean and Hogge--the more dynamic of the two whips--soon developed considerable esprit de corps. Attempts by Coalition Liberals to draw them away from Asquith and into a new Liberal or Center party headed by Lloyd George were unavailing, but disillusionment with the official leader, his seatless lieutenants, and his lethargic machine was growing. It was at this time that frustrated Liberals outside Parliament initiated the movement that evolved into the Liberal Summer School; and some of the Wee Free M.P.'s were attracted to the idea of a new independent Liberal party under Maclean, Lord Grey, or even Lord Robert Cecil, a respected anti-Lloyd George Tory. Disappointment among the Wee Frees was muted when Asquith's protege, Sir John Simon, attempting a Parliamentary comeback in the Spen Valley by-election of December 1919, lost out to a Labourite.

It was clear that if Asquith did not soon return to the Commons, his restless following might disperse in several directions. There were even some--though not all--prominent Conservatives who wanted Asquith back in the House as a bulwark against the "red specter" of Labour.

Partridge's handsome cartoon focuses upon two of Asquith's difficulties as a candidate in the Paisley by-election of February 1920. The electorate contained many female mill hands, and it was believed to be moving leftward. Would a pillar of old fashioned Liberalism, and a former opponent of women's suffrage, win the confidence of these predominantly working class voters? Perhaps to his own surprise Asquith easily trounced his Labour opponent and crushed the Coalition's candidate. It turned out to be his last real victory. "Wait and

A WOMAN OF SOME IMPORTANCE

(*Mr. Asquith and the Paisley Mill-hand*).

"HOW ARE YOU VOTING, MY PRETTY MAID?"
"WAIT AND YOU'LL SEE, KIND SIR," SHE SAID.

see" had first been uttered by Asquith as a threat during the 1910-1 fight over the Parliament Bill and-- very much out of context--was used against him during the dark days of the war.

THE RETURN OF THE EX-CHAMPION

Although Bernard Partridge implies in this cartoon that Asquith and his Wee Frees were at the receiving end of Lloyd George's Coalition punches, the opposite was closer to the truth. By mid-1920, and certainly before the end of the year, the Coalition was in trouble internally and externally, and the Asquithians had taken the offensive against it. The government's controversial Irish policy gave its Liberal opponents a lively issue, but trade and international questions were exploited as well.

Hostility toward the "Coalies" exploded at the National Liberal Federation's Leamington conference in May 1920, when several Coalition ministers in atten- dance were virtually driven from the hall. The inci- dent sparked a veritable civil war in the constituency associations, which outside Wales generally was won by the Asquithians.

Curiously, the return of Asquith to the House of Commons depolarized the Liberal feud within Parliament. The former prime minister was both a less partisan and a less effective spokesman for the orthodox Liberals than his stand-in, Sir Donald Maclean. Although he resolutely opposed Liberal reunion unless the Coali- tionists repented, and made some telling points against Lloyd George's Black and Tan War in Ireland, the "ex- champion" was too badly out of shape to win many points from the titleholder. At the same time Asquith's pres- tige was too high for him to be dethroned from the Liberal leadership, which many of his disenchanted followers believed would help reunite the party and bring down Lloyd George.

THE RETURN OF THE EX-CHAMPION.

Mr. Lloyd George. "WELCOME BACK! I'VE BEEN WANTING A SPARRING PARTNER TO GET ME INTO CONDITION; AND YOU'RE THE VERY MAN."

Only a bold prophet would have predicted in 1915 or 1916 that Ramsay MacDonald--despised former chairman of the Parliamentary Labour party and founder of the pacifist Union of Democratic Control--within less than a decade would be the official opposition leader and prospective prime minister. MacDonald's phoenix-like restoration was little more remarkable than the ascendancy of the Labour party itself, thanks to the enlargement of the electorate and the opportune split in organized Liberalism.

Most Liberals, and political observers generally, expected that Labour's assumption of the opposition leadership after the 1918 election was temporary. It was supposed that the Liberals--under this name or some other--after healing their schism would again become a party of government. The collapse of Liberalism at the local level, which may have begun before the war, cast some doubt on this outcome but was widely ignored. Also discounted was the defection to Labour, often via the Union for Democratic Control, of numerous radical Liberals disgusted by their former party's official support of the war.

By 1922, when the Lloyd George Coalition was approaching its end, working class reaction against those parties and individuals identified with the war practically guaranteed the return of a large Labour bloc at the next election. Whether it kept the opposition leadership depended on its being first past the post in enough constituencies over Liberals of all kinds. If there were more Liberal than Labour M.P.'s after the election, nominal Liberal reunion in order to become the official opposition was a probability.

Partridge's cartoon implies that Asquith and Lloyd George acquiesced to MacDonald's leapfrogging by fighting each other with separate machines. Would Liberalism have done better in 1922 if united? The answer to this question cannot be obtained simply by adding together official and National Liberal seats and votes, because a genuinely unified Liberal party fighting this general election would have produced quite different results from two factions separately fighting all and sundry as well as each other. Labour's impressive by-election record between 1919 and 1922, and its capture

30

INTO THE LIMELIGHT.

of votes in industrial constituencies in November 1922,
point to Ramsay MacDonald's becoming opposition leader
in any event.

THE SHEEP-TROT

Although Lloyd George still toyed with the idea of
a Center party incorporating moderate and democratic
members of all the old parties, after the 1922 general
election he put out cautious feelers to the Asquithians
for Liberal reunion. As Partridge's cartoon under-
scores, Asquith received this offer coolly, his un-
yielding lieutenants yet more so. Not a man to be
rebuffed, Lloyd George drew back, while not discouraging conciliatory gestures by any of his followers
willing to risk Asquithian snubs.

Although there were plenty of these, there were
also many instances of the flocks gamboling together,
Several M.P.'s of both groups asked for double whips,
petitions for reunion were circulated in the House of
Commons, the Liberal peers agreed upon Lord Grey as
their common leader, and the merging of divided constituency associations proceeded apace.

The cartoonist assumed his educated readership
would be familiar with Strephon and Amaryllis, rustic
characters in poems by Sir Philip Sidney and Edmund
Spenser. Asquith's reply to Lloyd George is of course
a play on "wait and see."

THE SHEEP-TROT.

Strephon George. "OUR RESPECTIVE FLOCKS SEEM DISPOSED TO GAMBOL TOGETHER: SHALL WE TWAIN NOT TREAD A MEASURE TOO?"

Amaryllis Asquith. "NAY, PRESUMPTUOUS SWAIN; I PREFER FOR THE MOMENT TO CULTIVATE AN ATTITUDE OF EXPECTANT HESITANCY."

Prime Minister Baldwin's declaration for protection and his call for a mandate on this issue were the fillips that at last brought the Asquithians and Coalies together, just months after the National Liberal Federation had flatly defeated a unity resolution. The Baldwin demarche also nailed the coffin lid on the Center party scheme, which Lloyd George--repulsed by his old Liberal colleagues--may have been plotting to revive upon a platform of imperial tariff preference.

The cartoon makes the point that repudiation of protection and acknowledgment of Asquith's leadership were prerequisites for Lloyd George's return to the orthodox Liberal sanctuary. The need to keep food costs low, upon which Lloyd George had always insisted even when straying from Liberal free trade orthodoxy, was the bridge by which the wanderer crossed back to his old allegiance.

Lloyd George's free trade declaration was in fact made at a dock-side news conference at Southampton after returning by sea from the United States. The swag-bag hefted by the returning mariner may allude to the National Liberal Fund, which the prodigal was expected to--but did not--hand over to the Liberal Central Association.

THE MARINER'S RETURN.

Mr. Asquith. "AND HAVE YOU TAUGHT YOUR PARROT TO SAY——"

Parrot (*chipping in*). "DOWN WITH PROTECTION! YOUR FOOD WILL COST YOU MORE! GOOD OLD ASQUITH!"

Mr. Asquith. "A MOST ADMIRABLE BIRD."

THE VELVET BOOT

Asquith and Lloyd George had quite different objects for keeping a minority Labour government in office. The older man wanted to leave it in until it had proven its incompetence, after which--he anticipated--the king would ask him to form a minority Liberal government that would be upheld by reasonable men of all parties. A return to the premiership, with Lloyd George once again a subordinate cabinet minister, would go far to compensate Asquith for his treatment in December 1916.

Lloyd George expected Labour to promote radical reforms that Liberals could endorse. There was also the possibility that, if the Labourites got into deep water, they might put him in charge of a bailing-out operation like the one he had conducted successfully during the war.

Neither of these prospects materialized. It soon became clear that Ramsay MacDonald had no intention of either stepping aside for the Liberals or introducing a comprehensive and imaginative radical program. Instead, he used the parliamentary session to discredit the Liberals and, possibly in collusion with the Conservatives' Stanley Baldwin, to prevent the return of Lloyd George to office and power.

Although they continued to disagree about policies and tactics, and their associates were at loggerheads over electoral strategy and the disbursement of the Lloyd George Fund, the two Liberal chiefs were agreed that another election--the third in two years--would do their party no good and might be disastrous. It was essential that MacDonald be kept in as long as possible: at least until the electorate was convinced beyond doubt of Labour's incapacity to govern.

"The Velvet Boot" is a superb example of Bernard Partridge's inventiveness and workmanship. The Liberals' dilemma of keeping the surly, ungrateful Labourites both in office and on the mark is exemplified in the confrontation between the timid bourgeois landlord and his glowering working class tenant. Labour's one significant domestic reform, its low income housing program, may also be part of Partridge's symbolism.

THE VELVET BOOT.

Mr. Asquith. "UNLESS YOU PROVE A MORE DESIRABLE TENANT IT MAY BECOME MY PAINFUL DUTY TO——"

Mr. MacDonald. "EVICT ME?"

Mr. Asquith. "NO, NO; BUT I MAY HAVE TO THREATEN TO GIVE YOU SEVERAL MONTHS' NOTICE."

THE BATTLE OF HASTINGS

This cartoon is included less for its indispensability to the saga of the Liberal party than for its wit and artistry. A burlesque of the Bayeux Tapestry (purportedly embroidered by William the Conqueror's queen), it chronicles the fate of Ramsay MacDonald's attorney-general, Sir Patrick Hastings, whose inept handling of the "Campbell case" helped bring down the 1924 Labour government.

The attorney-general's withdrawal of the indictment of a Communist editor, J. R. Campbell, alleged to have incited British troops to mutiny, resulted in a Conservative censure motion that MacDonald insisted must be a question of confidence. The prime minister refused to accept a Liberal amendment to submit the matter to a select committee of the House, thus defusing the issue. With the Conservatives ready to support their amendment, the Liberals were in the unhappy position of having to vote down a government they wanted to stay in office. The Labour cabinet apparently was willing to be ousted so that the Liberals could be done to death in the ensuing election.

In various segments of this intricate drawing we espy Campbell's agitation, prosecution, and defiance, as well as the contretemps in the House between Baldwin (left, with pipe), Asquith, MacDonald (appropriately escutcheoned), and the fallen Hastings. Note the bottom panel with its mocking Justice, tipsy scales, judicial cap and bells, and revolutionary cloche.

THE BATTLE OF HASTINGS.
(After the Bayeux Tapestry.)

BACK TO THE LAND

To many country house and Clubland denizens among Punch's readers, Lloyd George's 1925-6 land reforms seemed to hark back to his anti-landlord campaigns of 1909-10 and 1912-4. This is clearly Partridge's interpretation. The pheasant alludes to Lloyd George's famous gaffe when, in a speech at Bedford in October 1913, he insisted erroneously that farmers' mangold crops were destroyed by gamekeeper-protected birds. The Welshman's depiction as a gun-toting squire may contain a thrust at his pretentions to land ownership at Bron-y-de, Churt, Surrey.

BACK TO THE LAND.

Pheasant. "HULLO! HERE'S THE OLD SPORTSMAN WHO MISSED ME IN 1909."
Mr. Lloyd George. "YES; BUT I'VE GOT A NEW GUN THIS TIME."

THE DILUVIANS

Any Lloyd George scheme could be counted on to stir up a furor in the Liberal party, but the land nationalization proposal in the Green Book was too much of a burden for several of the Welshman's most dedicated partisans. Among them was Sir Alfred Mond, former Coalition Liberal minister and for years an unswerving Lloyd Georgite. Mond had already disagreed with his chief over the use of the Fund, believing that a larger portion of its income should have been spent upon the party during the critical 1924 campaign.

Partridge implies, as did Lloyd George, that the Liberal party in the twenties was at sea and needed a tow "back to the land." What better mechanism than a revival of the Liberal land campaign interrupted by the war? Many Liberals, including Mond, accepted the strategy but were appalled by Lloyd George's latest plans and tactics, the latter including creation of an extra-party Land and Nation League better financed and equipped than the "old firm" itself.

The symbol of the ark, with its "Noah" (Lord Oxford and Asquith) relaxing complacently in the captain's cabin, probably is a pun on the increasing reliance of the older generation of Liberals upon free trade and other nineteenth century shibboleths as contents of an inviolable Ark of the Covenant. This vessel was to be guarded from profanation, even at the risk of electoral disaster and extinction as a major party.

About two weeks after this cartoon was published, Sir Alfred Mond defected to the Conservative party.

THE DILUVIANS.

Mr. Lloyd George. "GIVE YOU A TOW TO ARARAT?"

Sir Alfred Mond. "THANK YOU; I'M ALL FOR GETTING BACK TO THE LAND; BUT— I RATHER MISTRUST YOUR CRAFT."

[Sir Alfred Mond, while expressing his eagerness for agricultural reforms, has severely criticised Mr. Lloyd George's new Land Scheme.]

A MARRIAGE HAS BEEN RE-ARRANGED

Following Lord Oxford and Asquith's retirement as Liberal leader in October 1926, Lloyd George quickly won control of the official party machinery. The biggest inducement to accept the Welshman's stewardship was his offer to subsidize the party from the income and capital of his Fund. In return, unfriendly party headquarters personnel--including some critical of the tainted source of the funds--were persuaded to retire. Some of these superannuated veterans immediately established an anti-Lloyd George Liberal Council, which a number of Asquithian stalwarts--headed by Lord Grey-- joined and maintained.

Partridge evidently did not believe that the "remarriage" of Lloyd George and the Liberal party-- actually the second since 1922--would be faithfully honored by either party. The "bridegroom" categorically refused to part with his Fund's capital, except in driblets, while the "bride" was reluctant to take his lead in matters of policy. The repartee chaffs at the contemporary dispute over revision of the Anglican Prayer Book, including the marriage vows. Looking down upon the scene is the Liberal paterfamilias, former Prime Minister Lord Rosebery. His letter to The Times of February 16, 1927, recalled the honors traffic of Coalition days, when most of the Lloyd George Fund had been accumulated.

A MARRIAGE HAS BEEN RE-ARRANGED . . .

The Bride. "WITH ALL THY WORLDLY GOODS (NEVER MIND HOW THOU GOTTEST THEM) DOST THOU ME ENDOW?"

The Bridegroom. "CERTAINLY NOT—ONLY A SHARE OF THEM. I ADOPT THE REVISED VERSION."

The Bride. "OH, THOU DOST, DOST THOU? THEN I DON'T OBEY."

THE SLEEPING BEAUTY SITS UP

Those who had written off the staggering and quarrel-riven Liberal party after its 1924 debacle were forced to take second thought during 1927, as its average by-election poll rose to nearly 30 percent of the three party vote. Partisans of Lloyd George attributed these gains to the Welshman's new broom. Disenchanted observers, including some former Asquithians, were more inclined to credit the greater efficiency of party headquarters under its neutral chairman, Sir Herbert Samuel.

Although once regarded as one of the Liberal "old gang" (see "The Babes in the Wood," above), Samuel had been employed by the Coalition as high commissioner of Palestine. Later he headed a royal commission on the coal industry that reached conclusions similar to those of Lloyd George's own Coal Inquiry. Lloyd George ratified Samuel's appointment to the headquarters post without much enthusiasm, as a gesture to his opponents and critics in the party. A Lloyd George lieutenant, Thomas F. Tweed, was commissioned to assist Samuel and keep him under surveillance.

THE SLEEPING BEAUTY SITS UP.

Liberal Party (*to the Fairy Prince Samuel*). "O LOVE, THY KISS WOULD WAKE THE DEAD!"

Tennyson: "*The Day-Dream.*"

[The success of the Liberal Party at two recent by-elections has been attributed to the return of Sir Herbert Samuel to its councils.]

THE RETURN OF ULYSSES

Like Bernard Partridge, Ernest Howard Shepard expected the readers of _Punch_ to know their literature. Here Shepard reworks the tale of the great adventurer Ulysses in terms of Lloyd George's odyssey during the Coalition years and after, as it might have been rendered on a pottery shard of the Homeric age.

Shepard's point is that command of the party machinery did not make Lloyd George the master of the Liberal party. Like Ulysses's Penelope, Liberalism would recognize the Welshman's legitimacy only when he had successfully bent the bow of leadership. Until he had done so, the party would be wooed by other suitors, not only among the Conservatives and Labourites but from other Liberal factions. The fleeing figures in the lower left of the panel may represent Asquithian suitors for party leadership, who in dudgeon had recently withdrawn to the political sidelines.

The occasion for this cartoon was a revival of press controversy over the Lloyd George Fund, and anticipation of the report of the Liberal Industrial Inquiry--financed by the Fund--which was expected to set forth Lloyd George's platform for the next election.

Shepard's portrayal of the Liberal party as a comely and scantily clad woman contrasts with Partridge's less charming feminine images of the party in two of the previous cartoons.

THE RETURN OF ULYSSES.

THE WANDERER. "WILL SHE RECOGNISE ME?"

WELSH WIZARDRY--A REVIVAL

The publication of <u>We Can Conquer Unemployment</u>, Lloyd George's program for beating the slump, was the background of this cartoon. The Liberal chieftain is pictured as a white wizard in a pointed Welsh bonnet determined, in the style of the old nursery rhyme, to sweep the cobwebs of unemployment from the economic sky. Lloyd George had been known as the Welsh Wizard since establishing his political ascendancy over Wales during the fight over the 1902 Education Act.

Sir Herbert Samuel, his expression mildly skeptical, has nevertheless attached himself securely to the wizard and his heterodox conveyance. Even Walter Runciman, bitter end Asquithian and charter member of the Liberal Council, finds enough merit--and electoral prospects--in the wizard's schemes to catch a ride on his broomstick.

WELSH WIZARDRY—A REVIVAL.

SIR HERBERT SAMUEL }
MR. RUNCIMAN   "OLD WIZARD, OLD WIZARD, WHITHER SO HIGH?"

MR. LLOYD GEORGE.   "TO SWEEP THE COBWEBS OUT OF THE SKY."

Although the Liberals had the only coherent plan for "conquering unemployment," their readiness to confront the nation's most serious problem proved not to be a convincing electoral asset. Only 59 constituencies were carried by Liberal candidates in the general election of May 30, 1929.

Labour had at last become the largest party, but it was still a minority party. A combination of Conservatives and Liberals could have precluded a Labour government from taking or long remaining in office. This would have necessitated cooperation between Stanley Baldwin and Lloyd George, confirmed political enemies. Although advocated by Winston Churchill and other Tories as in 1923-4, nothing came of the notion of an anti-Labour pact.

Similarly, Ramsay MacDonald dismissed any idea of an agreement with the Liberals and, when Baldwin resigned, formed a second minority administration. He had no kind words for Lloyd George's economic policies, indeed hinting that they had been mostly stolen from Labour.

Lloyd George's critics sometimes charged that his Napoleonic image--derived from the war--stood in the way of Liberal electoral success, or of any interparty agreement or alliance unless, perhaps, there should be another great national crisis. Here the cartoonist is suggesting that the former "man of destiny" may have become a discounted has-been.

THE MAN OF DESTINY

NO
REASONABLE
OFFER
REFÚSED.

NOTHING DOING.

THE PARTY CHEST

Lloyd George's basic strategy for the Liberals during the 1929-31 Parliament was to cooperate with the Labour government in return for enactment of some form of transferable ballot. Only the latter, he now believed, would guarantee the survival of a politically potent Liberal party. Ramsay MacDonald was equally determined to retain the "first past the post" arrangement that, he was convinced, had enabled Labour to oust the Liberals from primacy in numerous industrial constituencies.

Since MacDonald needed Liberal votes to carry legislation, his strategy was one of foot-dragging. Lloyd George was promised an electoral reform bill in the future after other measures with priority had been passed with Liberal help.

Soon after the 1929 election MacDonald insisted that groundwork for electoral reform must include an investigation of political funds that could influence elections. Partridge's cartoon picturesquely lays bare Lloyd George's dilemma, and indeed the Labour government's. A strong spotlight on the controversial Lloyd George Fund would do nothing to encourage Liberal party solidarity. The Welshman knew that unity was essential if his party was to give the government the backing it needed in the Commons. MacDonald must have been equally aware of Lloyd George's plight, which could intensify his own, but seemed to prefer weakening the Liberals and embarrassing his rival to working with him to advance a common program.

THE PARTY CHEST.

Mr. MacDonald. "THIS IS OUR NEW DESIGN, SIR. I UNDERSTAND THAT YOU FAVOUR DRESS-REFORM?"

Mr. Lloyd George. "I DO; BUT I SHOULDN'T CARE TO EXPOSE MY CHEST LIKE THAT."

[The Prime Minister has stated that any consideration of electoral reform would include an inquiry into the use of "huge central funds" employed for party purposes.]

THE RETURN OF THE PRODIGAL

During the evolving political crisis of 1931 the Liberal Parliamentary party split three ways. As early as March, the Liberal group led by Sir John Simon declared its rejection of Lloyd George's strategy of cooperation with Labour. Simon also stated publicly that the nation's free trade tradition must be reexamined.

When the Labour government fell in August, Lloyd George was in the hospital. The deputy chairman of the Liberal Parliamentary party, Sir Herbert Samuel, led the non-Simonite Liberal M.P.'s into the National government being formed by Ramsay MacDonald. Several of the Samuelite Liberals became ministers. The Simonites independently supported the National government, but were given no ministerial posts.

The third break in the party came in October, when Lloyd George refused to accept Samuel's decision, as acting Liberal chairman, to participate in the National government coalition fighting the general election. After the election, the Samuelite and Simonite Liberals --increased in numbers--sat on the government benches, but Lloyd George and three other Liberal M.P.'s (all relatives of his) crossed over into opposition. Several prominent Simonites now joined the officially protectionist National government as ministers.

Although granted an unusual concession--the "agreement to differ"--the remaining Samuelite ministers were never comfortable in a protectionist cabinet. After some eleven months of equivocation, Samuel and ten other Liberal ministers bowed to conscience and outside pressure and resigned from the government on September 28, 1932. But over a year was to pass before Samuel and most of his M.P.'s followed Lloyd George across the floor in November 1933.

In Punch's issue of the week after the ministerial resignations, Partridge draws Samuel and Lloyd George as prodigal son and somewhat less than warmly welcoming father. Unlike the Biblical parent, this one has no intention of slaughtering a fatted calf to celebrate the reunion. This cartoon should be compared with that of November 14, 1923, in which Lloyd George is portrayed as the reformed wanderer from the free trade

THE RETURN OF THE PRODIGAL.

FARMER GEORGE. "HULLO, SAMUEL! SO YOU'VE COME BACK, HAVE YOU? WELL, I HOPE YOU'VE BROUGHT YOUR OWN VEAL SANDWICHES WITH YOU."

path. The 1932 cartoon may also be jesting at Lloyd George's pretensions to being a practical farmer, as well as the strict dietary rules of Samuel's Jewish religion.

THE NEW HEALERS

Lloyd George's "new deal," unveiled to the British public early in 1935, was patently modeled upon Franklin D. Roosevelt's American reconstruction program of the same name. But it also drew heavily on the Liberals' Yellow and Orange Books and the economic proposals that Lloyd George, with little success, had tried to persuade the Labour government of 1929-31 to act upon.

Although Lloyd George was invited to submit his proposals to the National cabinet, neither an invitation to join the government--which he may have counted on--nor a favorable reaction to specific recommendations was forthcoming. The attitude of press and public opinion ranged from bored to indifferent. Partridge's cartoon suggests that the Welsh medicine man's spiel has fallen on deaf ears, unlike that of his American counterpart. Although Roosevelt's panaceas were beginning to meet conservative resistance, as well as to be upstaged by others more radical or visionary, the United States president at least had been in a position to experiment and initiate action.

THE NEW HEALERS.

FEARLESS FRANK. "ALL MY CROWD SEEMS TO BE MELTING AWAY."
DYNAMIC DAVE. "WELL, I HAVEN'T GOT ONE AT ALL YET!"

COUNCIL OF FACTION

Bernard Partridge again has recourse to a nursery rhyme to illustrate the alliance of convenience between Lloyd George, Sir Herbert Samuel, and the apostate Labourite Lord (Philip) Snowden during the 1935 election campaign. It was the objective of all three politicians to defeat, or more realistically reduce the majority of, the National government dominated by Ramsay MacDonald, Stanley Baldwin, and Neville Chamberlain. Lloyd George's nonpartisan Council of Action, officially endorsed by Snowden but not by Samuel, was the imperfect instrument by which a "progressive" majority of the House of Commons, drawn from all three parties, was to be elected.

The cartoonist plays somewhat loosely with the facts when he puts Samuel aboard the crazy ship "Jolly Mixup," but he succeeds very well in capturing the confusion and discord of those occupying the middle ground between official conservatism and the trade union-manipulated socialism of the Labour party. The observant reader will also be struck by the cartoonists' changing images of Lloyd George, from the steadfast national leader of the first drawings in this section, to the tousle-haired rabble rouser of the last two.

COUNCIL OF FACTION.

"THREE WISE MEN OF GOTHAM
WENT TO SEA IN A BOWL.
IF THE BOWL HAD BEEN STRONGER
MY TALE HAD BEEN LONGER."—*Old Nursery Rhyme.*

[To commemorate the triple alliance—on the microphone—of Sir HERBERT SAMUEL, Lord SNOWDEN and
Mr. DAVID LLOYD GEORGE.]

PART THREE

Seven Essays

THE MURDER OF THE LIBERAL PARTY: A HISTORY LESSON*

This essay is an almost verbatim transcript of a fifty-minute lecture to an undergraduate history class. It is a deliberate oversimplification--but not, I think a distortion--of a complicated chapter of political history.

I am going to tell you a murder story. The crime was unpremeditated, but it left the victim just as dead as if it had been carefully planned. The victim was a great political party, a national institution whose experienced, talented, broad-minded, and far-sighted leaders, if they had held office, might have lessened the effects of the economic depression of the 1930s and possibly even prevented the Second World War.

The victim of the crime was the British Liberal party, and there were three "murderers." The name of the "first murderer" was Herbert Henry Asquith. The name of the "second murderer" was David Lloyd George. There was also a "third murderer." This was the British voter, who in effect gave the victim the coup de grace--an act of mercy, as we shall see.

The murder of the Liberal party might not have succeeded if the victim had not been debilitated by previous illnesses. The Liberal party was the great reform party of nineteenth century Britain. Its leaders gave the country a succession of new or recon-structed institutions: a reformed Parliament, a greatly expanded electorate, a new organization of municipal government, a renovated judicial structure, modernized taxation, the beginning of a national education system, army reform, land reform, mine and factory legislation, legalization of trade unions, and many other signifi-cant institutional changes that transformed Britain into a modern nation.

---

*This essay was originally published as "The Murder of the British Liberal Party" in The History Teacher, III (May 1970), 27-36. It is reproduced by permission of the Society for History Education.

By 1885, the Liberal party and the country were ready for another great leap forward into the field of social reform. The British working class, newly enfranchised by the Liberals, were pressing for old age pensions, workmen's compensation for industrial accidents, minimum wages, maximum hours on the job, safer and pleasanter working conditions, and other benefits that we associate today with the welfare state. There were two bold men in the party who would have led it along this road: Sir Charles Dilke and Joseph Chamberlain. Neither man, unfortunately, became leader of the Liberal party. Dilke's career was cut short by a bizarre scandal. Chamberlain bolted the party over the issue of Irish home rule--which he opposed. He affiliated himself and a group of his followers with the Conservatives, and in so doing gave the latter a much needed stimulus.

The Liberal party was severely weakened by the loss of these two promising leaders. If either man had become Liberal prime minister and carried through the social reforms he and many other party members were pressing for during the 1880s, the Liberal party might have survived as the party of the moderate left governing Britain today. The political murder we are about to investigate might never have had a chance to occur.

The Liberal party was further weakened by the long overdue departure of its greatest nineteenth century leader, William Ewart Gladstone. Gladstone, whose remarkable ministry of 1868-74 had carried through many of the institutional reforms mentioned above, should have retired--at the age of sixty-five--in 1874. However, the headstrong old man hung on to the party leadership for another two decades. Instead of transforming the Liberal party into an instrument of social change, as either Dilke or Chamberlain certainly would have done, Gladstone--relict of the earlier stage of laissez-faire Liberalism that had completed its work by the late 1870s--dragged his unwilling party after him in pursuit of a mirage. This was the political liberation of Ireland, for which the British people were not yet prepared and in which the British working class had not the slightest interest.

For nearly twenty years, this Grand Old Man, energetic and domineering despite his advanced age, whom everyone admired but had become exceedingly bored with, diverted the Liberals from their true mission. When Gladstone finally was shunted into retirement at eighty-five, there followed a further crisis of the Liberal party, a ten-year struggle for leadership among his power-thirsty lieutenants. This was finally settled, after much bloodletting, in 1905 when Herbert Henry Asquith emerged as the coming man in the party. Three years later he succeeded to the official leadership and, since the Liberals were then in power, to the prime ministership.

The Liberals, returned to office after a long opposition by the periodic swing of the political pendulum, now began to make up for lost time. Under Asquith's able guidance, a group of younger Liberal leaders, David Lloyd George the most conspicuous but also including Winston Churchill and several other very capable men in their thirties and early forties, carried through a long overdue series of far-reaching social reforms. These included pensions, minimum wages for miners, sickness and unemployment insurance, a steeply graduated income tax, heavy inheritance taxes, a system of labor exchanges to fight unemployment, and other necessary and useful legislation. There was also the famous and heatedly-fought constitutional revision which checked the power of the Conservative-dominated House of Lords. The great Liberal ministry of 1905-15 finally conceded to the British working class many of the gains first sought over two decades before.

But in the meantime the disgruntled left wing of the Liberal party associated with the trade union movement had grown tired of waiting. It had broken away from the parent party and established a new Labour party, financed by union funds and dedicated to the gradual socialization of the British economy. The new Labour party was not much of a success, simply because when the Liberals finally did get a reform ministry into office in 1905, it began to fulfill most of what the Labourites and the working class in general wanted done at this stage.

Like many third parties, the Labour party was in the unfortunate predicament of seeing one of the major parties steal its program. By 1914, the Labour party was faltering. If a peacetime election had been held in 1914 or 1915, the Labour party might have lost up to half its forty-odd M.P.'s. Indeed Labour really had been kept alive for a decade by an electoral alliance with the Liberals, who used it as a kind of satellite party to win votes in heavily working class constituencies. This alliance, for various reasons, had come apart by 1914. If there had been an election then, the Liberals probably would have fought Labour and possibly destroyed it.

The important thing about the prewar Labour party was not its strength or its influence, both of which were very limited, but the mere fact that it was there, that it existed as an alternative reform party should anything happen to embarrass and discredit the Liberals.

We come now to our main event. The dramatis personae need some introduction, which must be abbreviated. Asquith--portly, bland, genial, a lover of good food and drink, a charming conversationalist and raconteur--after a brilliant career at Oxford, had done well as a barrister and been enticed into politics by Gladstone. More importantly, he had been initiated into High Society by his second wife, a social gadfly with important connections in the highest circles. It was these social-political connections, even more than his considerable ability, that accounted for Asquith's final emergence over his rivals as Liberal party leader.

While he was prime minister in peacetime from 1908 to 1914, Asquith was an exceptionally competent leader of the party and the government. An astute parliamentarian, able committee chairman, and efficient administrator, he skillfully manipulated his remarkable colleagues, one of the most talented groups of men ever to govern Britain. Asquith's enormous success as Liberal leader before the war contrasts so sharply with his later failures that the change seems incredible.

The driving spirit of the Liberal ministry was not Asquith, but David Lloyd George. This extraordinary Welshman, so very unlike most of his affluent and polished cabinet colleagues, came from a humble home--he was an orphan raised by a shoemaker uncle--and after succeeding as a lawyer, rose to prominence in the Liberal party solely through tremendous drive and an incomparably sharp and devious mind. Lloyd George had a computer-like brain, absorbing everything that he saw or heard, recalling it instantly when needed, and intuitively fitting together all the elements needed to make lightning decisions. It is probably no exaggeration to say that no other British statesman has possessed Lloyd George's raw intellectual ability.

This exceptional mental agility had no solid foundation in character. Lloyd George lacked formal education except for the "three R's" and a smattering of technical legal knowledge, plus the religious indoctrination that he had superficially imbibed as a child and youth in rural Wales. The latter was quickly rubbed away when he entered the great world of London politics and society. Thus we have in Lloyd George the dangerous combination of tremendous brain power and practically no fixed principles. Indeed, there were many political enemies of Lloyd George, and even some close associates, who regarded him as close to being an unprincipled scoundrel.

Asquith understood this dark side of Lloyd George's personality very well. He saw it, made allowance for it--Asquith was very tolerant--and protected Lloyd George from his own shortcomings. In 1913, Asquith saved Lloyd George from the fate of Sir Charles Dilke when the Welshman became involved in a shoddy financial scandal, the Marconi affair, involving the unethical use of inside information available to Lloyd George as a cabinet minister. Asquith knew that Lloyd George was of great value to the Liberal party because of his shrewd insight, his ability to simplify complex issues, his talent as a mediator of disputes, his gift as a public speaker--close to demagoguery--which no other prominent Liberal had, and his unmatched power to drive the party forward, a power Asquith lacked but knew the Liberals needed if they were to stay in power. Asquith probably had no intention of ever allowing Lloyd George to become party leader, a post for which he considered him unfitted by any proper standards of ethics or conduct.

The great Liberal ministry was interrupted by the First World War, a war that might not have happened if Asquith and his colleagues had given as close attention to foreign affairs as to domestic. The domestic troubles had seemed far more pressing until that fatal August of 1914 brought an abrupt end to the prewar world and the pending crises in Ireland and in labor relations that had absorbed the cabinet for months. An official moratorium on party politics was agreed upon and a three-party coalition cabinet replaced the Liberal ministry early in 1915.

This war was unlike any in which Britain ever before had been engaged. The problems of mobilization and training of manpower, supply, transportation, and

organization of the homefront were wholly unprecedented. These problems were too much for the old-
fashioned, unimaginative Asquith to cope with successfully, although at first he did his best. But these
difficult matters and the immediate decisions they
required were the very food on which a mind like Lloyd
George's thrived.

This man, once erroneously considered a paci-
fist--he had strongly opposed the Boer War and frowned
on heavy peacetime spending for armaments--within
months transformed himself into a guiding spirit of the
British war effort. Unlike Asquith and most of the
other rather complacent Liberal ministers, Lloyd George
was by temperament a fighter. War gave him an outlet
for his energies and skills that no peacetime pursuit
ever could have provided. Only Churchill shared this
enthusiasm for a war, and Churchill soon was removed
from the cabinet as a scapegoat for blunders in war
strategy.

Unfortunately for the Liberal party, the newfound
power that Lloyd George was able to grasp as minister
chiefly responsible for the war effort gave him fancies
and ambitions that earlier he either had not had or had
been willing to sublimate. In short, Lloyd George saw
that the circumstances were ripe for a power play that
would give him the supreme leadership of the British
government, in fact if not in name.

Lloyd George's ambition was heightened by a growing awareness that Asquith was no longer fulfilling the
demands of his office. Asquith was increasingly
disheartened and disillusioned by the misery and death
on the battlefield, which was startlingly brought home
to him in the summer of 1916 by the loss of his eldest
son, a promising young lawyer and politician. Under
Asquith's faltering leadership, further weakened by
this personal tragedy, the British government and its
war program lost momentum. As this happened, a peace
movement began to gain ground both within and outside
the government. Simultaneously, patriotic and nation-
alistic forces associated with the Conservative party,
and rallied by the powerful newspaper publisher, Lord
Northcliffe, demanded the removal of Asquith and his
replacement by a more effective prime minister.

Asquith, accustomed to years of authority in the
Liberal party, believed he was indispensable to the
party, which still, of course, controlled a majority in

the House of Commons. He therefore discounted and closed his mind to the intrigue that was developing to oust him and substitute Lloyd George as prime minister. Lloyd George, who was sincerely patriotic--one of his few consistent principles--was frankly worried by the peace movement. Perhaps with reason, he feared that Asquith might be captured by it and try to end the war on terms favorable to the enemy.

Combining quite legitimate apprehension about Asquith with personal ambition for power, Lloyd George joined forces with the plotters, nearly all of whom were Conservatives who before the war had been among his severest critics. Among them were Andrew Bonar Law, Sir Max Aitken (later Lord Beaverbrook), Sir Edward Carson, Lord Milner, and Leopold Amery. There seems little doubt that some of these conspirators, while inspired by truly patriotic motives, also saw the situation as an excellent opportunity to discredit the Liberal party for years by tagging it with responsibility both for lack of preparedness before the war and ineptitude in managing it. By making Lloyd George prime minister, they would remove from the Liberal party its ablest politician, since Asquith would never take him back after such a betrayal. He might even be absorbed into the Tory party as Chamberlain had been thirty years before.

In early December 1916, this festering intrigue came to a head. In concert with his new political and journalistic allies, Lloyd George gave Asquith an ultimatum demanding that he be made head of a special war council that would take complete control of the war, while Asquith would remain in office as a figurehead prime minister. Asquith, at first seemingly acquiescent, suddenly changed his mind and tried to force Lloyd George out of the government. Apparently the prime minister abandoned his original plan to compromise with Lloyd George when some of his Liberal friends, who intensely disliked the Welshman, reminded Asquith of the Marconi incident and offered other evidence of the man's untrustworthy and dangerous qualities. Asquith therefore determined to fight back. Thereupon the Conservative leaders, some of whom were privy to Lloyd George's plot, threatened a full-scale government crisis unless Asquith resigned.

Asquith did so, possibly thinking that the plot would fail and he would be returned to office. But Lloyd George and his fellow conspirators had prepared

71

their ground well. Just under half the Liberal and Labour M.P.'s were persuaded that the success of the war effort required a government controlled by the Welshman. Combined with a solid Conservative bloc critical of Asquith, this gave Lloyd George more than enough votes to defeat him if there was a showdown in the House of Commons. When Asquith grasped the true situation, he saw that he was beaten and went quietly into opposition. Lloyd George became prime minister of a new Coalition ministry of Conservatives and dissident Liberals. It is noteworthy that a number of obscure Liberal M.P.'s who backed Lloyd George were given undersecretaryships and other minor government posts that they would not have gotten in ordinary circumstances. They were, in effect, paid off.

In four days of skulduggery, the historic Liberal party had been cleaved in two, temporarily as most thought at the time, permanently as events were to prove. The murder had been committed.

There remain the questions, which of the two Liberal leaders was primarily responsible for the schism, and did it have to happen? Most students of this affair have placed the principal blame on Lloyd George. I do not agree. Lloyd George did not want to destroy the Liberal party.* His object was control of the government to win the war. He singlemindedly pursued this goal, one by-product being the destruction of the party. A second one was the destruction of Lloyd George's peacetime political career, because once the war and postwar reconstruction were over, the Welshman was ditched unceremoniously by his ungrateful Conservative allies and never returned to office.

Although Lloyd George's intrigue indirectly resulted in the destruction of the Liberal party, it was actually Asquith's refusal to accept Lloyd George's ultimatum that was the immediate cause. If Asquith had been willing to act as titular prime minister, or perhaps to take a peerage and an honorific office like lord chancellor, there would have been no party split at this time, and possibly not at all.

We must ask, was Asquith justified in deciding to

---

*I now (1982) have some reservations about this assertion.

fight Lloyd George and suffer the possible consequences? As noted, Asquith may have thought he could
defeat the rebel. But if he believed this, his political wisdom had grown very dim. If, on the other hand,
he knew he would lose the struggle, he must also have
known that the Liberal party of which he was the leader
was, at best, doomed to years of weakness and frustration. Thus Asquith either was guilty of gross political incompetence, or he was prepared to sacrifice the
party for the sake of his personal honor and pride. In
either case, I would say Asquith was the real "murderer" of the Liberal party, and Lloyd George merely an
accessory.[1]

The sequel is well known and need not detain us.
The Labour party, waiting in the wings, came out of the
war in a very strong position politically, because it
bore no responsiblity for either the causes or the
effects of the conflict. Once Lloyd George's personal
prestige as "the man who won the war" had faded, as it
was bound to, the electorate was given the choice of a
powerful Conservative party, strengthened by the anni-
hilation of its traditional Liberal opposition; an
aggressive, optimistic Labour party appealing strongly
to discontented workingmen and newly-enfranchised
women; and two weak Liberal factions attached to the
two rival leaders, more intent on fighting each other
than winning Parliamentary elections. The British
voter, always a sportsman, decided in due course to put
the mortally wounded Liberal party out of its misery.
In so doing, unfortunately, he retired into private
life some of the best administrative brains in Britain,
with consequences the country is still suffering.

ASQUITH: THE LAST BIG WHIG*

In his War Memoirs, Lloyd George declared magnanimously that no British prime minister--save possibly Gladstone and Disraeli--was better endowed mentally for a political career than Asquith, his onetime chief and subsequent adversary. It was entirely "superior talent and political aptitude," the Welshman contended, that raised to distinction this son of a Nonconformist Yorkshire weaver, a man who--unlike Sir Edward Grey and most of his other Liberal colleagues--"had neither wealth nor rank to help him."[1]

An Oxford education at Balliol under Benjamin Jowett was the first step in liberating Asquith from a Nonconformist lower middle class background not greatly unlike Lloyd George's.[2] His second marriage, to the brilliant socialite Margot Tennant, completed Asquith's transition to the world of social eminence and severed any lingering connection with his humble origins, which, in Lloyd George's opinion, he seemed to be trying all his life to forget.[3] The death of his first wife, who had disliked Society and according to Asquith had been a restricting rather than a stimulating influence on his career,[4] and his remarriage were perhaps decisive in fixing the character of the future prime minister as a solid and contented member of the Establishment.

Speaking of Asquith in 1917, F. E. Smith--himself no intellectual sluggard--remarked to Archibald Salvidge that the "old man has got more brains in his little finger than you and I possess in the whole of our two heads." A contemporary historian who has studied Asquith's career minutely is of no doubt that he had the intelligence to easily outstrip any and all of his fellow ministers in cabinet discussion.[5]

Although Asquith's mental powers, in his prime, are nowhere denied, their nature has been debated. His

---

*This essay is a revision of "The Last English Whig: Lord Oxford and Asquith," published in the Duquesne Review, XI (Spring 1966), 1-14. The copyright to the original article is the property of the Duquesne University Press.

mind has been described as quick, observant, penetrating, judicious, and imperturbable, but not speculative, imaginative, or introspective. John Maynard Keynes wrote that Asquith's mind was built to deal with given facts. He "had no intellectual fancies to lead him astray."

Asquith's official biographers spoke of his photographic memory, even for the trivial, always an invaluable gift for a legal and political career. It was Asquith's exceptional capacity to absorb and retain, according to Lord Beaverbrook, that made it possible for him to accomplish so much public business while simultaneously devoting so much time to conversation and social life. His ability to write chatty letters to women friends while presiding over involved cabinet meetings has been remarked on.

In the opinion of a shrewd political journalist, H. N. Brailsford, Asquith's matter-of-factness and lack of philosophical doubts allowed him to concentrate his attention effectively on precise objectives. Referring to the storm aroused in the Liberal party by Asquith's censure of Lloyd George's conduct during the 1926 general strike, Wickham Steed noted that Asquith remained perfectly calm through it all. "He had done what his judicial mind and his sense of duty had convinced him was right, and he cared little what might be crushed by the sledgehammer blow he had struck." Earlier in his career, Asquith had been nicknamed "The Hammer" for his relentless single-mindedness in parliamentary debate.

A social psychologist studying the British political elite concluded that Asquith's talent was narrowly legalistic: that while gifted in analysis and deduction, he was "non-intellectual" in the sense of being unable to view a question from all sides and visualize the remote causes and consequences. By temperament and training, Asquith had become a "reasoning machine," in whom "the instinctive . . . had been driven underground."

Many writers have noted Asquith's lack of interest in abstract ideas and avoidance of idealism. A. G. Gardiner said that ideals were of interest to Asquith only when they seemed to offer the basis for concrete achievement. Brailsford maintained that his political philosophy was limited to "party commonplaces," while Lloyd George contended that Asquith was most impressed by "traditional ideas garbed in aphoristic jargon."[11] A frequent criticism of Asquith was that he clung obstinately to outworn party shibboleths which he lacked the will or energy to reevaluate.[12] This apparent distrust of unfamiliar ideas, perhaps partly due to a lawyer's unwillingness to speculate, partly to conventionality, led to charges of complacency and conservatism. C. P. Scott, for example, felt that Asquith was too cautious to be a true Liberal, while Sir Alfred Mond spoke of him as "barred from greatness by . . . the lack of adventure." Asquith's "trenchant dialectic," wrote Harold Begbie, could not conceal the fact that he was "entirely without creative power . . . a cistern and not a fountain."[13]

On the other hand, Gardiner argued that while lacking initiative and inventiveness, Asquith was not hostile to novel concepts and methods:

> He is the constructive engineer of politics, not the seer of visions. He leaves the pioneering work to others. . . . No great cause will ever owe anything to him in inception, but when he is convinced of its justice and practicability, he will take it up with a quiet undemonstrative firmness.[14]

As Gardiner suggested, Asquith's intellectual caution must not be confused with timidity. His authorized biographers observed that in all his major decisions from early in his career, "the voice of caution was silenced, and his actions determined by a . . . touch of the gambler's temper." Margot Asquith concurred: "Though modest, he was arrogant, he never had any doubt that in the end his will would prevail. . . . Like myself, he admired those who live dangerously." Brailsford also spoke of Asquith's self-reliance and occasional arrogance, while Lloyd George called him a "natural optimist." Asquith's resoluteness may have been fostered by the unimpeded success of his career up to the First World War. Sir John Marriott suggested that possibly he would not have been so smugly self-confident if he had encountered more obstacles in his climb to the top, and went on to remark that fortune might not have deserted him so suddenly if his rise to power had been more arduous.[15]

As a result of his Balliol training and the atmosphere of the restricted circle within which he moved after reaching maturity, Asquith became something of a social and intellectual snob. Cameron Hazlehurst has made the point that Asquith's social exclusiveness-- partly attributable to his second wife's influence-- deeply conditioned his roles as prime minister and Liberal party leader. Ever critical of Margot Asquith, Lord Haldane regretted London Society's capture and "corruption" of her husband, and the resulting deteri- oration of his previously "serious" and "stern" outlook on life.[16] As one writer maintained, during Asquith's later career there was "a faint dilettantism about him, a faint want of earnestness, even in a crisis."[17] This trait is illustrated by one of the prime minister's ways of relieving strain and anxiety during the war: the translation of Kipling's poetry into classical Greek verse.[18]

Asquith was especially attracted to erudite aris- tocrats like Lord Curzon and well-bred men of affairs like John Morley, whose "charming manners and delight- ful talk, his spacious and discursive way of approach- ing even small things" were "after Asquith's own heart." Contrariwise, Asquith was repelled by aggres- sive public men like Lord Milner, whom he felt was "commonplace" and lacking in "flavour and fragrance";[19] businessmen-politicians like Bonar Law, whose "origin, his training, his equipment, his prejudices, his very appearance and outfit excited every antipathy in Mr. Asquith's mind";[20] and unconventional personalities like Theodore Roosevelt, whose "vehemence repelled the unexcitable Englishman" and for whose "mannerisms and his tendency to be sentimental and platitudinous" Asquith had "an instinctive dislike not far removed from contempt."[21] Asquith's near-loathing of profi- teering businessmen--if not the profit motive itself-- has been noted by his biographers.[22]

Asquith was harshly accused during the war, and even before, of lethargy and indolence. This alleged characteristic may have been more apparent than real, and certainly did not exist during his early career. Asquith's official biographers recorded that during his early days in Parliament he worked "colossally." The change in working habits seems to have followed his second marriage: "In later life this strenuous but effortless asceticism was relaxed, and [thereafter] he could not be reckoned, except when necessity called, an early riser." Spender and Asquith further called attention to their subject's "change of life" when they remarked that "until the age of about forty his frame was spare and his face pale, contrasting with the full habit of body and hale complexion with which the public later became familiar." (A later biographer, Roy Jenkins, deduced from photographs that the marked change in Asquith's appearance occurred when he was about fifty.)[23]

Even in later life, there is much evidence that Asquith's "laziness" was a myth resulting from misunderstanding of the man's working habits. Lord Beaverbrook's observation on Asquith's phenomenal retentive powers has been cited. Asquith's official biographers believed that the extreme rapidity and ease with which his mind worked left him considerable spare time that he could devote to personal interests, giving rise to the misconception that he was shirking his job. They concluded that his political career, especially during the eight and a half years of his prime ministership, was marked by such intellectual exertion and emotional tension that "his determination that what little leisure it allowed should be unmixed" was fully justified.[24]

A friendly journalist admitted that there was a definite strain of hedonism in Asquith's nature: "He hoarded neither life nor money, but spent both with a free hand and a great gusto of enjoyment."[25] Lord Vansittart, who as a rising Foreign Office official saw much of the Asquiths before and during the war, and Prince Lichnowsky, the prewar German ambassador, provided two vivid pictures of Asquith the epicure. Vansittart described Asquith as "hospitable, even matey after dinner . . . as the port ran its laps." Lichnowsky recalled Asquith as "a jovial bon viveur, fond of the ladies, especially the young and pretty ones, [and] partial to cheerful society and good cooking," whose "good health and excellent nerves had been steeled by devotion to the game of golf."[26]

Long golfing weekends and afternoon bridge games infuriated Asquith's wartime critics, but enabled the prime minister to unwind.[27] So did indulgence in spirits to the degree, according to General Haig, that "his legs were unsteady, but his head was quite clear." Asquith's heavy after-dinner drinking even before the war had more than once caused Winston Churchill and other colleagues to "squirm with embarrassment," but the prime minister was "serene, efficient, undisturbed" the next morning.[28]

Despite his conviviality, Asquith had few close male friends. Marie Belloc Lowndes, the Liberal hostess-novelist, believed that he had no intimate friends of the same intellectual caliber as himself.[29] This observation was made after the unhappy ending of his long intimacy with Haldane, identified by Asquith's official biographers as "possibly the closest" of his friends.[30] Edwin Montagu was said to have been the only male member of the next generation, outside Asquith's family, on anything like familiar terms with him, although Roy Jenkins has disclosed that Asquith was more interested in Montagu's young wife than in her husband.[31]

While, because of his impersonality and aloofness, few people were really close to him, and he was never a man to open his mind to others,[32] Asquith was the recipient of intense respect and loyalty from most of his associates. A magnanimous man who placed honor, integrity, frankness, and tolerance at the top of his scale of values, Asquith was generally appraised as being "straight," even by military men who did not ordinarily grant such a virtue to politicians.[33] Civil servants had the highest trust in his word.[34] He appreciated the special gifts of talented colleagues like Lloyd George and Churchill, and was pleased to see them recognized by others, even when his own qualities suffered by contrast.[35]

Asquith is represented by Mrs. Lowndes, a Society hostess who saw much of him, as being unable to feel malice or resentment.[36] If he had such sentiments he never verbalized them, and was angered by being told of ill feelings or plots against him.[37] There is no evidence that Asquith ever expressed antagonism toward a colleague on personal grounds. When he did show anger, which itself was quite rare, it was invariably over an objective issue of policy.[38] It has been suggested that Asquith's calmness was superficial and deceptive, and that beneath the surface he was sensitive and easily hurt.[39] One writer believed that Asquith's poor health in his last years due to arterial deterioration was the inevitable result of years of suppressed emotions.[40]

Asquith's record as prime minister has been the subject of much controversy, and numerous interpretations have been offered. Since his performance as head of peacetime and wartime governments produced such contrasting results, it has been customary to compare his behavior as a "peace minister" and a "war minister." An authority on the British prime ministership asserted that "it is not an exaggeration to say that Asquith was one of the most successful peace-time Premiers of this century." One of Asquith's biographers went farther, contending that before the war he was an even more successful head of government than Gladstone.[41]

W. L. Guttsman, comparing prominent figures in the British political elite in the early twentieth century, believed that the secret of Asquith's strength as prime minister was his ability to hold together a team of strong-willed personalities both as an efficient chairman and as arbiter between individual members. Lord Cecil of Chelwood, who served under Asquith in the first wartime coalition, testified that Asquith was "an excellent chairman, quick to understand any point raised, unfailingly courteous to all his colleagues, but apparently regarding it as no part of his duties to initiate solutions of any difficulty or make suggestions for a new departure of policy." Winston Churchill recalled that Asquith was habitually silent during cabinet discussions, summing up judicially after all views had been presented.[42] Any dynamism in the cabinet had to come from his colleagues, and with the wealth of human resources at his disposal there was no lack of it.

As prime minister, Asquith never forced events, but rather avoided a showdown, if possible, by postponement or compromise. When decision was absolutely necessary, he would move only after careful inquiry, weighing of evidence, consultation with experts, and tentative experimentation with alternative solutions.[43] After this painstaking preparation and biding of time that exasperated his more impetuous colleagues, he would decisively throw his weight in one direction or the other.[44] Once his decision was made, he would adhere to it unshakably. This behavior, while producing few serious mistakes during Asquith's peacetime government, tended to be uninspiring and brought charges from critics that the prime minister's decisions in the end were always forced upon him by circumstances and usually took the line of least resistance.[45] His defenders replied that Asquith's deliberation permitted him to reduce problems to the essential and the practical and to "dismiss the irrelevant and the inopportune."[46]

Powerful supporting evidence for the overall success of Asquith's leadership as a "peace minister" was his ability to surmount one major governmental crisis following another in swift succession for six years: the budget crisis, the quarrels over naval expenditures, reform of the House of Lords, the miners' strike of 1912, the Ulster revolt, and finally entrance into the First World War. Part of his success must be accredited to his extraordinary patience and his belief in the moderating influence of time. His implicit approach to crisis seemed to be to "let men talk, give them time to blow off steam and cool down, wait for a favourable wind and keep the atmosphere as far as possible dispassionate and minds open and accessible."[47]

This method of leadership seemed to be generally adequate to the demands of peacetime, but in war emergencies succeeded one another so unrelentingly that decisions had to be made with much greater speed and precision, and temporizing became not only inadvisable but dangerous. The pressure under which action had to be taken was increased tremendously, and delay and compromise ceased abruptly to be the virtues they once had been. Even Asquith's apologists believe that he was miscast as a wartime prime minister, although they are not prepared to dismiss him as a failure.[48] His detachment, his lack of initiative, his tendency to encourage lengthy investigation and discussion, and his proclivity to postpone decisions on urgent matters certainly impeded, even if they did not--as his enemies asserted--paralyze the war effort. Calm deliberation and dispassionate judgment were ill-suited to times requiring a willingness to assume risks and to try venturesome expendients offering a reasonable chance of success.[49] As Lord Cecil suggested with characteristic British understatement, "cabinet discussions under [Asquith] were models of propriety and decorum but a little wanting in that liveliness and resource necessary to cope with the prodigious difficulties with which we were faced."[50]

J. A. Spender wrote that "it may be assumed that any Prime Minister during the Great War was a predestined victim of the failure to achieve victory within the expected time," and went on to add that Asquith's character and methods made him a particularly easy victim. "He did not create the impression of being a visionary, dynamic leader," stated an historian of the Liberal party, but instead projected an image of "habitual fumbling and indecision."[51]

Asquith's impersonal, unemotional, purely cerebral

approach to public affairs had never endeared him to the masses. Lack of warmth and magnetism probably would have kept him from ever becoming a really popular figure, even if he had wanted to be one, but seeking public favor was always farthest from his mind. "It was not merely that he did not cultivate popularity; he disliked it, distrusted it and fled from it."[52] Asquith had "no sense of theatre,"[53] and abhorred "any kind of historical self vindication."[54] Already wavering in their attachment to the Liberal party, the public, after two unsuccessful years of war, demanded a national leader able to give them action, color, and the appearance of results. Lloyd George of course fulfilled this role. A bitter critic of the Welshman declared that although Asquith as war minister had done all that had to be done without "fuss," it took the "perpetual excitement" generated by Lloyd George to persuade the public that results were being achieved. Although the first part of this assertion may be challenged, there can be no doubt of the second. A journal not ordinarily friendly to Asquith aptly summed up his public relations problem during the war when it observed editorially on his death that "it is a disquieting commentary on the age of democracy that men combining dignity, reticence and judicial temperament seem unable to command . . . a following in times of public excitement."[55]

Spender observed that a prime minister of Asquith's reserved disposition needed an organized party with an active press behind it "to blow his trumpet and repel the attacks on him." Asquith had such a party and press in peacetime, but during the war a party truce was observed and the Liberal press, no longer bound by party discipline and loyalty, occasionally joined in the criticism of the government. Anyhow, the generally decorous Liberal press was overwhelmingly "outtrumpeted" by the shrill blasts of the "popular" newspapers. Gardiner remarked that Asquith "ignored the popular Press, hated its appeals to the passions of the mob and incurred its sleepless animosity."[56] While it is not strictly correct to say that Asquith ignored the newspapers--his handling of the controversy between Churchill and Lord Fisher in May 1915, for example, was probably influenced by fear of press reaction--Byrum Carter was close to the truth when he maintained that of all the twentieth century British prime ministers, Asquith had the least appreciation of the need to conciliate the press. The thought of deliberately trying to manipulate it for his own purposes does not seem to have entered his mind.[57] In the words of Gardiner again, Asquith "would as soon have thought of consulting his footman about policy as of making terms with the Northcliffes and Beaverbrooks of the Press."[58]

A prime minister who did not even read newspapers regularly, and who intensely disliked press interviews,[59] Asquith remained silent in the face of increasingly vociferous press attacks. He neither made any effort to approach his press critics personally, nor sent colleagues to try to influence them in his favor, nor even answered them directly. In reply to comment on his inaction, Asquith said that he preferred to leave matters up to "public judgment." But, since he made no response to his critics, the public had no way of knowing his side of the case. Carter believed that "Asquith's failure to attempt to gain press support is the most substantial demerit that must be placed against him in evaluating his effectiveness as a democratic leader."[60]

Although Asquith cannot be classed as a notably successful democratic leader, there is no doubt that as prime minister he had a unique ascendancy over the House of Commons based on integrity, intellect, and communicative skill. Brailsford contended that before the First World War Asquith enjoyed more real power over Parliament than any Liberal prime minister since Gladstone split the party over home rule in 1886.[61]

Since rhetoric was a major factor in establishing a reputation as a parliamentary leader in Britain, Asquith's oratory must have been effective, though opinions have differed on its quality and style. Carter made the standard assertion that the House of Commons preferred Asquith to Lloyd George as a debater, although the latter was far more powerful as a public speaker. On the other hand, Lord Samuel maintained without qualification that Asquith was "the most impressive speaker of his day." A recent writer suggested that in his maiden speech Asquith "assumed at once the authoritative tone of a front bencher," and ever after was "accepted . . . at his own valuation." Lloyd George thought that Asquith was less effective as a parliamentary speaker after his return to the House in 1920 than before 1918 because earlier he "had been accustomed to rise with a burst of applause from his supporters. Now there were but few cheers and he had to address a huge unfriendly mass of opponents."[62]

An expert on parliamentary speech observed that
Asquith's oratory, while it could not uplift or disturb
an audience, had great persuasive power. His appeal
was always moral and intellectual, never emotional.
This writer used the simile of Asquith as "an old Roman
senator composedly addressing the conscript fathers,"
an image frequently evoked by editorial writers and
cartoonists. More colorful is the picture of Asquith
the orator drawn by the cartoonist David Low, who described how "one could forget the matter of his speech
in fascination at the voice, suggestive of rich port
wine, issuing from the firm lips moistened with a ner-
vous recurring flick of the tongue, like a dignified
old lizard."[63]

Asquith's voice has been described as mellow and
resonant, harmonizing with his lofty manner and "long
trailing words," often of Latin derivation. [64] These
words were used with economy and precision, for "Asquith never used two words where one would do." [65]
Critics, however, felt that the superficial elegance
and carefully contrived balance of Asquith's speeches
barely concealed a poverty of ideas: "One might search
through his speeches from beginning to end without
coming across a real thought."[66]

It is difficult to locate Asquith's precise place
in the spectrum of opinion within the Liberal party of
his day. Steed's identification of Asquith as radical
in ideas, whig in temperament may be close to the mark
though oversimplified. [67] Asquith himself maintained
that he was just as good a radical as Lloyd George, [68]
and indeed the latter, writing as a correspondent for
Welsh newspapers in the early nineties, described
Asquith as "the hope of the rising generation of Radicals."[69] At that time Asquith must be considered
slightly left of center within the Liberal party, along
with R. B. Haldane, Edward Grey, Sydney Buxton, Arthur
Acland, and Thomas Ellis, all members of a group of
earnest young M.P.'s seeking to continue the social
reform program abandoned by the party leaders after the
secession of Joseph Chamberlain. Asquith was recognized as the leader of this ginger group, which from
1886 onward promoted advanced labor, housing, and educational legislation. [70] But after Asquith took office
as home secretary in 1892, although he effected various
progressive measures, at no time--any more than later
when he was prime minister--could he be considered a
pace-setter. At this time also he began to exhibit
certain definite conservative tendencies, especially in

his attitude toward organized labor.

Asquith's firm treatment of certain strikes while home secretary, and again while prime minister, was severely criticized by labor spokesmen. His authorized biographers contended that although Asquith sympathized with the strikers, many of whom he thought to be under- paid and overworked, he believed the first obligation of the government was to preserve order. This same attitude was shown during the General Strike of 1926, when Asquith's unreserved support of the Baldwin gov- ernment led to his final break with Lloyd George. In view of Asquith's temperament, training, and associa- tions, it was hardly surprising that, in Gardiner's words, "his mind revolted against revolutionary who would break violently with the past. . . . Liberalism meant to him the wise equilibrium between the forces of stagnation and the forces of convulsion."[71]

It was his Burkean emphasis on gradualism that clearly separated Asquith from Lloyd George and other true radicals. R. C. K. Ensor argued that the quarrel between Asquith and Lloyd George was simply a continu- ance of the ancient struggle between whig and radical in the Liberal party, and that the two men were intel- lectual reincarnations of Gladstone and Chamberlain.[72] However, this interpretation deemphasized the long and fruitful cooperation between the two, something that never had occurred in the case of the nineteenth cen- tury politicians.

Asquith's official biographers concurred, noting that until the First World War the combination of Asquith and Lloyd George, each compensating the other's deficiencies, seemed likely to dominate British poli- tics for many years. It was differences over war policies that proved to be the "ultimate tests" of the partnership, revealing temperamental differences that were "bound to clash." But "clashing" had occurred in mild form from time to time before the war, and had not resulted in a disruption of the combination. Something more was needed. As Lloyd George remarked wistfully to his and Asquith's mutual friend, Kathleen Scott Young, in 1923,

There had never really been any reason for the estrangement, only the fools around [Asquith]. . . . [Lloyd George] said it was a terrible pity, for he and Mr. Asquith were such excellent comple- ments to each other. "I could supply some things he has not, and, God knows! he could supply plenty of things I have not."[73]

The last dozen years of Asquith's life contrasted sharply and pathetically with the uninterrupted success of his earlier career. One disaster, personal or public, followed another: the death in the war of his oldest and most gifted son, his fall from power as prime minister, rejection in the "coupon election" by a constituency that had returned him for over thirty years, defeat--largely due to political animosity--for the chancellorship of Oxford, the humiliating Paisley upset of 1924 that ended his long tenure in the House of Commons, and--probably most embarrassing to As- quith--"the impoverishment which was the penalty of the sacrifice of a great professional career to the public service and of his own indifference to the calculations of self-interest."[74] It must have been galling to a man of Asquith's pride to have to depend on an annual income of £3500 from his millionaire friend, Lord Cowdray, during his last years.[75]

There was little of satisfaction for Asquith after 1916. The apparent revival of his fortunes indicated by his reelection to Parliament in 1920 soon was shown to be illusory. Asquith derived no personal gratifica- tion from his service in the postwar Parliaments, and was accorded nothing like the respect he had had before the war. In the early twenties, in the words of Lord Percy of Newcastle, "he seemed to have lapsed into the habit of almost consciously caricaturing his old parli- amentary manner--rather ludicrously so sometimes." "Altogether a somewhat querulous and very old, old man," C. P. Scott--six years older than Asquith--in- dited in his diary.[76]

Even Asquith's official biographers admitted that during the last decade of his life, his "mind was rarely 'extended'; there was a visible slackening, not so much of its fibre, as of the will to use it," accounted for partly by the strains and disappointments of politics, partly by the shock inflicted by the death of his son Raymond.[77] Yet Asquith to the end met such blows of fortune with dignity and fortitude.

A severe critic conceded that Asquith, "half a child and half a man of the world," was called upon to lead his party and to govern in exceptionally troubled times, whose problems were so difficult that any statesman would have been hard put to devise solutions.

In quieter times Asquith might have "drifted before the winds of prosperity and guided the country with skill and dignity in the same direction." But in the actual circumstances Asquith was too lacking in idealism and imagination to take the kind of bold liberal stand a man like Gladstone might have taken successfully, while at the same time devoid of the artfulness and daring that enabled "men like Disraeli and Bismarck [and Lloyd George?], with few ideals and no principles, to control events instead of being controlled by them."[78] Another writer, while prepared to grant that Asquith had been a quite acceptable "peace minister," believed that "the War was evidently beyond his real strength. . . . He had none of that mixture of drive, resourcefulness and demagogic power which the great conflict demanded of its statesmen."[79]

The final word, like the first, may be left to Lloyd George. Interviewed by the Manchester Guardian on his eightieth birthday, the Welshman declared of the man he had overthrown that he "was no War Minister. . . . He was not a man of action." Yet, "he was an extraordinarily able man, a man of the soundest judgment."[80] Thus the last great radical epitomized the last big whig.

LLOYD GEORGE: "THE GREAT GOD PAN"*

The only Welshman to be prime minister of Britain was described impressionistically, as she first saw him in 1911, by the sagacious woman who became his private secretary, confidant, mistress, and eventually second wife and countess:

> His image as I saw him then is graven on my mind: the sensitive face, with deep furrows between the eyes: the eyes themselves, in which were all knowledge of human nature, grave and gay almost simultaneously--which, when they scrutinised yours, convinced you that they understood all the workings of your heart and mind, sympathised with all your difficulties, set you in a place apart. The broad brow; the beautiful profile--straight nose, neat insolent chin, and a complexion as young and fresh as a child's. . . . But there was something more even than this which distinguished him from all other men I had ever met--from all whom I ever did meet thereafter--a magnetism which made my heart leap and swept aside my judgment, producing an excitement which seemed to permeate my entire being.[1]

Sir Geoffrey Shakespeare, a member of Lloyd George's secretariat during the postwar Coalition, remarked more prosaically that Lloyd George was quite short--only five and a half feet--but with a powerful frame and chest and a large head whose flowing mane of hair, white by then, gave him a distinguished, leonine appearance. But again the man's eyes most deeply impressed the observer: "They were blue and of remarkable depth. They looked right through you."[2]

The stocky, stubby-legged little man bore himself with assured, almost cocky self-confidence, yet did not appear bumptious or vulgar. To Sir Oswald Mosley, Lloyd George's "slight legs under the massive torso

---

*This essay is a revision of "David Lloyd George, 1863-1945: A Reassessment," published in the Duquesne Review, X (Fall 1965), 81-107. The copyright to the original article is the property of the Duquesne University Press.

surmounted by a magnificent head rather [suggested] the
great god Pan . . . at his best." It was this likeness, according to Mosley, that gave Lloyd George his
famous nickname, "the Goat," alluding to both his
sexual and political light-footedness.[3] To other,
censorious members of his generation, the dapper politician was the Bounder from Wales.

Well-groomed and careful of his appearance almost
to the point of vanity, Lloyd George--despite lifelong
hypochondria--enjoyed a robust physique and excellent
health until he was past eighty. At seventy-one, he
was described by a physician as having the "physical
and mental machinery" of a young man. Sir Geoffrey
Shakespeare believed that Lloyd George's strong constitution was one of the keys to his success in public
life, endowing him with unusual energy, powers of
application, and resistance to fatigue. The ability to
sleep at will, whether natural or acquired, was also an
important gift for a hyperactive politician, permitting
the Welshman to snatch cat naps during the day and
awaken refreshed, and to retire early without fear of
insomnia. As a result, Lloyd George "never seemed to
be bowed down by the strain of work or the press of
events. The more desperate the situation, the more
buoyant and resilient he became." Lloyd George himself
thought that his ability to doze in the middle of the
day was "one of [my] greatest blessings," enabling him
to surmount the "terrible strain" of the war.[4]

Lady Lloyd George claimed that "it was the alert
quality of L. G.'s brain that made him a leader of men;
and not only a leader but a driver." His ebullient
temperament and restless, penetrating mind made Lloyd
George the wonder and delight of some people, but the
bugbear of others. Lady Lloyd George remarked that
even those close to her husband found him "not an easy
person to live with," while those "who preferred an
easy life or had only a moderate amount of vitality
. . . were debilitated, even exhausted, by his presence." Shakespeare felt that much of the distrust
Lloyd George aroused was due to his exceptional mental
agility. "His very resourcefulness made him the object
of suspicion to the slow-witted or reactionary.[5]

Lloyd George's mental processes were intuitive and
imaginative rather than logical or deductive. "His eye
ranged ahead of the obvious," Winston Churchill declared in his eulogy to the dead statesman. "He was
always hunting in the field beyond." Similarly, Lady

Lloyd George compared her husband to an "expert chess player" who "could see and plan many moves ahead-- always aware of what his opponent would do under certain circumstances, knowing his reactions before even the man himself was aware of them."[6]

Reliance on impression, intuition, and imagination, combined with lightning comprehension, did little to encourage patience and accuracy. Many contemporaries noted Lloyd George's restlessness, intolerance of routine, and scorn of detail.[7] A prewar critic remarked of Lloyd George that "he imagines that imperfections are remedied if only they are not discovered." Writing several months before Lloyd George became prime minister, a sympathizer admitted his lack of "balance, restraint, accuracy or administrative capacity," but believed that these failings were more than outweighed by "courage . . . quick insight and enthusiasm."[8]

Impatience and indifference to detail did not, in Lloyd George's case, mean lack of industry or application. When a task interested or seemed important to him, he was indefatigable. He was "incapable of half-doing a job of work. If anything, he did it too thoroughly, as everyone around him knew to their cost." In sharp contrast to Asquith, his predecessor as prime minister, whom he criticized for becoming entangled in London Society, Lloyd George did not--at least before 1922--allow personal or social activities to interfere with his work as a politician. "His code was that the job was the thing. It came first, and personal considerations afterwards."[9]

Lloyd George's elder son, in an extremely frank and critical memoir, conceded his father's brilliance and energy but argued that he fell short of greatness because of a deficient sense of responsibility. Richard Lloyd George maintained that his father was reckless, capricious, and selfish, in large part because he had been spoiled in childhood by his over-solicitous mother and uncle. This indulgence in childhood may have contributed to Lloyd George's impetuosity, opportunism, ruthlessness, and autocratic tendencies as an adult. Giovanni Costigan summed up the Welsh statesman's grown-up personality as "infantile."[10]

References to Lloyd George's dictatorial behavior, both in and out of office, are numerous. An exposé published in 1913 accused him of seeking dictatorial power by popular vote and labeled him "an outstanding peril" to British political institutions. Sir Geoffrey Shakespeare admitted that Lloyd George rode roughshod over people who opposed or disagreed with him and was "quite ruthless in achieving his aim if he believed his cause was right." A discerning editor thought that Lloyd George failed as a political leader in normal times because his domineering temperament made it impossible for him to work with the "committee mind" characteristic of British politics. Much the same conclusion was reached by Shakespeare, who added that one reason why Lloyd George never acquired team spirit was that unlike most of his colleagues he had never attended an English public school. "His voracious appetite for personal power undermined the all-important trust of colleagues," wrote a Canadian political scientist. "He had dazzling wit and constant ingenuity, but the speed and uncertainty of his maneuvers aroused the fears of followers."[11]

What made Lloyd George exasperating to conventional British politicians was not so much his relentless drive, forcing aside human as well as material obstacles, as the devious methods he often employed to secure his objectives. One of the historians of the Liberal party has described the Welshman as "a compulsive, obsessive intriguer." Thomas Jones, Lloyd George's brain truster and biographer, believed that it was his "preference for circuitous methods" that most undermined confidence in him. According to Jones, Lloyd George was almost Borgia-like in his dependence on secretive, oblique, and disingenuous tactics.[12] It was, moreover, difficult to bind him to definite statements or promises, and he frequently "forgot" commitments he had made.[13] In seeking to explain and perhaps excuse his subject's dubious methods, Lloyd George's authorized biographer pointed out that he "was a Welshman with a Welshman's code . . . [whose] principle was to spare people's feelings and avoid putting them out of countenance; indeed, to bring a touch of artistry into social dealings."[14]

Lloyd George's "crookedness" naturally led to charges that he was wanting in principle. "He had no principles at all, only emotions," charged the Tory editor, Sir Colin Coote, who added that the Welshman was "the greatest cad who has ever been a great man." "Lloyd George was probably no more ambitious than many another politician," historian Michael Kinnear has written, "but whether he deserved it or not, he was widely regarded as a self-seeking plotter." Comparing him to Asquith, one political scientist evaluated Lloyd George as "essentially an opportunist, who had few fixed principles but infinite capacity for adapting to circumstances." "He has got the cunning of a monkey and the shrewdness of a bookmaker," gibed the novelist Edgar Wallace on one occasion.[15]

In contrast, Sir Dingle Foot contended that Lloyd George was capable of deep loyalty, but to causes rather than to individuals or organizations. The Welshman's essential integrity was similarly defended by his second wife when she declared that "once he gave his heart to a cause, he never failed it."

In his personal relations, Lloyd George mixed a unique combination of ruthlessness, cynicism, impudence, and charm. An "old and trusted colleague" told Marie Belloc Lowndes, the author and Liberal hostess, that he had never known a man with so poor an opinion of human nature as Lloyd George, who was "convinced that every man had his price, and that it was only a question of finding out what that price happened to be." On the other hand, Lord Beaverbrook testified that Lloyd George took a "lenient and charitable view of human frailties," while the Welshman's son referred to his "tenderheartedness" and "generosity," though these qualities occasionally were alloyed with "unconscious cruelty" and "meanness." Lloyd George's mistress thought that he was "much too sensitive for a man, much too tender-hearted," but again we learn that he could be "fearfully hard too."[16]

Most commentators on Lloyd George, even those doubtful of his morals, have attested to his warmheartedness and geniality. Malcolm Thomson observed that "people reared in Tory circles, accustomed to hear Lloyd George denounced as a tub-thumping scoundrel of the most repulsive kind, were amazed on meeting him to find a courteous, humorous and understanding person." A disenchanted journalist identified Lloyd George as "the pleasantest of the distinguished men I have met. I never for a moment supposed he was entirely sincere, but he was never pompous or patronizing or distant."[17]

Not everyone was captured by Lloyd George's spell. "There was . . . one type of person," wrote Thomson, "who never liked or trusted him--the cold, humourless doctrinaire." Lloyd George's irrepressible verve only made him more unpalatable to "these costive spirits, of

whom there were a number in the Liberal party." These
serious souls never ceased to question his competence,
morality, and propriety.[18] "His sense of fun sometimes
led him to the danger point, for the line between the
solemn and the ridiculous was for him very finely
drawn, and his comments at the gravest moments were
often unpublishable."[19] Harold Macmillan recalled that
it was often hard to persuade Lloyd George not to make
a gibe, even when it was bound to cause trouble. The
Welshman's effervescence and irreverance, according to
a perceptive social historian, may have handicapped him
with the English public, who tended to identify sober-
ness with statesmanship and perhaps doubted that Lloyd
George had the "gentlemanly" qualities needed by a
minister of the Crown.[20]

The reverse side of her husband's charm, according
to Lady Lloyd George, was "an insolence which endeared
him to those who were not the subjects of it." Sir
Geoffrey Shakespeare noted that Lloyd George's "favour-
ite method [of political attack] was to kill by ridicule; as no one likes to be ridiculed in public, he
left behind him much angry resentment, and the objects
of his attacks seldom forgave him." Derisive barbs
shot by the prime minister at Lord Curzon and other
Tory ministers were said by one commentator to have
helped bring down the coalition and precluded its ever
being reconstituted.[21]

Famed as a conversationalist and raconteur, Lloyd
George--unlike Winston Churchill--was always an atten-
tive listener, constantly alert for information or
ideas he could use for his own purposes. "His ideas,
plans, projects and visions came from and needed con-
tact with people," remarked Lord Swinton. "The greater
the stimulus from others the more fertile were his own
ideas." At his best in small, intimate gatherings, "he
made everyone feel that their own contribution to the
conversation was of intense interest and of exceptional
brilliance." The subjects of these conversations were
invariably politics and public affairs, of which Lloyd
George never tired and to which he was rather narrowly
restricted by the limitations of his education. Literature and the arts were almost entirely outside the
range of his knowledge and interest.[22]

Lloyd George was privately sensitive about the
deficiencies, both social and educational, of his lower
middle class background, but his envy of the privileged
was mixed with contempt for wellborn persons who mis-

94

used or did not take advantage of their opportunities. His dislike of snobbery and pomp was revealed again and again in his conversation and personal letters.[23] Lady Lloyd George wrote that her husband "to the end of his life was ill at ease and uncomfortable in the houses of the great. He shrank from their gatherings and their dinner-parties, avoiding them whenever possible." In a conversation with Tom Clarke in the early thirties, Lloyd George bitingly observed that "I was never one of them--the Eton-Balliol gang . . . like Grey, full of exclusive pomp of whiggery. . . . I did not like them and they did not like me . . . the vulgarian . . . the man of the people." There is no doubt that the "Eton-Balliol gang" never warmed to Lloyd George, in part because his background was alien and seemed inferior to theirs, in part because--as Malcolm Thomson put it--he was "an almost indecently clever little fellow . . . not altogether sound." Lord Haldane, himself only on the fringe of the "gang," connected these two sources of distrust and dislike when he once spoke of Lloyd George as "an illiterate with an unbalanced mind."[24]

As a cabinet minister and later as prime minister, Lloyd George was so different from the typical British career politician of his day that he seemed almost from another country. With his Welsh background, in a sense he was.

While serving as a subordinate minister in peacetime between 1905 and 1914, Lloyd George won public acclaim and the grudging respect of hostile colleagues for his powers as a negotiator and conciliator dealing with financial, business, labor, and other interest groups. The Welshman capitalized upon these skills during the early months of the war to obtain extraordinary concessions in the public interest from trade unions and manufacturers. Sir Geoffrey Shakespeare believed that both then and later when he had become prime minister, Lloyd George "was at his best presiding over a committee or receiving a deputation, in which conflicting views had to be reconciled."[25]

In communicating with such a group, Lloyd George did not treat it as a collective entity but addressed himself to each individual member, listening intently and sympathetically to each point of view and then volubly taking the offensive to develop a consensus or win over opponents to his own viewpoint. In the words of a civil servant who saw much of Lloyd George, he "dealt with his visitor as a snake charmer deals with a snake. He talked to him with many gestures, in his most genial and persuasive manner, hardly allowing [him] . . . to get a word in."[26] Lloyd George's open-mindedness and freedom from the prejudices and shibboleths of party orthodoxy, which at other times made him suspect, on these occasions facilitated his search for a common ground and made possible amicable and productive approaches to opponents and critics, many of whom came to him as enemies and left as friends.

Lloyd George's infinite capacity for hard work distinguished him from most of his associates in the prewar Liberal government, including Prime Minister Asquith, who felt that their social obligations imposed upon them a long weekend and "gentlemen's hours" in the office and the House of Commons during the week. During the war, it was Lloyd George's tireless devotion to his job that marked him off so sharply from Asquith and the rest of the "old gang." Every hour of the day was gainfully employed by Lloyd George, even meal times and recreation. The "political breakfast," attended by ministers, M.P.'s, and civil servants, was an invention of Lloyd George, and lunch and dinner also were used frequently to conduct business. The golf games which Lloyd George played solely for exercise--unlike Asquith, who took the game quite seriously--often were interrupted by impromptu discussions with fellow players. Weekends, devoted to sports, card games, and polite talk by Asquith and his friends, were filled by Lloyd George with conferences with cabinet colleagues, diplomats, administrators, experts, and sundry other figures in public life. Even holidays, which Lloyd George frequently cut short because he felt bored or out of touch with events, were monopolized by conversations about current affairs.

Like Asquith, Lloyd George had an unusually retentive memory which was invaluable to him in his profession, but he employed it in an altogether different way. A man who disliked reading except for pleasure, Lloyd George refused to work through the lengthy and complicated documents that were devoured by Asquith and instead obtained his information from oral interviews, discussions, and conversations. He was especially skilled in asking leading questions that would quickly get him to the root of the matter he was interested in. Unlike most ministers, Lloyd George was never satisfied merely to take the official views of civil servants, but invariably checked these against the positions of businessmen, labor leaders, journalists, economists, and others outside government who had special knowledge or who could speak with authority for an interest group. "He paid attention to the views of the humblest persons, which often irritated experts."[27] In this way he received many valuable suggestions and acquired a much wider perspective than the conventional government official.

After the war began in 1914, Lloyd George the troubleshooter and spark plug of the cabinet gave way to Lloyd George the human dynamo, who seemed at times to be conducting the war single-handed--and took great pains to convey this impression. It was now that Lloyd George's team spirit, never very strong, faced its sternest test, which ultimately it failed. Yet his very disassociation from the Asquith team, combined with his partly concocted reputation as a miracle-working minister of munitions, made Lloyd George the obvious alternative prime minister when Asquith seemed to falter:

> The backbenchers [of both major parties] . . . clung firmly to the belief that he was not one of the "Old Gang" under whom they had groaned for the first two years of the war. This was Lloyd George's decisive asset. . . . He was enough of a "rogue" to eclipse demagogues like Pemberton Billing and Horatio Bottomley.[28]

Once in the driver's seat, Lloyd George created the image of action and leadership that Asquith had failed to project. As his wartime adviser Thomas Jones remarked, Lloyd George "had the drive which stretched the powers of his Ministers and secretaries to the utmost and there was no question who was the central animating dynamo." To the sardonic Lord Esher, Lloyd George was "like a fire burning in the midst of a frozen world" of civil and military bureaucrats.[29] The apathy bordering on defeatism that had pervaded the Asquith government gave way to churning energy and inspired optimism.

The author of one of the most searching studies of the British prime ministership stated that experience has shown that a prime minister effective in peacetime is often an unsatisfactory wartime leader, and conversely.[30] Asquith and Lloyd George are the best modern examples. The dynamic, aggressive, impatient Lloyd George, tirelessly demanding results and furious at any delay or excuse, galvanized the government in war but encountered mounting opposition once the emergency was over. A partial return to the conciliatory methods effectively employed as a subordinate minister did not bring similar success to a prime minister who had exercised dictatorial power for several years, and in so doing had developed behavior patterns suggesting "incipient Caesarism."[31] The suave mediator had become increasingly arbitrary. The great experimenter, who in the wartime crisis had ruthlessly tried one expedient after another until he got what he wanted, seemed in peacetime to be merely impetuous and wavering. Lloyd George's "over-elasticity of mind" now became as much of a disadvantage as Asquith's phlegmatic calm had been six years earlier.[32] Finally, the man whose sharp contrast to the "old gang" had ensured his ascendancy to power now found this distinction a liability. The distrusted outsider was judged by the Establishment to be "expendable; and when the crisis was over, he was expended."[33]

It was said of Lloyd George that he was the first British prime minister who "instinctively understood the modern press" and used it to mold public opinion.[34] While still a subordinate minister, he had tried to create favorable press reactions to his personality and policies, cultivating Lord Northcliffe and other publishers and editors by giving their papers inside information. Northcliffe being the most powerful of the press lords, Lloyd George made a special effort to obtain his support, and they cooperated much of the time between 1909 and 1918.

However, Byrum Carter exaggerated when he spoke of Lloyd George and Northcliffe as "cordial friends."[35] The Northcliffe press's criticism of the government in the 1915 munitions controversy paved the way for the formation of the munitions ministry Lloyd George wanted, and his appointment to head it; and Northcliffe's relentless campaign against Asquith facilitated Lloyd George's succession to the prime ministership. But throughout this period both men had different long range objectives, and it is most likely that each always used the other strictly for his own ends. While they were working in harmony during most of Lloyd George's wartime administration, Northcliffe was given direct access to the prime minister's office and, according to Tom Clarke, then a Northcliffe editor, the publisher's staff could "ring up" Lloyd George at any time for the latest news.[36] But Northcliffe did not always grant Lloyd George's requests for aid--for example, he refused to help Lloyd George get rid of General Haig--and Lloyd George certainly never allowed Northcliffe to dictate policy to him, as the publisher tried to do several times. When Lloyd George was powerful and secure enough to dispense with Northcliffe, and the latter had become more of an embarrassment than a useful ally, he was promptly jettisoned.

The opportunism and questionable ethics of the Lloyd George-Northcliffe relationship were matched in many of Lloyd George's other press connections. Publishers, editors, and journalists were used as needed, sometimes rewarded with places on the honors list or even posts in the government, and cast aside when their usefulness was at an end. Whenever a significant policy demarche was in the offing, Lloyd George would negotiate with important publishers for their support, either personally or through emissaries. With the endorsement of a shifting group of powerful newspapers, and through them the approval of readers who looked to the papers for political guidance, Lloyd George was able to maintain a unique hold on public opinion without the backing of a party press such as earlier political leaders could always rely on.

Only somewhat less important in swaying the public than his command over the press was Lloyd George's oratorical talent. Byrum Carter rated Lloyd George as "the finest speaker of his day" as a public orator, but much less effective in the House of Commons. Opinions differed on Lloyd George's skill in parliamentary debate. He usually was considered inferior to Asquith, although Lord Beaverbrook asserted that "before his downfall [in 1922] he dominated the House of Commons. There was none to equal him." Sir Geoffrey Shakespeare maintained that Lloyd George's style was more suited to the platform than the House of Commons, but that he was a first class parliamentarian who "marshalled his arguments with great skill. . . . He knew instinctively how to concentrate on his strong points and how to gloss over his weak ones." Carter concluded that the House was always anxious to hear Lloyd George's colorful forays against his opponents, but did not hold him in the same high respect as speakers like Asquith or Sir John Simon who depended on logic and reasoned analysis: "Exaggeration, emphasis, and emotional appeal enabled him to capture a crowd, but the same glibness seemed to have displeased the House." Lloyd George's speeches in the House of Commons also may have been too colloquial for its taste. Sir Alfred Mond remarked in a letter in 1922 that it was a "pity that a man who can be so fine, spoils so many of his speeches by vulgarisms."[37]

On the platform, however, Lloyd George could not be surpassed. "Emotional, dramatic, rhetorical, and never too long, he was always the incomparable actor with a perfect sense of theatre."[38] Observers were struck by his "histrionic powers" and his "hands of an actor. In moving his arms or hands he could describe a whole scene and bring it to life."[39] "His face . . . was something between an incomparable drama and a high-class vaudeville act," recalled George Dangerfield. "Emotions chased themselves across it like wind across a rain puddle, breaking it up into a hundred images."[40] Lloyd George possessed a voice described by one writer as "seductive and vibrant," by another as "soft, rich and musical, and flexible in its range."[41] The most striking feature of Lloyd George's oratory was his use of descriptive imagery. He was said by one student of rhetoric to have "absolutely no equal" in the employment of "a boundless store of metaphors, similes and pictures."[42]

Like many professional orators, Lloyd George suffered from what a psychohistorian has called "perpetual stage fright." He both loved and feared speaking, and for days before a major address would be anxious and depressed. These symptoms disappeared almost as soon as he mounted the platform.[43] Although Lloyd George took infinite pains to construct his prepared speeches--absorbing himself in his subject by reading and talking about it and picking the brains of experts--if necessary he could abandon the verbatim draft which he had memorized and deliver a rousing extemporaneous talk. Hecklers were never a problem; few were willing to cross swords with a speaker so able and willing to use "exaggeration, ridicule and abuse to cut and smite opponents."[44]

Ever the shrewd operator, Lloyd George early in his ministerial career took the advice of his friend, the publisher Sir George Riddell, and reserved his most important speeches for Saturday afternoon. This ensured that they would be reported in three different groups of newspapers: Saturday evening, Sunday, and Monday morning.[45]

When a speech was a great success, producing a positive response from both audience and press, Lloyd

100

George was buoyed up for days afterwards. An unfriendly critic suggested that at such times the Welshman became infatuated with his own eloquence: "Such men as . . . Lloyd George . . . begin to feel for the cheers of their audience, sacrificing sense for applause, and, when they gain the cheers for which they have a drunkard's craving, convincing themselves they have displayed statesmanship."[46]

Much more than any other contemporary British politician, Lloyd George was free of binding commitments to party shibboleths. Although he always declared himself to be a Liberal, and never joined another party, he interpreted Liberal party doctrine as freely as possible throughout his career. His son tagged him as an eclectic who never hesitated to borrow novel ideas from the widest range of sources, whether they be British Labourites and Fabians, German and Swiss Social Democrats, or American New Dealers. Sir Robert Boothby remarked admiringly that Lloyd George was "never wedded to any of the quack nostrums which so often do service in purely party politics. He had a penchant for ad hoc solutions provided they would work."[47]

Lloyd George's independence of party discipline and disregard of standard Liberal tenets aroused the distrust of fellow Liberals from the start to the end of his political career. During the Liberal government of 1892-5, soon after he entered Parliament, he was suspected of plotting to organize Welsh Liberals into a Welsh nationalist faction modeled after the Irish Nationalists and utilizing similar obstructive tactics to press for Welsh autonomy. Lloyd George's defiance of the Liberal government in demanding action on purely Welsh issues was believed by many Liberals to have hastened its downfall.

Lloyd George's characteristic pragmatism led him early into close personal relations with Conservatives, and later Labourites, who might be willing to aid his plans. This lack of party exclusiveness, along with his open-mindedness on such fundamental Liberal doctrines as free trade, pacifism, and internationalism, led many progressive Conservatives to believe that he might be persuaded to join forces with them in support of a constructive program in the manner of his one-time hero, Joseph Chamberlain. From Lloyd George's friendly contacts with successive groups of "Tory democrats" emerged proposals for alliances in 1910, 1922-3, and 1935; while the actual Lloyd George-Conservative Coalition of 1916-22, although produced by the war crisis, could not have been formed, and could not have continued after the war, if Lloyd George had been a less flexible partisan. Labour party leaders were more guarded in their approaches to Lloyd George, but on at least three occasions--in 1926, 1930-1, and 1932--there were serious possibilities of an entente.[48]

Lloyd George's cavalier behavior within the Liberal party and his repeated feelers to politicians outside the party clearly show that he was never a party politician in the typical British sense. He never truly practiced, and perhaps never really understood, the duties and obligations of a party man. He used his status in the Liberal party, itself derived from his unique public reputation, to advance his own schemes, many of which were trumpeted forth in personal manifestoes without the prior approval, or even knowledge, of his party associates. The Welshman's political style, according to Kenneth Morgan, "was a mixture of Wesley and Rousseau, of the nonconformist conscience and the general will." This "un-British" behavior was compounded by Lloyd George's tendency after 1916 to regard himself as standing above parties as a national strong man. "Temperamentally and ideologically," John Campbell has written, "the image of the man above party suited Lloyd George only too well. . . . But it was fatally at odds with the British way of politics."[49]

Such conduct by a man who claimed to be, but rarely acted as, a legitimate party leader inevitably created a gulf between him and his colleagues, while simultaneously destroying the confidence of members of other parties interested in working with him but fearing his disruptive effects. It was this distrust, according to Leopold Amery, that prevented what might have been a useful understanding between Stanley Baldwin and Lloyd George in the mid-twenties to work for an imperial development program based on enlightened protectionism.[50]

Another reason why Lloyd George found it easy to work with members of other parties was the contradictory and fluctuating nature of his beliefs. The man who made common cause with Liberal and Labourite pacifists in the Boer War and nearly resigned from the government over British entry into the First World War was transformed into the pugnacious war leader demanding a "knock-out blow" against the enemy. Although Lloyd George never was a believer in peace at any price, in his early career he clearly opposed war as an instrument of national policy. By 1922, he had reached the point of intriguing for a war against Turkey as a strategem to unify the country behind his government.[51] The champion of international peace and the rights of small nations had become--at least temporarily--a bellicose nationalist.

Equally ambiguous were Lloyd George's opinions about economic systems and class rivalries. A ceaseless critic of private enterprise capitalism, whose outbursts against that system were frequently demagogic and at times incendiary, Lloyd George nevertheless would have no part of any program substituting some other basic form of economic organization. To A. J. Sylvester he once described the first Soviet Five Year Plan as "one of the most wonderful experiments the world has ever seen," but attributed its success to the "hardworking [Russian] people" since Communism was "not practical." His son maintained that in Lloyd George's case a distinction must be made between social rebel, which obviously he was, and social revolutionary, which he was not. In fact, said Richard Lloyd George, his father, while detesting social privilege, was essentially an institutionalist who once told him that he had "a respect--a reverence, you might say--for institutions of authority." Lloyd George explained to his son that his favorite historical character was Abraham Lincoln, because Lincoln had been both a champion of the oppressed and a deep respecter of his country's traditions and culture.[52]

W. S. Adams argued that Lloyd George, though prepared to use revolutionary language as a political weapon, was never anything other than a constructive reformer anxious to meet the legitimate demands of the working class in order to strengthen the nation and avoid social disturbance. Adams believed that Lloyd George probably all his life had smoldering visions of a great revolutionary upheaval, engendered by his childhood hatred of the privileged classes which he never entirely outgrew, but that in adulthood he quickly came to realize that this "cure" would be worse than the disease. Moreover, said Richard Lloyd George, his father was strongly attracted to revolutionary personalities--be they socialist agitators, Irish rebels, or fascist dictators--who, like himself, "could blaze a trail or make a loud individual noise." Probably it was this charisma that accounted for Hitler's fascination to the elderly Welshman, not delusion or senility

103

as Giovanni Costigan suggested.[53]

Until late in his career Lloyd George's radicalism carried conviction to the underprivileged and aroused fear and hostility among the possessing classes. But at the same time, the essentially conservative character of his actual reforms, especially the disappointing few enacted during his postwar premiership, proved to knowledgeable members of the Establishment that capitalism and property really had nothing to fear from him. Adams made the point that Lloyd George's demagogic speeches tended to increase in violence and revolutionary phraseology in inverse proportion to the benefits bestowed on the working class by the reforms he was sponsoring. Perhaps Winston Churchill was most nearly right when he protested to Lloyd George that "you are not against the social order, but against that part that gets in your way."[54]

This is not to say that Lloyd George's radicalism was a sham. Sir Robert Boothby was probably correct when he said that Lloyd George was governed all his life by two unchanging instincts: deep patriotism and hatred of oppression.[55] Lloyd George's patriotism, originally felt only for his native Wales, in time came to include Britain and the British Empire, until in the thirties he was almost as imperialistic as Churchill. His radicalism began as a loathing of the Anglo-Welsh landlord, but long after his hostility to England had faded away, "the landlord as an enemy remained firmly fixed in the 'myth' that sustained him emotionally."[56]

On the other hand, Lloyd George was not a leveler or egalitarian. Believing strongly in the destruction of vested privileges and the opening of opportunities to the masses, he also became convinced that the large corporation and the big businessman were essential to national economic progress. By the end of the First World War, Lloyd George had acquired the highest respect for "captains of industry," many of whom had served in his government, and went so far as to defend their right to large war profits.[57] Lloyd George "makes friends too easily with . . . Mammon . . . and sells some quality of his soul for political power," wrote Philip Gibbs, the war correspondent.[58] Yet this cordiality to the corporate rich did not prevent him from urging improved relations with Soviet Russia, from denouncing the mine owners and the role of the government in the 1926 General Strike, or from advocating government intervention in the economy when private

104

business could not cope with economic crisis. Tom Clarke held that Lloyd George's Liberalism rejected privilege and leveling together and was fundamentally a program of control over the anti-social impulses of both the few and the many.[59]

Lloyd George's radicalism was deeply rooted in the countryside, and he never fully understood the problems or the psychology of the urban workingman. Philip Snowden recognized this, and once remarked to Sir James Grigg that Lloyd George was a political anachronism because he would not cast off the "searing hatred" of his youth against the Welsh landlords and dispassionately view the needs of a modern industrial society.[60] Lloyd George's reaction to the urban working class was sympathetic but shallow. He was aware that the workers faced severe hardships but, not being a serious reader, was largely unacquainted with the standard literature of economics and sociology. The knowledge of urban and industrial conditions commanded by the Webbs and the Fabians was only vaguely grasped by Lloyd George, and such conditions were never personally experienced by him as they had been by city-bred Liberals like Charles Masterman and Herbert Samuel. Lloyd George apparently never read Marx, and his naive social philosophy seems to have been conditioned to a large extent by repeated reading of Victor Hugo's sentimental novel, Les Misérables.[61] His son speculated that Lloyd George's career as a social reformer may have had its birth when he tasted the sordidness of London slum life as a volunteer constable helping to search for the mass murderer, Jack the Ripper.[62]

Lloyd George's unfamiliarity with the details of social problems led him to oversimplify the answers to such problems and to display greater optimism about their solution than was realistic. This may partly account for the failure of his postwar administration's program of social reforms. Ever the pragmatist and man of common sense, Lloyd George scorned intellectuals-- "professor" was one of his favorite terms of contempt-- and except for his brief collaboration with the Liberal Summer School economists in the twenties, preferred the advice of "hard-headed" businessmen and financiers. He took an equally dim view of most leaders of the labor movement, excepting only a few skilled politicians like Philip Snowden and J. H. Thomas. Lloyd George's impatience with trade union leaders may be partly explained by the imperviousness of many of them to either his charm in negotiation or his demagoguery on the platform.

105

One of Lloyd George's detractors, writing in 1913, made what was then a bold prediction:

> Mr. George will never again be anything but a private Member of Parliament--always picturesque but generally a nuisance--if only the nation will quickly take stock of his methods.[63]

Nine more years of cabinet service, six of them at its head, elapsed before this prophecy became fact, but it is a valid description of Lloyd George's role in public life after 1922. For over twenty-two years he sat in the house of Commons without holding office, part of the time as leader of a faction-ridden party, the rest as a kind of political ghost, evoking vivid memories of his years of authority but never again entrusted with the tools of power. It is generally acknowledged that Lloyd George went into decline sometime after 1922, but there is no agreement on the cause. Sir Alfred Davies, a Welsh civil servant, wrote that

> a friend of mine, who, like myself, knew [Lloyd George] well, and served him and the nation in highly responsible office during the First World War, dated the deterioration in character and morals--which, by common consent, marked the last two decades of his life--as beginning about the year 1925.[64]

Richard Lloyd George emphatically asserted that his father's principal trouble after--and even before-- leaving office was a series of "extramarital relations with young women" which made him "a rather pathetic and foolish figure." As a result of his "pursuit of the sensual," Lloyd George became bored, querulous, and "morbidly preoccupied with himself." Lord Beaverbrook confirmed that Lloyd George's "increasingly bad temper" and growing tendency to carp at his associates and adversaries were among the reasons for his eclipse in the twenties and thirties. Lloyd George's son added that his father, once so eager to sound out all ranges of opinion, became so intolerant of criticism that "he deliberately surrounded himself with those who were content to nod their heads with the predictable regularity of rockinghorses." The indomitable man of action, whom Asquith's procrastination had driven to fury, now found excuses and rationalizations for not making a greater effort in politics. When his children reminded him of his obligations as a statesman, he replied that he had had enough of the burdens of office and deserved a rest.[65]

Rich from the sale of his books and syndicated newspaper articles, and increasingly preoccupied with the maintenance of his country estate, Lloyd George perhaps had become too comfortable to be a vigorous politician. "He was content to vegetate in luxury, surrounded by bevies of female retainers." These women friends finally drove his faithful and long-suffering wife--who as staunch supporter and shrewd, sympathetic critic had been invaluable to Lloyd George in his earlier career--to quietly separate from him and live apart in Wales. For the better part of two decades Lloyd George lived a kind of double life, with an official family in Wales and a ménage in Surrey which his son Richard compared to an "Eastern harem."[66]

Distracted by the pressures of "sycophants, fools, flatterers, [and] scheming women, so that important affairs began to get out of focus,"[67] Lloyd George was "like a powerful motor which is thrown out of gear, 'races,' and may cause and suffer damage."[68] A social historian observed that the cartoonist David Low, who before 1922 had drawn Lloyd George as a "fiery, inspired, active leader," in the late twenties and thirties depicted him "as a little old woman wearing absurd hats, a ridiculous figure of fun without power."[69]

Other commentators have placed much of the blame for the deterioration of his political fortune on his notorious "party fund" amassed during the Coalition. Thomas Jones remarked pointedly that Lloyd George "commanded advertising experts, special trains, packed halls, responsive newspapers. He piped and the audience danced, but they did not vote for him."[70]

After 1931, when he resigned as leader of the Liberal party, Lloyd George began to pour the income from his writings into his Surrey estate and to give more attention to agriculture than to politics. Although, according to Lord Beaverbrook, the project was never really a success--Lloyd George apparently having no more talent for managing his own farm than he had for managing the factious Liberal party--he was "endlessly interested" in new farming methods.[71] Thomas Jones portrayed him as he appeared in the mid-thirties:

Carefully dressed in homespun, his white locks falling on his flowing cloak, pet dogs at his heels, he delighted to walk his guests over the "blossoming desert," to expatiate on his experiments with this apple or that raspberry, and to argue from his particular demonstration plot to its possible imitation all over the country.[72]

The picture of the aging Lloyd George as a rusticating pseudo-squire, almost a caricature of the Tory landlords he had damned as a young agitator, was but one aspect of the truth. He continued to maintain an active interest in all current events and commented on them acidulously in speeches in and outside Parliament, interviews in the British press, and articles in foreign, especially American, papers--being paid huge sums for the last. Lloyd George's articles in the foreign press were generally critical of the government in power, were widely denounced as mischievous and even disloyal, and were sometimes cited in Parliament as damaging to the national interest. Thomas Jones admitted that Lloyd George's writings at times were dashed off too rapidly to acquire perspective, but maintained that in general they were "acute and fearless." Sir Robert Boothby justified Lloyd George's occasional extravagences in speech and writing while out of power as natural reactions "when a great man sees the main achievements of his life in increasing jeopardy."[73]

Lloyd George's extraordinary career, second only to Disraeli's among British prime ministers in defying convention and normality, will always fascinate and puzzle historians. Was he an inspired statesman or a self-seeking charlatan, or--most likely--some compound of both? C. L. Mowat was misled when he stated that the Welshman "was the sort of man people admired or loathed; there were no half measures . . . in people's opinion of him." It was the very paradoxicalness of Lloyd George's character, methods, and objectives that made him so irritating to many informed people. They could never decide whether he was a brilliant innovator or a half-educated tinkerer, a dynamic crusader or a brazen demagogue, an honest man or a rogue--because he was all these things at one time or another. "He is extra-many sided," wrote Thelma Cazalet-Keir, "and that is why the average person who is only two- or three-sided finds it hard to understand [him]." The perplexity Lloyd George created in the minds of respectable British men of affairs is amusingly suggested by this quotation of Stephen Spender speaking of his uncle, J. Alfred Spender, the Liberal journalist:

> When my uncle . . . talked about Lloyd George, I began to wonder whether that statesman was not a demonic spirit nurtured within the soul of the Liberals, like the frightful nightmare of some maiden aunt. My uncle would tell how this terrible man whose real name was not Lloyd George at all but just plain George, who had not been to Balliol and knew no Latin or Greek, had by a series of betrayals gained the most powerful position in the Liberal party and then destroyed it. . . . George, he said, could never understand the arguments for and against Free Trade, and had to be coached in these whenever he made a speech defending this bastion of Liberal policy. When George was first in Liberal Party or Coalition Cabinets, the Asquithians would keep him in his place by quoting Homer and Vergil at him. But George, when he became prime minister, took revenge by holding up Cabinet meetings while he quoted verses from the Welsh bards "in a language which no civilized person has ever understood or wanted to understand," my uncle would exclaim ferociously.[74]

Yet this same J. Alfred Spender made many generous references in his writings to Lloyd George as a capable and constructive Liberal politician--when held in restraint by Balliol men, of course. Mowat was closer to the truth when he said of Lloyd George that "he was a genius with a double-dose of everything, good and bad; he could do as well with his left hand as with his right." Lord Milner took note of the ambiguities in Lloyd George's makeup when he declared at a private dinner just before the 1918 armistice that the prime minister's "methods are dubious, and his manners are often intolerable, but he has a genius and an insight and an absolutely amazing courage, which place him, in my opinion, high among the great rulers of our race."[75]

W. J. Brown, a Labour M.P. who knew and was intrigued by Lloyd George, believed that the latter's career was made possible by the coincidence of the man and the moment. The early twentieth century in Britain was a period when political democracy had been substantially achieved, but social and economic democracy were far from attained and there was still no strong political party that really could be counted as democratic.

Lloyd George, as a self-made demagogue of exceptional talent, was in a position to exploit the no longer suppressible working class demands for social reform and to serve the Liberal party elite by channeling these demands along acceptable paths. There was both sincerity and self-interest in Lloyd George's designs. He "made himself the mouthpiece of the deep and strong yearning of the poor for security and social justice." At no other time would Lloyd George's particular personal qualities have been politically effective, Brown argued. By 1922, circumstances had changed. The Liberal party was no longer the party of change, but had been supplanted on the left by a Labour party that could claim to be truly democratic and representative of the working class. Lloyd George, who might successfully have fought Labour for the support of the mass electorate if the times had been normal and if he had been in full control of the Liberal party, had blurred his position as a spokesman of the poor by his wartime and postwar association with the Conservatives. Lacking a strong party behind him and no longer trusted by the workingman voter, Lloyd George was written off by the public. He had been bypassed by history.[76]

Thomas Jones also believed that "personal success depends upon a fortunate conjunction of public events and personal qualities," and that while "Lloyd George turned many events into opportunities for his own advancement . . . there were other events 'in the nature of things' which defied him," notably the eclipse of the Liberal party which, according to Jones, "was proceeding apart from anything he could do to hasten or delay the process."[77]

While Jones's conclusion about the fate of the Liberal party has been debated, there is no doubt that he was right when he stated in the same passage that "Liberalism was being dissolved from the right by Baldwin." Numerous writers have lamented the failure of Lloyd George to reconstruct the Liberal party or, alternatively, to combine his talents with those of Stanley Baldwin in a fusion party or a coalition. Leopold Amery, as noted above, regretted the inability of Lloyd George and Baldwin to unite in support of a bold movement for imperial reconstruction based on preferential tariffs. Sir Robert Boothby was convinced that with Baldwin beside him to manage the internal affairs of a fused Liberal-Conservative party, Lloyd George could have shared a partnership as successful as the one he had had with Asquith before the war and with

110

Bonar Law during it. The complacency of the twenties
and the appeasement of the thirties never would have
been tolerated with Lloyd George at the head of the
government.[78]

Tom Clarke thought that Lloyd George "could have
saved at least the label for Liberalism" and kept a
vigorous third party in existence during the thirties
to act as a goad to the Conservatives and a brake on
Labour if he had been given the chance by Baldwin and
other party leaders. Clarke believed that Lloyd
George's opponents acknowledged the usefulness of such
a party, but found it impossible to trust Lloyd George.
There was no one else with the necessary ability,
energy, and demagogic skill to lead it. Lloyd George
was the only Liberal of his day "with the supreme
qualities of imagination, drive, and leadership. He
had the 'common touch,' the essential . . . crowd
magnetism. He was warm. The others were cold."[79]

Bitterly disappointed over his father's failings,
both moral and political, Richard Lloyd George still
believed that he was the only leader of his day with
the ability and--possibly more important--the "enormous
personal prestige with all classes" needed to solve the
critical social and economic problems of the postwar
years. Only Lloyd George could have won over to support of expensive reforms the financiers and businessmen who admired him for averting a financial panic at
the beginning of the First World War and for his
masterful organization of munitions and shipping during
the war.[80]

All such ambitions were of course beyond his
power, largely because he had neglected the advice
given him early in his career by another frustrated
political rebel: "Take care always to have the Party
machine behind you. Nothing can be accomplished
without this."[81] By splitting with Asquith in 1916,
Lloyd George cut himself off from the party machine,
with its liabilities but also, in the British political
system, its indispensable advantages.

LLOYD GEORGE'S LUCRE: THE NATIONAL LIBERAL FUND*

One of the more controversial features of the turbulent career of David Lloyd George was the political fund which he raised during his Coalition government of 1916-22, and subsequently used to maintain a personal political headquarters and support a variety of political and semipolitical activities. The magnitude of this fund, and the munificence with which Lloyd George doled it out at his pleasure, won for him during the twenties the questionable distinction of being the "Monte Cristo of party finance."[1] The scandal-tainted origins of the fund, one of the perennial topics of London political gossip in the interwar years, led a former ministerial colleague of the ex-prime minister to label him as "the shepherd of the Liberal party—and its crook."[2]

Much of the internal bickering that weakened the Liberal party during the twenties was roused by Lloyd George's possession of this fund, and his unwillingness to turn over the capital to the party treasury. Although the Lloyd George Fund was used almost entirely for nonpersonal objectives, such as the employment of a large office staff, the financing of elaborate policy studies, and the underwriting of nationwide political campaigns, it was an endless source of suspicion and criticism of Lloyd George by members of all parties.

I

The Lloyd George Fund was raised in much the same way as earlier, and later, funds of the official Liberal and Conservative parties. In the pre-1914 Liberal party, fund raising was one of the responsibilities of the chief whip, who headed the Liberal Central Association, the national party headquarters. Aided by his junior whips, by the permanent secretary of the National Liberal Federation, by Liberal peers, and by past

---

*This essay is a revision of "The Lloyd George Political Fund," published in Research Studies, XXXV (September 1967), 198-219. The copyright to the original article is the property of Washington State University.

and present Liberal Members of Parliament, the chief whip raised the money needed to conduct election campaigns and cover other party expenses. He did so informally and unsystematically, and--subject to the veto of the party leader--disbursed the money at his discretion. The Liberal party leader rarely had any direct connection with raising party funds, and usually knew little about their precise origins. Neither did most other ranking members of the party hierarchy, and indeed the top Liberals often preferred to remain ignorant of the occasionally sordid task of soliciting funds.[3]

Not all Liberal funds passed through the chief whip's office. For example, in 1891 Francis Schnadhorst, the inscrutable secretary of the National Liberal Federation, pocketed a £5,000 political gift from Cecil Rhodes and made no accounting of it to the chief whip. Similarly, Lewis Harcourt, son of a former party leader and himself a future cabinet minister, in 1903 received a donation of £10,000 from the South African millionaire, Joseph B. Robinson (who would figure later in the Lloyd George honors scandal of 1922). Instead of turning this money over to Chief Whip Herbert Gladstone, as the latter requested, Harcourt allocated it among various Liberal party organizations and affiliates of his own choice.[4]

Like the Conservaties, the prewar Liberals had large and mysterious contributions furnished by an assortment of powerful business interests and wealthy individuals seeking favors or good will from a present or prospective Liberal government, or recognition for public or political services in the form of a peerage, baronetcy, knighthood, or decoration. The granting of honors for helping the government to carry on by financial support of the party in power, or hopefully soon to be in power, had been a legitimate feature of party government for over two hundred years. It was when this customary method of party fund raising seemed to be abused, or drew political attention to itself, that talk arose of a "sale of honors."[5]

On several occasions before 1914 Liberal party officials came under heavy attack for egregious grants of honors. In 1894, as rumors of sordid deals circulated, Sir Wilfrid Lawson, a radical Liberal M.P., moved unsuccessfully that future announcement of honors must be accompanied by reasons for the awards. The following year a major scandal broke when the outgoing

114

Rosebery administration awarded two peerages and a baronetcy for questionable services, financial and electoral, to the Liberal party. The recommendation in 1909 of the exclusive Order of the Knights of St. Patrick for Lord Pirrie, a Belfast industrialist contributing to Liberal funds, brought down the wrath of King Edward VII upon Asquith's government.[6]

A proposal of honors for deserving Liberal journalists--initiated by Winston Churchill in 1912--was turned down by Prime Minister Asquith, partly, some said, because of attacks by radical editors upon the Liberal party's patronage system. "What would be the state of the Liberal party chest," the Manchester Guardian had asked rhetorically in 1910, "if it depended on the voluntary subscriptions of the rank and file?" H. W. Massingham of the Nation denounced "the Achilles' heel of Liberalism, which is the secret Party Fund," putting him in the same camp with ex-Lord Chancellor Loreburn, whose opinion was that the Liberal party organization was "kept going solely by the sale of honours."[7] Another source of radical criticism of the Asquith government was the excessive number of junior ministerial posts given to big contributors of party funds or their relatives.[8] Arthur Ponsonby, a former private secretary to Prime Minister Campbell-Bannerman, who would later secede to the Labour party, wanted the 1913 manifesto of his proposed Radical Group of M.P.'s to include a "condemnation of all 'Honours.'"[9]

To a greater degree than the Conservatives, the Liberals were liable to charges of "selling" honors because they were forced to extract the funds needed to conduct propaganda and elections from a diminishing number of rich men. Not only Gladstone's endorsement of Irish home rule but Liberal promotion of innovative measures generally induced hundreds of wealthy landlords and businessmen to cross over to the Conservative side. The Liberal party, which after the Conservative split over free trade in the 1840s had been more affluent than its rival, had become markedly poorer by 1900. According to one estimate, only 27 percent of the Liberal members of Parliament in 1906 were men of great wealth, compared to 35 percent of the Conservatives.[10] Most of the Liberal war chest for the crucial 1906 election was contributed by twenty-seven rich men, the majority of them North of England industrialists.[11] Many wealthy men continued to be Liberals, and some would do so long after the party's fortunes had collapsed. As late as the 1935 election, the presence of "very rich Quakers and Jews" in the Liberal party would be noted. But from the 1880s, special inducements such as honors had to be used increasingly to raise Liberal funds.[12] This partly explains why scrupulous Liberal fund raisers such as Lord Gladstone and Sir Robert Hudson were accutely sensitive to charges of exploiting honors, and would react so severely to the Lloyd George Fund.

II

The Lloyd George Fund began to be accumulated soon after Lloyd George succeeded H. H. Asquith as prime minister in December 1916. Since Lloyd George was now persona non grata with the official Liberal party, he no longer had access to its party funds. Nor was he prepared to turn over donations made to him or his Liberal associates to either the Liberal party fund or the fund of the Conservative party, his partner in the new Coalition. It was therefore agreed by Lloyd George and Bonar Law, the leader of the Conservative party, that any political contribution made to Lloyd George, to the whips of his Coalition Liberal parliamentary group, or to any other member of his Liberal faction would be kept by the Coalition Liberals, while all donations made directly to the Conservative party organization would be retained by it. The granting of honors was to be done by Lloyd George and Bonar Law jointly, from nominations submitted by their respective chief whips. Such nominations would be based to a large degree on contributions to the political funds, in the traditional fashion, but--in theory at least--neither Lloyd George nor Bonar Law would know precisely who had contributed, or how much, and would make their final choices on relative merit. They would function in exactly the same way as previous prime ministers, except that decisions on honors would be joint instead of individual.[13]

The systematic collection of Coalition Liberal funds started about March 1917, when Frederick Guest succeeded Neil Primrose as Coalition Liberal chief whip. Guest, a cousin of Winston Churchill, has been described as a "genial playboy" who displayed remarkable skill in negotiating delicate political deals.[14] One of Guest's duties was to prepare a campaign war chest for the Coalition Liberal M.P.'s in the event

116

that the Conservatives should abandon the Coalition and force an election. The "touting" of honors by the Coalition Liberal whips was so vigorous during the spring of 1917 that a body of Conservative privy councillors addressed a letter of complaint to the prime minister on March 25. Under the leadership of Lords Halsbury, Selborne, and Salisbury, right wing Conservatives, an admonitory resolution was piloted through the House of Lords in August 1917. Like the abortive Lawson resolution of 1894, this one requested the prime minister to state publicly the reason for conferring each honor, but it went on to insist that he "satisfy himself" that there was no direct connection between awards of honors and political contributions.[15] The slight extent to which this resolution was obeyed is indicated by the fact that the Coalition Liberals, having broken with the official Liberal party before the 1918 election, were able to field some 150 candidates in the election with funds acquired during the preceding two years.

Once the split with the Asquithian Liberals had become final, the Coalition Liberals had to intensify their fund raising activities to support their separate party. The staff of the chief whip's office was expanded to include several additional junior whips and a large number of itinerant agents whose sole job was to negotiate donations in return for honors. Among the most successful of these "touts" was Sir William Sutherland, M.P., whose sales territory was London's "clubland." Another was the mysterious Arthur Maundy Gregory, a former private detective and secret service agent who catered specially to war profiteers. Gregory, later employed by the Conservatives and said to canvass for Papal honors as well, posed as a newspaper publisher and operated from a lavishly furnished suite of offices near Parliament Square. Easily the most disreputable of the several Lloyd George honors brokers who grew wealthy from their agent's commissions, Gregory came into possession of numerous shady secrets that enabled him to wield considerable influence behind the political scene before his prosecution for fraud, conviction, and bankruptcy in 1933-4.[16]

The details of these deals were left to the brokers and were not inquired into too closely by either the Coalition Liberal chief whip or the prime minister, although the former, at least, must have been wise to who was giving what. On one occasion in 1919 Guest wrote to Lloyd George hoping that the prime minister would "rely to a certain extent on my discretion" in accepting the enclosed honors list. A year later the chief whip warned his superior to "burn as soon as read" his annotated list of recommendations for King's Birthday Honors, adding that he was making "a tremendous effort" to persuade people to contribute to the Coalition Liberal fund and some of the donors were on the list. As one hostile critic later observed, "it is always easier to disavow what one has not been told,"[17] but this was no different from the practices of earlier party leaders. The principal distinctions between the Lloyd George Fund and previous political funds were the vastly greater sources of wealth to be tapped as a result of wartime profits, the unprecedented greed of middle class war profiteers for titles and decorations, and the adroitness of the Coalition Liberal honors brokers in pandering to this cupidity. These were distinctions of degree, not kind.

The use of honors by the Coalition whips, both Liberal and Conservative, to build up their party funds during this exceptionally lucrative period is substantiated not only by the considerable increase in the number of honors awarded by the Lloyd George Coalition in comparison with previous governments, but by a change in the backgrounds of the recipients. Whereas the Asquith Liberal and Coalition governments had created on the average eleven peers a year, the Lloyd George Coalition created fifteen. The average annual creation of baronetcies rose from twenty under Asquith to forty-three under Lloyd George. There was an even greater increase in the average annual conferments of knighthoods and decorations.[18] The number of honors at the prime minister's dispensation was considerably augmented by the establishment in the summer of 1917 of the Order of the British Empire and the Companionship of Honor. The O.B.E., of which over 25,000 were awarded during the Lloyd George era, was burlesqued in the music halls as the "Order of the Bad Egg."[19]

The possibility that the marked upswing in the average annual grant of honors was due to the rewarding of distinguished servicemen and public servants for wartime accomplishments was disposed of when the vocations of the new peers, baronets, and knights were scrutinized. A controversial article by Harold Laski claimed that the percentage of peerages bestowed on businessmen and newspapermen (principally newspaper proprietors, managers, and shareholders) rocketed from 21 percent during Asquith's prime ministership to 49 percent during Lloyd George's. The increase in the proportion of baronetcies granted to businessmen and newspapermen was reported to be comparatively slight (74 percent to 78 percent), but the share of knight-hoods to have risen from 25 percent to 40 percent. The proportions of the three classes awarded for public services, including military and naval distinction, were said to have dropped, respectively, from 79 per-cent to 51 percent, 26 percent to 22 percent and 75 percent to 60 percent.[20]

The awarding of honors to newspapermen in unex-ampled numbers was a much-discussed and criticized practice of the Lloyd George government, complained of as early as 1917 by King George V and denounced in a famous speech to the House of Lords by the "die-hard" Conservative Duke of Northumberland during the honors scandal debate of 1922. Exposés of this practice in the rightist National Review showed that few newspaper proprietors friendly to the Coalition escaped this kind of recognition. Not only did such cronies of Lloyd George as Aitken (Lord Beaverbrook), Dalziel, and Rid-dell, previously un-coronetted, receive the ermine, but many already ennobled newspaper owners--for example, Northcliffe and Rothermere--were given a boost upward in the peerage. Numerous proprietors of important and sympathetic provincial papers received baronetcies and knighthoods.[21] These newspapermen were rewarded less for their gifts to party funds than for their editorial support of the government, but as men of wealth some of them undoubtedly made such gifts.

Although both the Liberal and Conservative sec-tions of the postwar Coalition did very well from the traffic in honors, the Coalition Liberal brokers were much the better salesmen, persuading even inveterate Conservatives to contribute to the Lloyd George Fund. The Coalition Liberal agents were also less scrupulous than their Conservative counterparts, promising honors to unsavory types at whom the Tory whips gagged. Early in 1921, the chairman of the Conservative Party Organi-zation complained to Bonar Law of "poaching" by the Coalition Liberal whips, and referred to a baronetcy granted to a "fellow [who] at the most critical stage of the War was discovered to be hoarding huge quanti-ties of food, and they had him up and fined him near-ly £1000."[22] The Lloyd George whips were said to have a standard tariff of rates for various classes of hon-ors: £12,000-£15,000 for a knighthood, £25,000-£35,000 for a baronetcy, and £40,000-£50,000 for a barony, with the proviso that genuine merit would re-

119

duce the price.[23] According to a Tory journalist
attacking the Lloyd George Fund in the late twenties,
"the old system of credit [was] as nearly as possible
abolished and cash on a spot basis substituted."[24]
There was evidence of collusion between the Coalition
Liberal whips and the senile treasurer of the Conservative Party Organization, Lord Farquhar, in which large
sums of money contributed to the Conservative fund were
secretly diverted into the Lloyd George Fund, possibly
in return for money gifts to the nearly-bankrupt Farquhar and successive promotions in the peerage.[25]

The deterioration in the quality of Lloyd George's
honors recipients, the disproportionate number of honors given to Coalition Liberals, and the unseemly manner in which the awards were made finally became intolerable to members of the "die-hard" wing of the Conservative party, who already were at odds with the prime
minister over Ireland and other questions. At various
times during 1921, the issue was raised in the House of
Lords by many of the same peers who had first complained in 1917. In the House of Commons it was kept
alive by Sir Henry Page Croft, a Tory of the far right
who had campaigned against misuse of honors in the 1918
election.[26] Rightist pressure was also brought to bear
upon the Conservative Central Office, to the dismay of
party officials already at loggerheads with their Coalition Liberal colleagues.[27] When three of the five
peerages to be granted in the King's Birthday Honors
List of June 1922 were found to be bestowed on very
rich men of questionable reputation--one of whom, Sir
Joseph Robinson, the South African mining speculator,
had recently been implicated in frauds--the "honors
scandal" burst into the open. As the king expressed
his "profound concern," a heated debate arose in both
houses of Parliament.[28]

The discussion in the House of Lords was especially frank. The Duke of Northumberland charged that,
while Conservative party funds languished, the Coalition Liberals had amassed over 1,000,000 since 1917,
and that in the same period scores of newspapers had
been "bought" by the government through grants of honors to strategically placed newspapermen. Lords Salisbury, Lansdowne, Carson, and Selborne were among the
other right wing Conservative peers who joined in the
attack on what Salisbury called the "swindling" tactics
of the prime minister's Coalition Liberal agents. (It
was even suggested the Lloyd George was sabotaging the
House of Lords by selling peerages to scoundrels.)[29]

120

In the House of Commons, despite former Prime Minister Asquith's defense of the traditional methods of raising party funds,[30] and Lloyd George's claim that he, like previous prime ministers, had no idea how much, if anything, nominees for honors contributed to such funds, the government was plainly embarrassed. Lloyd George, after an earlier refusal, had to agree to a royal commission to recommend changes in the honors procedure, in order to head off Conservative demands for a select committee of inquiry into the past scandal. The "Welsh Walpole"--as he was designated by the rightist National Review--conceded to the House of Commons that "mistakes have been made" in the selection of honors recipients, but he added that "the percentage, in spite of the exceptional pressure, has been as low as in any previous period."[31]

Besides the donations made to the Lloyd George Fund for the purpose of buying honors, others were made for less selfish motives. In the words of Lloyd George himself, writing to his friend Lord Reading in August 1929, many of the contributions

> made through my Whip to me when I was a non-Party premier [were] to be used for such political purposes as I thought desirable to spend them upon. At that time there was a very large body of non-partisan opinion which rallied around me and was convinced that my direction of affairs was essential, not only to the winning of the war, but afterwards to the clearing up of the mess that follows war. This opinion was particularly concerned about the unrest throughout the world and was very apprehensive that Bolshevik doctrines might overthrow Society. They trusted me to see the country through this period of anxiety. Party considerations never entered their minds. It was entirely a matter of personal confidence.[32]

Lloyd George's crusade against Bolshevism was neither steadfast nor consistent. As early as January 1919, Chief Whip Frederick Guest had to warn his master that his "readiness to fraternise with the Bolsheviks" was creating anxiety among his supporters and might lead to political trouble, including by implication a decline in political contributions.[33]

Not only was money conferred on Lloyd George to fight the abstract menaces of "Bolshevism" and "socialism," but also to forestall the more concrete possibility of a Labour party victory. This was to be done by keeping in power a Lloyd George government, whether based on a Liberal-Conservative coalition or on a new Fusion or National party such as Churchill, Lord Birkenhead, and other friends of the prime minister envisaged. The prevention of a Labour government's gaining office was among the reasons for contributing to the Lloyd George Fund urged upon prospective donors in a letter said to have been written by an agent of the Coalition Liberal whips and freely quoted by the Duke of Northumberland in his House of Lords speech of July 17, 1922. Attention was called to this purpose of the fund by Churchill during the 1929 election campaign, when he complained of Lloyd George's subsidizing the Liberal party from the fund. A fund that had been raised "for the expressed and avowed purpose of enabling both Liberals and Conservatives to make common cause against Socialism," Churchill claimed, "is now being used for the purpose of securing the return of as large a number of Socialists as possible." (Churchill was referring to three-cornered contests in which votes for weak Liberal condidates might result in Labour pluralities.)[34]

According to Lloyd George, it was this original stipulation of the use of the fund that made it altogether impossible for him to turn its capital over to the Liberal party, for if he did former Coalition Liberals who had become Conservatives might initiate a lawsuit. "Were I to abandon my control of this Fund and hand it over to the organisation of any political party, I should be betraying a trust," Lloyd George remarked in his letter to Lord Reading. But, he continued, "that does not mean that I am not within my rights in making grants from time to time for the promotion of political ends which are consistent with its creation." Lloyd George interpreted the subsidies to the Liberal party as consonant with the intentions of the fund's donors, although Churchill viewed them as "a breach . . . of moral faith." So did the ultraconservative National Review, one of whose staff writers wondered in 1928 whether the former Coalition Liberal Chief Whip Frederick Guest, who had been responsible for collecting much of the Lloyd George Fund and had since affiliated with the Conservatives, "proposes to acquiesce in such a situation."[35] But apart from occasional fulminations against their former chief, neither Churchill nor Guest took any steps to restrict Lloyd George's use of the fund.

One of the early uses to which the Lloyd George Fund was put was the purchase of newspapers to serve as mouthpieces for the Welshman and his Coalition Liberal group. Most of the London and much of the provincial Liberal press had opposed the ousting of Asquith as prime minister and remained bitterly critical of the Lloyd George regime. The papers controlled by the "press barons"--Northcliffe, Rothermere, and Beaverbrook--had approved the coup against Asquith, but their support of Lloyd George was capricious and unreliable. The only London daily that Lloyd George both respected and counted on for disinterested support was the independent Liberal Daily Chronicle, owned by Frank Lloyd and edited by Sir Robert Donald, a neighbor and occasional golfing partner of the prime minister. Even this paper began to irritate Lloyd George when it rebuked him for his vendetta against Generals Robertson and Haig, and it infuriated him by appointing as military correspondent General Sir Frederick Maurice, whose charges that the prime minister had falsified military information threatened to wreck his government in May 1918.

While Lloyd George and Donald were still on good terms, the Welshman had hinted to the editor that some of his wealthy friends might buy the paper and publish it in his interest. This was in January 1917, when Neil Primrose was still Coalition Liberal chief whip and before Primrose's successor, Frederick Guest, had begun his successful drive to raise a huge fund for Lloyd George. One possible buyer of the Chronicle was Sir William Lever, the soap magnate, a former Liberal M.P. and an enthusiastic supporter of the Lloyd George government. Later in 1917, after Guest had begun to amass the fund, Lloyd George had again approached Donald, suggesting to him that he would like to use part of his growing fund to buy the Chronicle from Frank Lloyd and make it the official organ of the Coalition Liberals. According to Donald's contemporary notes, the editor was not encouraging.[36]

Thereafter Donald was not consulted, as negotiations for purchasing the Chronicle were conducted between Frank Lloyd and Lloyd George's representatives, Chief Whip Guest and Sir Henry Dalziel, Coalition Liberal M.P. and chief shareholder of Reynolds's News.[37] The negotiations were speeded up after the appearance

in September 1918 of a Chronicle editorial chastising
Lloyd George for his "small minded" attitude toward Sir
Douglas Haig.[38] Frank Lloyd himself was disturbed by
Donald's increasing hostility to the government, and
early in October 1918 readily agreed to the sale of the
Chronicle and its sister paper, Lloyd's Sunday News,
for £1,650,000 to a corporation known as United Newspapers, Ltd. A majority of shares in the corporation
was held by the administrator of the Lloyd George Fund,
Chief Whip Guest, while a substantial minority was divided up among such affluent supporters of Lloyd George
as Dalziel, Andrew Weir (later Lord Inverforth), Lord
Inchcape, the Marquess of Bute, and James White, "a
notorious Lancashire company promoter."[39] Donald--
after an unsuccessful attempt to buy the paper him-
self--immediately resigned as editor, while General
Maurice and a number of other employees transferred to
the staff of the Asquithian Daily News. Soon after the
Lloyd newspapers were purchased, United Newspapers
acquired controlling interests in the Edinburgh Evening
News, previously a leading pro-Asquith paper, and the
Yorkshire Evening News. The well-equipped office of
the latter in Leeds was turned into a northern publication office for the Daily Chronicle, where special
editions were prepared for circulation in the tradi-
tionally Liberal north of England and Scotland.[40]

Although Lloyd George had no personal association
with United Newspapers, other than the ownership by
himself and his family of a small number of shares in
the company, its papers completely reflected his political views. In the words of a critical journalist, the
Daily Chronicle, under its new editor, Ernest Perris,
became "the official organ, the defender through thick
and thin, fair and foul, of Lloyd George and his Coalition."[41] In return, the Lloyd George government made
every effort to assist the Chronicle by arranging for
it to receive "scoops," to the annoyance of the Northcliffe and Beaverbrook editors who previously could
count on these favors.[42] Despite, or perhaps because
of, this favoritism, the Chronicle added little to
Lloyd George's political strength, while losing the
reputation for integrity it had earned under Sir Robert
Donald's editorship.[43] The "ownership" of a leading
newspaper by a prime minister seemed to many observers
a dangerous threat to an independent press, a charge
made several times in the House of Commons between 1918
and 1922 by the tart-tongued Asquithian M.P., W. M. R.
Pringle. Nevertheless, the Chronicle maintained its
1918 status as the London Liberal daily with the larg-

est circulation, surpassed only by Northcliffe's <u>Daily Mail</u> and Beaverbrook's <u>Daily Express</u>. With Sir Henry Dalziel as its first chairman and managing director--followed in 1921 by Philip Kerr, Lloyd George's former private secretary, and in 1922 by Charles A. McCurdy, Guest's successor as Coalition Liberal chief whip--the <u>Chronicle</u> adhered to a progressive editorial policy, advocating radical programs Lloyd George would have liked to carry through but was prevented from doing by the political exigencies of his Coalition.

Between 1918 and 1921, United Newspapers made money for the Lloyd George Fund and for its other shareholders, including Dalziel who resigned as chairman and manager and retired from the newspaper business in 1921. The next head of the company, Philip Kerr, while reflecting Lloyd George's political views more closely than Dalziel, was a poorer businessman and was replaced after leading shareholders complained about the deteriorating financial condition of the papers. [44] At this point Lloyd George invested more of his fund in the company and, after resigning from the prime ministership, took an active interest in the papers' management. In his letter to Lord Reading of August 1929, Lloyd George stated that

> when the [<u>Daily Chronicle</u>] was in low water . . . I put the whole of my strength and experience in the newspaper business into improving the value of the investment. I took in hand the supreme direction of the business policy of the enterprise, and owing to great savings, changes and improvements which were the direct result of my intervention, the property increased enormously in value so that I was able to sell it at several times the sum I paid for it.

As he indicated to Reading, Lloyd George had considerable practical experience as a newspaperman. In addition to acting as correspondent for the <u>Manchester Guardian</u> and other papers while a young politician, he had founded his own Welsh newspaper companies in the eighties and nineties to support his political concerns. Later, the Welshman had been deeply involved in a successful plot to acquire the London <u>Daily News</u> for the pro-Boer interest during the South African War, and had been a director of the <u>News</u> until becoming a cabinet minister. [45] Lloyd George's reputation as a brilliant manipulator of the press while an office holder was notorious. However, little of this formidable background in journalism had been on the business side.

It is open to question whether the financial success of the Daily Chronicle and its sister papers after 1922 was due to the expertise of Lloyd George, his son Gwilym who represented him on the board of directors and acted for a time as business manager, and Charles McCurdy—or to a generally rising market for newspaper properties. There is no question that United Newspapers, Ltd., was sold in 1926-7 for approximately £2,900,000, an increase in value of 75 percent over the 1918 purchase price.

Lloyd George's reasons for selling the Chronicle and the associated papers were many. They included dissatisfaction with the dull contents of the Chronicle and the Sunday News, disagreements with the editors over policy and with his son over management and personnel, family opposition to his plan to appoint his mistress—Frances Stevenson—to a directorship, and his wish to increase the cash holdings of his fund to strengthen his hand in bargaining with the Asquith Liberals. As early as 1922, Lloyd George had tried to acquire Geoffrey Dawson, former and future editor of The Times, as editor of the Chronicle in place of Perris, who the Welshman charged "spends too many of his evenings at the Kit Kat Club."[46] In 1923 there was a bruising quarrel with an old crony, F. G. Kellaway, summarily dismissed as a director to make way for Gwilym.[47] An offer to buy the Chronicle in 1924, reported to Lloyd George by Frederick Guest, was turned down, but two years later, following a major dispute with McCurdy (whom he accused of being "lazy and flabby"), the Welshman took Lord Beaverbrook's advice to sell his fund's 614,003 shares in United Newspapers to a syndicate headed by Sir David Yule and Sir Thomas Catto, wealthy Liberal businessmen.[48] These shares accounted for all but 2,495 of the shares issued by United Newspapers, showing that the Lloyd George Fund since 1918 had bought out all of the major investors and most of the small ones.[49]

United Newspapers, now owned by the Yule-Catto syndicate, was reorganized in July 1927 as the Daily Chronicle Investment Corporation, with Lloyd George's old friend, Lord Reading, recently retired as viceroy of India, as chairman. Reading's presence undoubtedly was intended to give Lloyd George a continuing voice in the Chronicle's management and policies. However,

Reading, who had no experience or interest in newspaper work, disliked the job and resigned a year later when William Harrison's Inveresk Paper Company bought the controlling shares in the Chronicle papers from the Yule-Catto combine.[50]

The Lloyd George Fund retained a connection, although a much reduced one, with the Chronicle newspapers by buying a large number of shares in both the Daily Chronicle Investment Corporation and the Inveresk Paper Company. This was, as it turned out, a mistake, because after the 1927 purchase and reorganization the newspaper corporation's shares were inflated and suffered badly from the depression.[51] The Daily Chronicle itself was floundering. In 1928 its advertising director warned Lloyd George that the Chronicle was not holding its own in the furious circulation wars of the late twenties.[52] The newspaper was in "a tremendous mess," Lloyd George wrote his wife in 1930, but Lord St. Davids--the Welshman's financial adviser and chairman of the fund trustees--was "putting his back into it."[53] This and other attempts at resuscitation were not enough in the face of competition from a rejuvenated Daily Herald--the Labour party organ--and in May 1930 the Chronicle folded and was merged with the Daily News.

Another newspaper that Lloyd George seriously considered acquiring control of was the august Times of London, whose future ownership came into question during the fatal illness of Lord Northcliffe in the summer of 1922. Between mid-June and early September, Lloyd George considered and rejected various schemes for taking over the ownership or editorial direction of The Times.[54] In none of these plans did the Lloyd George Fund play a major part, because a very large portion of it was tied up in the United Newspapers chain, and the rest needed to be held in reserve for the forthcoming general election and future elections.

There also remained a possibility that a Fusion or National party, long discussed, might be formed by a combination of the Coalition Liberals and those Conservatives who valued Lloyd George's leadership. Such a party would depend heavily on the Lloyd George Fund. Still another possible use of the Lloyd George Fund during the summer of 1922 was a scheme to maneuver Lord Birkenhead, a close associate of Lloyd George, into the leadership of the Conservative party, then held by Austen Chamberlain. There were rumors that money was

being subscribed to ease Birkenhead's way, until he
rejected the plan. A likely source of at least part of
this subscription was the Lloyd George Fund, since a
Conservative party under Birkenhead's leadership would
have been more amenable to fusion than one under a
leader less sympathetic to Lloyd George.[55] After abandoning hope of becoming Tory leader, Birkenhead became
involved in the Times intrigues and unsuccessfully
tried to form a syndicate to capture it, apparently in
competition with the simultaneous efforts of Lloyd
George.[56]

Before Northcliffe's death, Lloyd George believed
he might be able to buy The Times, with its comparatively small circulation, for only £250,000, and had
made arrangements with David Davies, the Welsh coal
owner, and other wealthy friends to raise the money.[57]
Lloyd George did not intend to use more than a small
portion, if any, of his fund toward accumulating the
purchase price of The Times. After Northcliffe's death
it was found that over £1,000,000 would be needed, much
more than Lloyd George had immediate access to either
in his fund or through trustworthy acquaintances.[58]
After some vacillation he stood aside while the paper
was purchased by John Jacob Astor, whose object was to
prevent The Times from becoming a Lloyd George mouthpiece.

IV

As long as the Coalition Liberals existed as a
separate parliamentary group, and later--between 1922
and 1923--as a nominally independent though largely
phantom National Liberal party, their whips administered the Lloyd George Fund in the same way as the
whips of other parties.[59] Lloyd George, of course, had
the final word about how the money should be used, to a
greater degree than other party leaders because much of
the money had been subscribed for him to use at his
discretion. In his 1929 letter to Lord Reading, Lloyd
George was to contend that he had no more control over
his fund than Asquith had over prewar Liberal party
funds, but this denial contradicted assertions made in
the same letter, some of them quoted above. The prospect of Lloyd George's losing absolute control over his
fund was a factor in the collapse of the scheme to fuse
the Coalition Liberals and the Conservatives. In the
spring of 1920 fusion had received the approval of

128

Bonar Law and the Conservative Chairman Sir George Younger, provided Lloyd George surrendered his fund as "gate money."[60]

The same difficulty arose when, during the 1923 election campaign, Lloyd George decided to reunite his National Liberals with the Asquithian Liberal organization. The National Liberal party was abruptly discontinued, without consultation of rank and file members, but no action was taken to merge the Lloyd George Fund with the Liberal party funds, as most Liberal organizers rather naively expected.[61] Instead, the Lloyd George Fund maintained its separate existence under the formal designation of National Liberal Political Fund, wholly separate from both the regular Liberal party and the scattering of local National Liberal Associations that still functioned in some constituencies. A committee was named by Lloyd George to administer the fund, consisting of three former National Liberal whips: Charles McCurdy, Sir William Edge, and Gwilym Lloyd George. The income from the part of the fund invested in United Newspapers, and from portions invested in other income-producing properties, was to be used to finance a separate Lloyd George political office at 18 Abingdon Street (Liberal headquarters was at 21 Abingdon), a bureau at the same address to assist ex-servicemen, and various policy studies of national problems that Lloyd George initiated in 1924. Income from the fund--and when necessary allotments from the capital--would also be used to support Liberal election campaigns, but solely at the discretion of the committee administering the fund: meaning, in effect, at Lloyd George's discretion.[62] According to Lloyd George, at the time of Liberal reunion Asquith uncomplainingly accepted his explanation that the conditions of the donations to his fund prevented him from combining it with the regular Liberal party treasury.[63]

Asquith's tolerance toward the Lloyd George Fund, which he had shown earlier during the 1922 honors scandal debate, was not shared by his lieutenants in the orthodox Liberal party. Lord Gladstone, the former chief whip and again provisionally in charge of the Liberal central office, denounced the fund as "the proceeds of corruption" and declared the Liberals to be "better without it."[64] (He would soon change his mind.) The indignant Mr. Pringle, suspicious as always of Lloyd George, insisted--like Sir George Younger during the discussion of Conservative-Coalition Liberal fusion--that the heretic must turn over his coffer as "gate money." Pringle and his colleagues, aware that very little of the Lloyd George Fund had been spent by the National Liberals in the 1922 election, would not have been human if they had not lusted after a political war chest reputed to be worth about £3,000,000 including its newspaper shares. With ill-concealed reluctance they accepted Asquith's decision that £100,000 would be all that Lloyd George would be asked to contribute to the 1923 election expenses, but they assumed this was merely a first installment.[65]

When it became likely during the early months of 1924 that the new Labour government would not remain long in office, Liberal party headquarters renewed negotiations with Lloyd George for a subvention from his fund to fight the imminent general election. The Liberal treasury was badly depleted by the expenses of two campaigns in the previous eighteen months. It had emerged from the tandem 1910 general elections with a big surplus, but most of this was gone by 1924, the few rich men who had contributed the bulk of prewar funds were losing faith in Liberalism, and--Frederick Guest was told by Geoffrey Howard of the Liberal Central Association--party headquarters was eating up the balance at the rate of £50,000 a year. The National Liberal Federation was partially self-supporting and had collected a sizable sum at a 1919 rally, but its resources were fast being drained and without help from headquarters it would soon have to curtail activities. Few local Liberal Associations collected enough subscriptions from members to carry on party work and pay the election expenses of candidates without large grants from the L.C.A.[66] It was painfully clear that without substantial aid from Lloyd George, the Liberal party could not field the 450 to 500 candidates needed to be considered a serious competitor for office. And without the prospect of the party's return to power, wealthy aspirants for honors could not be enticed back into it.[67]

While in the House of Commons Labour Prime Minister Ramsay MacDonald nudged the Liberals toward a breach with his government that would result in their slaughter by the electorate, L.C.A. officials fruitlessly dickered with "the mysterious twister at No. 18" (in Sir Robert Hudson's words). Lloyd George evidently was convinced that the Liberals could not hope to win a majority following a dissolution by MacDonald, and should concentrate on retaining the 156 seats they held. He also was very dissatisfied with the organization and methods of Liberal headquarters, believing that his money would be wasted unless changes he urged were made. "The returned prodigal," as Lord Gladstone called him, passed the spring and summer of 1924 complaining of the poor work done by the Asquithian organizers, trying to insert his own people into the official machine, and laying down conditions for parting with his assets totally unacceptable to Gladstone and his long-suffering colleagues, Sir Robert Hudson, Sir Donald Maclean, and Geoffrey Howard.[68] Both Gladstone and Hudson blamed much of Lloyd George's perverseness on "Freddie Guest [who] is alleged to be [his] evil genius." Guest not only had collected most of the original Lloyd George Fund and continued to advise the Welshman on his newspaper properties and other fiscal matters, but like Churchill and Birkenhead was seen as still hankering after a Fusion party.[69]

The prolonged bickering over the amount of Lloyd George's subsidy held up Liberal preparations for the election campaign. Not until early October--and only after an appeal by Asquith to Lloyd George--could even the minimum 300 candidatures to which the Welshman agreed be guaranteed.[70] In the end only 343 Liberal candidates stood for election, barely enough to produce a majority if, incredibly, every one were elected. Only £50,000 was donated by Lloyd George, less than half of what the Liberals wanted, and much of this was earmarked for local contests of former National Liberals. Whether correctly or not, Liberal organizers and agents believed that the disastrous outcome for the party of the October 1924 election was due to shortages of candidates and funds which greater generosity by Lloyd George could have remedied.[71]

The profound animosity of the Asquith Liberals toward Lloyd George, held in check since the 1923 reunion in the hope of grabbing all or part of his fund, now burst out into the open. At a meeting of defeated Liberal candidates held shortly after the election under the chairmanship of the now-seatless Pringle, Lloyd George was roundly denounced for his niggardliness. It was even intimated that his withholding of election funds was intended to wipe out his enemies in the party,[72] a conjecture supported by the massacre of Asquithian Liberal M.P.'s at the polls. It began to be widely bruited about in Liberal circles that Lloyd George, with his separate fund and personal headquarters, which in 1924 had published an elaborate policy study of the ailing British coal industry and now was at work on a new land inquiry, would openly challenge official Liberal headquarters and the newly ennobled Lord Oxford and Asquith for the party leadership.

Although Lord Oxford himself characteristically discouraged discussion of the Lloyd George Fund,[73] his followers pressed the whispering campaign against the Welshman while simultaneously petitioning their foe to loosen his purse strings. During the summer of 1925, three devoted Asquithians (veterans of "the old aging gang," in Lord Gladstone's words)--Sir Donald Maclean, president of the National Liberal Federation, Vivian Phillipps, chairman of the Liberal party's Organization Committee, and Sir Robert Hudson, party treasurer--reopened negotiations with Lloyd George. The goal this time was a three-year annual subsidy of £60,000 from his fund to help cover the expenses of Liberal headquarters, which Lloyd George provisionally conceded. Phillipps also rather bluntly suggested that Lloyd George contribute a much larger sum to the Liberal Million Fund, the campaign chest that the newly-created Organization Committee was trying to collect for the next general election.[74] After investigating the Million Fund's machinery and personnel, Sir William Edge, one of the administrators of the Lloyd George Fund, advised his chief that his contributions to the Liberal party treasury should be kept as low as possible.[75]

The campaign for the Million Fund proved to be a fiasco. In theory this fund was to be raised mostly from small voluntary contributions by the rank and file--an innovation in British political fund raising[76] --but it was assumed that a number of big donations would be needed to put it over the top. These were not forthcoming. This was partly attributable, as Edge suggested, to the incompetence of the fund raisers, but in greater part to the embarrassing question, raised by potential donors, of why the Liberal party needed one million pounds when one of its leaders had access to at least a couple of million. As early as February 1925, the party treasurer acknowledged that the "Fighting Fund hasn't got going," and nearly two years later only £80,000 had been contributed or promised.[77] As Sir Robert Hudson ruefully noted, small subscribers earmarked their gifts for their local associations, while those who might have been large donors held back because of the presumed availability of the Welshman's largesse. Worse yet, a high proportion of subscrip-

132

tions took the form of pledges that never matured. The Million Fund also competed with the nearly moribund treasury of the National Liberal Federation for access to the dwindling Liberal sources of money. "The Million Fund isn't going," Hudson complained to Lord Gladstone, "but it has stopped all other central funds."[78]

Although the Liberal fund raisers would cheerfully have read Lloyd George out of the party but for his wealth, they could not very well do so as long as there was the slightest chance of his helping their impoverished party. They were also mindful of Lord Oxford's injunction that the party could hardly stand another open schism. Renouncing Lloyd George and his political chest might have encouraged gifts to the Million Fund, but in the process the party would risk bankruptcy and dissolution.

Before 1925 was over this prospect seemed to be looming anyway. Lloyd George's conditions for the subsidy to Liberal headquarters included party support of his land policy, enunciated in the Green Book policy study, which many moderate Liberals viewed as "socialistic." Angered by this chilly reaction to his latest enthusiasm and put out by Phillipps's demand for a large gift to the Million Fund with no strings attached, Lloyd George abruptly withdrew his subsidy offer and set up a Land and Nation League at his personal headquarters, now at 25 Old Queen Street, to campaign for the Green Book schemes independently of the regular party organization. In taking these steps the Welshman assented to the advice of--among others--Frances Stevenson, his secretary-mistress, Sir William Edge of the Lloyd George Fund, and labor leader J. H. Thomas, an old friend. These three were emphatic that he would be a "lunatic" to entrust any more of his fund to "fools" like Vivian Phillipps and his colleagues, who had "misused what money they had, and cannot raise any more."[79]

This action by the man he hated and for months had to kowtow to during the subsidy negotiations threw Phillipps into a rage, which he vented in a public diatribe against Lloyd George. In a speech to a party meeting at Hull on November 20, Phillipps pointedly accused Lloyd George of showing lack of party loyalty by his stinginess in contributing to party funds, and of wrecking the Million Fund by propagandizing for his controversial land program. He obliquely hinted that the Welshman was trying to bribe and corrupt the party for his own ends.[80]

Phillipps's bitter speech, together with a simultaneous row between Lloyd George and the editorial staff of the Liberal journal the <u>Nation</u>,[81] for some weeks threatened to split the party anew. In the end the patience and diplomacy of Lord Oxford, the refusal of fellow Asquithians to join Phillipps's open attack on Lloyd George, and the willingness of Lloyd George to be mollified smoothed over the disagreement about funds and paved the way for a compromise on land policy.

Of course all this harmony was superficial. Except for some help to Liberal candidates in selected by-elections,[82] Lloyd George gave no further financial aid to the official party organization for over a year, while furnishing the Land and Nation League with such abundant resources that it virtually supplanted the nearly destitute Liberal Central Association as the chief propaganda organ of the party. His enemies, despite their silence in public, also were active. While Walter Runciman, an old adversary, conspired with Vivian Phillipps to launch a new Radical party opposing Lloyd George,[83] Lord Cowdray, Lord Grey, Gladstone, Maclean, Hudson, Pringle, and other bitter-end Asquithians debated the "excision" of Lloyd George from the existing Liberal party. In the end they reluctantly agreed that no such "surgical operation" was practical in the face of Lord Oxford's opposition and the party's indigence. On the latter score Hudson was quite blunt: "As for money, the answer is simple, there ain't none."[84]

V

The year 1926 opened with a fragile détente between the Asquith and Lloyd George sections of the Liberal party. It closed with the latter in virtual control of the party machinery and the former either acquiescing or withdrawing in dudgeon to the political sidelines. This denouement came as the result of developments wholly unexpected at the beginning of the year, when Lloyd George's Green Book was the chief divisive issue in the party, and Lord Oxford applied all his renowned powers of persuasion to achieve an agreed-upon land policy at a special party conference in February. Despite his success, Oxford was disappointed at the patent failure of the Million Fund, which he had hoped would give the party "complete independence in matters of public policy" from the

Lloyd George Fund.[85] He feared that in any major policy disagreement in the future, Lloyd George with his ample resources would be able to call the tune.

This problem arose in acute form in May when Lord Oxford and his intimate associates broke decisively with Lloyd George over the stand the party should take toward the General Strike. Although the dispute was unrelated to the Lloyd George Fund, it quickly awakened all the latent antagonism associated with the fund. It was rumored in Asquithian circles that Lloyd George's sympathy for the strikers was the first move in his defection to the Labour party, which in return for the support of his fund and newspapers would endorse his land policy and make him agriculture minister in the next Labour government. This story apparently was given some credence by Lord Oxford himself.[86] Efforts by Sir Charles Hobhouse, Ramsay Muir, and other Liberals not closely associated with either warring camp to resolve the deadlock were hampered by the impassioned public statements of dedicated Asquithians such as journalist A. G. Gardiner, who in a speech in Birmingham called the Lloyd George Fund

> a source of personal influence which can be directed to any occult end, an imperium in imperio, as sinister and disruptive in its possibilities as it is . . . unprecedented in the whole history of British political life.[87]

Such strong language by Lord Oxford's friends could not hide the painful fact that the official party machinery, which they still controlled, was nearly bankrupt. The Organization Committee in late September estimated that it could keep party headquarters in full operation for about six months, but after that it would either have to shut down principal party functions or appeal hat in hand to Lloyd George.[88] Lord Oxford, in failing health and utterly disgusted by the months of intraparty wrangling, felt that he could make no further personal compromises and decided to resign the party leadership, both for his own peace of mind and to leave the party free to decide whether or not to accept Lloyd George's money and policy leadership. Stating in a confidential letter to his friends that he was "resolved not to take any part, direct or indirect, in a sectional controversy in the Party, either about Leadership or funds,"[89] Lord Oxford took dignified final leave of the party battles.

Even before Lord Oxford's retirement at the end of October, Lloyd George, through his assistant Thomas F. Tweed, organizing secretary of the Land and Nation League, had made overtures to the Liberal Organization Committee, offering to assume responsibility for financing Liberal candidates in rural constituencies as part of the land campaign. In response to this offer the Liberal Administrative Committee--parent body of the Organization Committee--on October 20 appointed a subcommittee under the chairmanship of Sir Charles Hobhouse, one of the leading peacemakers in the party, to confer with Lloyd George or his representatives not only on the rural candidacies scheme but on the conditions for merging the Lloyd George Fund with the regular Liberal funds. [90]

The Hobhouse Committee--whose chairmanship Hobhouse accepted with the understanding that he would have considerable latitude in negotiating--held six meetings with Lloyd George's aide, Tweed, in late October and early November 1926. The discussions ranged over the whole subject of Liberal party organization and finances. After some preliminary sparring, Lloyd George, through Tweed, offered to place the whole income of his fund at the disposal of the Liberal party, on condition that the expenses of the Land and Nation League and the newly launched Liberal Industrial Inquiry should be the first charges on the income, and that the party machinery should be reorganized with the dismissal of certain functionaries unfriendly to Lloyd George, particularly Vivian Phillipps. It was pointed out that due to the poor results of the Million Fund drive, the budget of party headquarters could not be subsidized from the income of the Lloyd George Fund in addition to the land campaign and Industrial Inquiry. Lloyd George then agreed to make up the balance from the liquid capital of his fund, which was about to be greatly increased through sale of the shares in United Newspapers. [91] These ostensible concessions did not deceive Phillipps, Hudson, and other old guard Asquithians whose immolation was demanded by "the little Welsher." "He has all along meant to starve us out," Phillipps wrote to Lord Gladstone, "and he has pretty well accomplished his purpose." [92]

On the basis of these talks, the Hobhouse Committee submitted its report to the full Administrative Committee urging compliance with Lloyd George's terms, subject to renegotiation after the next general election. A majority of the Administrative Committee approved the Hobhouse report on November 24, but a determined Asquithian minority insisted that only an unconditional offer of funds from Lloyd George should be accepted, and that Phillipps and the other party organizers objectionable to Lloyd George must not be sacrificed. In deference to this minority, which included the veteran party treasurer, Sir Robert Hudson, the Administrative Committee directed Hobhouse's subcommittee to negotiate further with Lloyd George in person.[93] In the meantime Vivian Phillipps and his allies counterattacked, threatening to "involve the party in a sort of civil war for the next two years" if Phillipps and his fellow employees of the L.C.A. were not allowed to retire gracefully, presumably after a generous financial settlement.[94] It was a compound of sympathy for Phillipps's position and fear of what he and his friends might do that evidently induced the Administrative Committee, now clearly leaning toward accommodation with Lloyd George, to drag its feet.[95]

Hobhouse reported to the Administrative Committee on December 15 that Lloyd George had agreed to withdraw most conditions for his financial support of the Liberal party. This support would include enough money from the income and capital of his fund to nominate a full slate of Liberal candidates in the next general election and to pay the expenses of the party machinery at least through the next poll. Lloyd George reserved the right to control the capital of the fund, which he maintained he was obliged to do by the terms of the original donations, and to withdraw or change the form of his aid to the party after the election. Since Hobhouse had urged on his own authority that Liberal headquarters should be reorganized,[96] it was clear that Lloyd George's dropping of conditions was a face-saving gesture to his opponents and that he expected his demand for changes in personnel to be carried out anyway.

The leading Asquithians were scarcely appeased by Lloyd George's tokens of good will and continued to show toward him what the disgusted editor of the Nation spoke of as "implacable hostility . . . amounting in one or two instances almost to a Freudian complex."[97] Several of them wrote letters to the press questioning Lloyd George's sincerity, accusing him of trying to buy the party, and castigating him for not handing over his entire capital—sometimes all in the same letter.[98]

Vivian Phillipps was in no hurry to relinquish his

post as head of the Organization Committee. He refused
to resign even after the Administrative Committee voted
on December 15 to accept Hobhouse's recommendation that
he and all other members of the Organization Committee
step down. However, following an interview of Lloyd
George by the full Administrative Committee on January
19, 1927, in which he dropped one more condition--the
precedence of the Land and Nation League and Industrial
Inquiry in claims on his fund--the Administrative Committee voted overwhelmingly to accept Lloyd George's
offer and to request the resignation of Phillipps and
the other Organization Committee members.[99] Two days
later, Sir Robert Hudson resigned as party treasurer
and honorary secretary of the Liberal Central Association, posts he had held for thirty-four years, in protest against the "capitulation" to Lloyd George.[100]

Lloyd George was now able to arrange the appointment of an Organization Committee dominated by his own
men, notably Thomas Tweed as organizing secretary.
Following completion of the sale of United Newspapers,
the Lloyd George Fund turned over to a friendly party
headquarters a contribution of £300,000, including
£40,000 for headquarters expenses.[101] The Welshman was
at last in effective command of the Liberal party
machine. The only obstacles to his complete control
were the lukewarm loyalty of many party officials and
the need to work with a "neutral" successor to Phillipps as Organization Committee chairman, the ex-As-
quithian Sir Herbert Samuel.

VI

The treaty between Lloyd George and the Administrative Committee produced yet another party schism. A
group of prominent Asquithians, led by Lord Grey of
Fallodon, on January 23, 1927, set up the Liberal
Council as a body of Liberals that would have offices
and funds completely separate from the official headquarters now financed and controlled by Lloyd George.
In a statement to the press, Lord Grey contended that
acceptance of an endowment from the Lloyd George Fund
put the Liberal Central Association under a moral obligation to Lloyd George, even though he claimed to
donate the money unconditionally. It was also intimated that the Welshman might very well withdraw his
aid to the party after the next election and leave it
high and dry, especially if it did not make significant

138

Parliamentary gains. In that event, the Liberal Council, several of whose members were wealthy, might step in and assume direction of the party.[102]

The Liberal Council did not pretend to be a separate anti-Lloyd George party--although Walter Runciman and a few others may have wanted it to become one--but it raised money, aided candidates, issued propaganda, and engaged in various other quasi-partisan activities. Its members, many of them elderly, were essentially Gladstonians of the late Victorian era, whose image of Liberalism was dated and quaint. The program of "Free Trade . . . drastic retrenchment . . . and licensing [reform]," suggested by Lord Gladstone, was hardly competitive with the dynamic twentieth century Liberalism enunciated in Lloyd George's policy studies.[103]

Although the Liberal Council was certain to divert some contributions that otherwise would have gone to the Million Fund--which Lloyd George hoped would be more attractive after he had put new life into the party machinery--it is unlikely that he was much disturbed by its competition, either political or financial. The chief executive officer of the Council was Vivian Phillipps, and one of its joint treasurers was Sir William Plender, neither of whom had been effectual as directors of the Million Fund in 1925-6. The Council got off to a slow start and never picked up momentum, even after the expertise of Lord Gladstone was drafted to fight "Funded Liberalism."[104] Despite the wealth of its membership, Gladstone's records indicate that donations were made reluctantly and commitments were difficult to fulfill. "Can you let me have a cheque, by return mail if possible," Phillipps begged Gladstone after the 1929 election, "as the account has to be squared by the end of the week."[105]

The Council organizers unwillingly conceded that for the moment Lloyd George held center stage in the Liberal party, that he was winning over the younger Asquithians who had not defected to Labour, and that their movement must become a trust company for "genuine Liberalism" until the Welshman died or retired, was discredited, or his "d----d fund" was exhausted.[106] Hope briefly revived after Lloyd George's setback in the 1929 election, only to fade once it became clear that Liberal headquarters was prepared to retain him as paymaster, dissatisfied though the pensioner might be with its dole. There was even a disinclination to "carry the baby" should they be asked to do so by Liberals "under the impression that the Council is much more affluent than it really is." In the end the Council leaders decided to "walk warily" until the younger generation of Liberals had tired of Lloyd George's nostrums.[107] For a year or two longer they kept up their verbal duel with the Welshman, and were generous with advice to British and foreign politicians inquiring about their quarrel with the "nemesis of British Liberalism" and his "cursed Fund."[108] Following the deaths of Gladstone in 1930 and Grey in 1933, the Liberal schisms over relations with the Labour party and support of free trade in 1931-2, and Lloyd George's withdrawal from the party leadership, the Council gradually faded into oblivion. An office was maintained until 1939 and a corporate existence as late as 1946,[109] but with its Welsh bugbear on the sidelines there was little reason to stay active.

VII

While most Liberals accepted Lloyd George's leadership of the party, and tolerated if they did not approve his subsidization of it, sniping at his fund increased. Involved were not only irreconcilable Liberals but members of other parties, especially right wing Conservatives who denounced both the origins of the fund and the uses to which it was being put. A new fusillade began on February 16, 1927, the very day that Sir Herbert Samuel took charge as head of the reconstructed party headquarters. A figure from the dim political past, the almost forgotten former Liberal prime minister, Lord Rosebery, addressed a letter to The Times recalling the honors scandal of 1922 and comparing it to "the worst times of Charles II or Sir Robert Walpole" (but not to his own administration's honors scandal of 1895). The "embarrassed old fogey," as Rosebery called himself in his letter, insisted that the Liberal party make public the amount, the sources, and the methods of acquisition of the Lloyd George Fund, although he must have been well aware of the answers to at least the last two parts of his query.[110]

Lord Rosebery's questions were taken up and repeated ad nauseam by such Conservative journals of the far right as the Morning Post and the National Review, while the pro-Lloyd George Liberal press retorted with rather uncharitable gibes at the private fund being raised by wealthy friends of Lord Oxford to relieve his

140

declining years.[111] Although most of the malicious gossip about the fund appeared in the Conservative press, some of the original purveyors apparently were disgruntled Liberals.[112] In late July 1927, Lord Rothermere's Daily Mail joined battle on Lloyd George's side, its attack on the "die-hard" papers climaxing in a brutal editorial on August 8 accusing them of "un-English" behavior in trying to discredit an ex-prime minister. Rothermere's press campaign in defense of Lloyd George evidently was part of a larger effort to boost the Welshman and the Liberals at the expense of Prime Minister Baldwin's wing of the Conservative party, with which the newspaper lord had fallen out.[113]

Lloyd George's patience in the face of continued press scrutiny of his fund finally snapped. Early in December 1927, he issued a blistering statement to the newspapers castigating the "cowardly slander privately circulated as to my use of the Party Funds." He went on to give a very simplified history of the fund, noting that the proceeds from the sale of United Newspapers had been turned over, along with the rest of the cash and securities belonging to the fund, to three trustees: Lord St. Davids, a personal friend; Sir John Davies, a former private secretary; and the Liberal chief whip, ex officio. These trustees replaced the committee of ex-National Liberal whips which had administered the fund between 1923 and 1927. These explanations did not satisfy Lloyd George's critics, who questioned whether the fund was a trust fund, a personal fund, or a party fund; whether either Lloyd George or his trustees—apparently mere rubber stamps—had the right to spend the funds of an extinct party; whether Lloyd George had touched any of the fund for personal use; and what would happen to the fund if Lloyd George were to die.[114] Lloyd George was compared to a rich but detested bridegroom whom the Liberal party had to marry to escape spinsterish impoverishment [see Cartoon 14] and to Chinese warlords, like "a certain Chiang Kai-shek," whose "affairs . . . are too shady for publication."[115]

What especially excited the fear and anger of Conservatives, Asquithian Liberals, and even some pro-Lloyd George Liberals in late 1927 and early 1928 were whispers that the Liberal party leader was again contemplating some kind of entente, alliance, or coalition with the Labour party. The National Review and other true-blue Conservative papers were outraged that money originally subscribed for anti-socialist purposes might be used by Lloyd George to work his way back to Downing Street at the head of a Liberal-Labour bloc.

Anxiety over the plans of the mercurial Lloyd George extended even to the new head of the Liberal Organization Committee, Sir Herbert Samuel. In February 1928, Samuel was inquiring of Lord St. Davids, chairman of the Lloyd George Fund trustees, whether "if Lloyd George became leader of the Labour Party tomorrow, could he take his Fund with him?" St. Davids replied that he would not permit this to be done, adding that if Lloyd George were to die he and the other trustees would regard the fund "as a Liberal fund to be used for the benefit of the Liberal Party." Although Lloyd George reportedly told Sir Charles Hobhouse that he planned to make arrangements for the continued payment, in the event of his death, of the subsidies promised to the Liberal party, there is no evidence that he actually did so.[116]

Lloyd George himself certainly believed that he rather than the trustees had effective control of the fund, even though on several occasions he claimed that the trustees made routine decisions on allocations for political purposes, that he never saw the accounts, and that they were collectively responsible for all investments, sales of securities, withdrawals, and payments. In his letter to Lord Reading of August 1929, Lloyd George stated that "I never interfere in any of their payments unless there is a great question of policy upon which I am consulted." Yet, as Ian Colvin pointed out, Lloyd George was legally regarded as the sole vendor of United Newspapers, and he evidently viewed the fund as so much his that he could change the trustees at will.[117] Events after the 1929 election--a disappointment for the Liberals--confirmed that in the final analysis the Welshman was the absolute master of his fund.

VIII

The expenses of the 1929 election cut heavily into the Lloyd George Fund. Between £400,000 and £500,000 were disbursed to cover pre-election expenses and the cost of political activities associated with the election campaign. Most of this amount came from the fund's capital, since the income, after taxes, was only about £30,000 a year. When the election was over, Lord

142

St. Davids informed Sir Herbert Samuel that the liquid capital stood at £765,000, while the rest of the fund was invested in shares, worth at least £1,200,000, in the Inveresk paper Company and in the Daily Chronicle Investment Corporation, successor to United Newspapers.[118]

From his shrunken but still very substantial treasure chest, Lloyd George continued to underwrite the expenses of the Liberal Central Association, though at a progressively diminishing rate, up to his break with the party in the fall of 1931 over participation in the National Government. Although he refused to guarantee Liberal headquarters a post-election income of £20,000, as Sir Archibald Sinclair had once urged, he evidently contributed almost that much to the L.C.A. during the fiscal year 1929-30.[119] Unlike the generous 1927-9 subsidy, however, the post-1929 election grants were one-at-a-time allocations, tied to immediate needs and requiring obedience to the paymaster if there were to be any more. Lloyd George demanded of Liberal headquarters economies, including the dismissal of redundant staff, that did not add to his popularity at 21 Abingdon Street. Requests for increased aid by Sir Herbert Samuel, Ramsay Muir, Harcourt Johnstone, Charles Kerr, and other party officials were answered brusquely and sometimes rudely--especially Muir's pleas that Lloyd George turn over to party headquarters a portion of his fund's capital.[120] In July and August 1929, Lord Reading tried to mediate between Lloyd George, Liberal headquarters, and the Liberal Council-- some of whose members, incredibly, still believed that the Welshman could be made to surrender his entire fund.[121] Nothing came of this attempt but Lloyd George's self-serving letter to Reading previously cited. Despite some conciliatory gestures by Lloyd George early in 1930, his wrangling with Liberal headquarters grew more embittered as his subsidies decreased, the Liberal parliamentary party broke apart over economic issues, and the Liberal Council sniped at him from the flanks. By the summer of 1931 his grants to the L.C.A. were down to about £2,000 per annum, and the finances of Liberal headquarters were so straitened that officials had to pay charwomen's wages out of their own pocket.[122]

It was not only disagreements between Lloyd George and fellow Liberals that tightened his purse strings, but the dwindling income from his corporate shares. So drastic was the impact of the 1929-32 depression, on the heels of the earlier newspaper stock slump, that Lloyd George had to cut salaries and dismiss staff in his own office and household. The old free trader was so worried about his investments that after the National Government came in, he hoped for the introduction of paper duties so that his Inveresk shares might gain.[123]

Despite his tongue-in-cheek approval of the National Government's protectionism, Lloyd George strongly opposed Liberal participation in the coalition. When the Liberals, led by Sir Herbert Samuel since Lloyd George's serious illness in July 1931, agreed to join Ramsay MacDonald in seeking a "doctor's mandate" from the electorate, Lloyd George terminated his subsidy to Liberal headquarters and made it plain that no Liberal candidate supporting the National Government would get any help from his fund.[124] Soon afterward, he dropped the Liberal chief whip as a fund trustee and laid down new terms that henceforth grants from the fund would be made only for "political purposes which would advance [the cause of] Liberalism in this country." He carefully stipulated that such disbursements were to be on instructions from himself, thus abandoning the fiction that the trustees were a decision-making body. Although the capital and income of the Lloyd George Fund (it now had this legal name in place of "National Liberal Political Fund") were severely reduced by depression, Lloyd George nevertheless was able to spend about £500,000 for his "new deal" policy studies and for the political activities of his Council of Action in the 1935 election campaign.[125] At one point, he even deliberated buying another newspaper.[126]

IX

After his last bid for power in 1935 as a nonparty statesman, Lloyd George sparingly used what remained of his fund to support his personal political headquarters, the ex-servicemen's aid bureau he had maintained since 1918, and the ghostly Council of Action. Disbursements were also made to selected candidates—Labour as well as Liberal—in by-elections up to the outbreak of war in 1939.[127] A scheme to bypass the Liberal Central Association and directly underwrite the office expenses of friendly Liberal M.P.'s did not materialize because of opposition from Harcourt Johnstone and other central office officials.[128] In late

1936, Lloyd George considered having Dr. Christopher Addison--an old friend and colleague with whom he had become reconciled since a bitter quarrel in 1921--appointed as an additional trustee of the fund. He changed his mind when it was pointed out that Addison, now a prominent Labourite, could object to Liberal candidates whom Lloyd George might want to support in by-elections. The Welshman also thought of adding his daughter Megan to the trustees, but abandoned the idea because of a family squabble.[129]

When the fund's two remaining trustees--Lord St. Davids and Sir John Davies--died in 1938 within a few days of each other, Lloyd George arranged for himself and his son Gwilym to be appointed their successors. He successfully resisted a lawsuit by one of Davies's executors to prevent transfer of the fund's legal control into his hands. It was at this time that the courts finally ruled that the presumed intentions of the original donors could never be precisely determined or enforced, and that the fund was Lloyd George's to do with as he pleased. In the words of a noted lawyer, Sir Wilfred Greene, he had the legal right to "gamble the fund away at Monte Carlo." The Welshman could have bought a pile of chips, for according to Gwilym Lloyd George's 1939 financial statement, the fund was still worth over £ 470,000.[130]

As Lloyd George passed into his seventies, uncertainty about the status of the fund began to worry his legal and financial advisers, as well as his dependents and the prospective beneficiaries of his estate. Veteran political henchmen, notably A. J. Sylvester, Thomas F. Tweed, and Walter Belcher, feared the loss of their livelihoods should the fund pass, as part of Lloyd George's estate, to his family. Following the 1938 legal decision that the fund was his property, Lloyd George himself began to be anxious about the enormous death duties his heirs would have to pay if the Board of Inland Revenue lumped the fund with his personal estate.[131]

At this juncture the last great furor over the Lloyd George Fund threatened to burst into public print, sparked by yet another attempt of the official Liberal party to get its hands on the income if not the capital of the fund. A Liberal inquest into party funds was fomented by Harcourt Johnstone and Sir Hugh Seely, financial angels to the party since Lloyd George had stopped his subsidies in 1931. This inquiry was initiated at about the same time that the Sunday Dispatch--possibly egged on by Conservatives angry at Lloyd George's vituperative foreign policy speeches in the House of Commons--planned a feature "stunt" on "Mr. Lloyd George's Secret Fund." Although the Dispatch article was at first suppressed, it was resurrected a few months later when it seemed possible that Gwilym Lloyd George, now a fund trustee, might be elected the next speaker of the Commons.

As on earlier occasions when the fund was tattled about in press circles, Lloyd George's agents were unable to untangle the complex skeins of rumor emanating from the many camps of his foes: Asquithians, ex-National Liberals, Tories, and lunatic fringe. They did not exclude the possibility that disgruntled former employees could have raided Lloyd George's files and be feeding data to his enemies. They may have neglected to suggest to their chief that one of his trusted lieutenants might be using the threat of massive publicity to force the old Welshman to transform the fund into a public trust, forever excluded from inheritance by his family. Whatever the truth, the whole plot evidently was aborted when Lloyd George made it clear that he would not hesitate to release information from his records perhaps even more damaging to his Liberal and Conservative persecutors than anything they could reveal. In any event, nothing more of consequence was published about the fund, and the hostile Liberal party investigation fizzled after Gwilym Lloyd George issued the financial statement already cited.[132]

Shortly before the outbreak of war in 1939, Lloyd George again weighed the possibility of aiding individual Liberal M.P.'s from his fund, the money to be channeled through the chief whip's parliamentary office rather than party headquarters; and again Harcourt Johnstone raised objections. When Johnstone resigned the L.C.A. treasurership upon becoming a minister in Churchill's war government, his successor--Chief Whip Sir Percy Harris--found the party till to be empty. It was revealed that Johnstone and a small coterie of wealthy friends had been paying the party's bills out of their own pockets. Chief Whip Harris approached Lloyd George in the spring of 1941, and again in 1942 and 1943, with requests for help, but there is no evidence that he responded in any systematic way.[133] Small political donations were made from time to time from the fund, whose capital was appreciating as the war economy prospered, and whose cash reserve exceed-

146

ed £75,000 in the spring of 1943. The last of these payments recorded in the Lloyd George Papers is a contribution of £50, to the Ffestiniog Liberal Association in North Wales, to help liquidate its debt. It was at Ffestiniog in 1886--nearly sixty years in the past--that Lloyd George had first been urged to stand for Parliament by Michael Davitt, after the young Welshman had introduced the Irish agitator to a wildly cheering crowd of tenant farmers and quarrymen.[134]

Lloyd George, according to his private secretary, A. J. Sylvester, wanted to spend as much as possible of his fund during his lifetime. Then it would neither be consumed by the death tax collector, nor pass to his son and fellow trustee, Gwilym Lloyd George, whose busy political career was taking him to the right while his father was moving back to the left. Death overtook the old politician before he could "blow it"--in Sylvester's words--and in 1945 Gwilym came into sole possession of perhaps half a million pounds in cash and securities. He informed Thomas Jones, writing his father's biography, that he too intended to do with the fund as he liked.[135] As in the past, precise information about the fund remained scanty and hard to come by. The executors of Lloyd George's personal estate were refused information, and little more was heard of the fund after the Board of Inland Revenue ruled that it was not part of the dead statesman's private property. Thus one of Lloyd George's fears came to nothing, but the other one--that Gwilym might use the fund in the Tory interest--may have proved more substantial. Gwilym Lloyd George became a prominent Conservative politician, was assigned several important ministerial posts, and topped his career with a peerage. What became of the fund after it passed to him may never be known, as Thomas Jones found that its records had been systematically destroyed.[136] The history of the Lloyd George Fund ended as it had begun: in speculation of one kind or another.

LIBERAL THINK TANK: THE SUMMER SCHOOL MOVEMENT*

    The progressive decline of the Liberal party as a
political force after the First World War was not par-
alleled by the withering away of intellectual Liberalism. There was, rather, a renaissance of Liberal
thought during the twenties that was in part a reaction
to the political sterility of organized Liberalism and
the ineptitude of Liberal party leaders: an attempt to
inject new life into the party from outside. Known
variously as the New Liberalism, the Cambridge School,
and--most frequently--the Liberal Summer School Movement, this Liberal intellectual revival flourished
between 1919 and 1931, reaching the apex of its political influence during the 1928-9 election campaign. The
combination of personalities comprising the Summer
School Movement gradually drifted apart during the
early thirties.

    The Liberal Summer School Movement gave a number
of Liberals of high ability, unable to pursue a parliamentary career due to the collapse of their party and
unattracted by either of the two dominant parties, an
alternative means of public service through participation in policy studies and discussions of major national problems. A Manchester circle, including Ramsay
Muir, Ernest D. Simon, and Edward T. Scott, joined
forces with a group of Cambridge intellectuals centered
around John Maynard Keynes, Hubert Henderson, and
Walter Layton. The products of this brains trust,
notably the Yellow Book of 1928 (Britain's Industrial
Future), were drawn on not only by the Liberal party
but by the two major parties, markedly influencing the
economic programs of contemporary politicians. Described by one writer as a "gallant and ambitious
attempt to drive in harness certain uneasy pairs of
horses, [such as] intensive national . . . development
and unadulterated free trade, [and] freedom of enterprise and drastic industrial 'rationalization,'"[1] the
Summer School Movement tried to reorient Liberal ideol-

---

*This essay is a revision of "The Liberal Summer School
Movement in Britain," published in Research Studies,
XXXIV (December 1966), 205-18. The copyright to the
original article is the property of Washington State
University.

149

ogy in the direction of state intervention and regulation while rejecting the doctrinaire socialism of the Labour party intelligentsia. This New Liberalism was more congenial than outright socialism to many Labourites who had once been strongly attached to Liberalism and resisted conversion to a wholly different ideology.

The end of the First World War left British Liberals bewildered and disheartened, not only by the collapse of their party but by the irrelevance of prewar Liberal dogma to postwar problems. The Liberal party seemed to lack constructive policies to offer a discontented younger generation, and thousands of young Liberals, who would normally have been a driving force in the party, were going over to the reorganized Labour party. Little was done to retard this exodus by orthodox party leaders who either confined their public remarks to vague generalities about Liberal principles and traditions or, if they became more concrete, harked back to the days of Gladstone and Bright and such antique doctrines as laissez-faire and free trade. Even the economic and social reforms of prewar Liberal governments, such as old age pensions, tax reform, and health and unemployment insurance, were deemphasized. Some Liberal leaders went so far as to discourage constructive new programs, arguing that the trend toward the Labour party was a flash in the pan and that the Liberals, as in the past, would return to power when the political pendulum swung from the Conservatives, provided the party was not split by radical policies.

After a year or two of such leadership Liberal intellectuals grew tired of attending party meetings merely to listen to old slogans. They felt there was little chance to return to power unless the party had a policy distinct from the other two parties, and that if the exodus of young members continued the Liberal party was in danger of becoming a mere remnant of loyal traditionalists. At the same time they felt that the public would be receptive to an alternative to Conservative timidity on the one hand and socialist formulas combined with trade union dictation on the other; and that the application of Liberalism to contemporary economic and social problems, such as unemployment and working class discontent, had only begun. It was agreed that mere negation of the policies of the other two parties was not enough, nor was assertion of an indefinite middle course between "reaction and revolution," since the Conservative and Labour parties clearly did not represent these extremes. However, there were no definite ideas as to what the lines of advance should be or what positive steps should be taken.

Nineteenth century Liberalism had received much inspiration from the teachings of the Benthamite Utilitarians, the classical economists, the Nonconformist reformers, and other groups of intellectuals and agitators sympathetic to the party but independent of official party control. One of the weaknesses of Liberalism immediately after the First World War was that such older sources of inspiration had dried up or lost touch with the party. There was no coherent body of timely Liberal thought comparable to that which the Utilitarians and Nonconformists had once supplied, no spontaneous, cooperative groups of thinkers and inquirers able to give form to the vague aspirations of Liberal intellectuals. During the immediate postwar years it seemed as if all active political and social thought was to be found only among the Labour party and its socialist allies, even though the public was clearly not prepared to accept sweeping socialist solutions to current problems. To fill this void the Summer School Movement began to take shape in an atmosphere of dissatisfaction mixed with enthusiasm and optimism.

It was felt that the main objectives of traditional Liberal policy had been reached with the reform of the House of Lords, disestablishment of the Welsh Church, and enactment of the Representation of the People Act of 1918. What was now needed was a completely new program for reorganizing industry supplementing the social reform legislation introduced by the Liberal government before the war. During the winter of 1918-9, a group of Manchester business and professional men, all Liberals, met frequently at the home of Ernest D. Simon, a local manufacturer and amateur authority on housing, to discuss industrial problems. Each endorsed the view that if he were a workingman he would be discontented with and anxious to change the existing economic order. In their successive discussions, members of this group formed some tentative proposals that were offered as resolutions at conferences of the National Liberal Federation. Most of these were coldly received by party leaders. Some had such an abstract and academic quality that they attracted little interest. Ramsay Muir, an articulate professor of modern history at the University of Manchester, was therefore asked to attend the meetings in order to help organize the thinking of the Simon group.

151

After about a half-dozen meetings with Simon and his friends, Muir in 1920 wrote and published a book entitled Liberalism and Industry, which fired the imagination of many hitherto disheartened Liberals. The enthusiastic welcome given this first serious attempt to apply Liberal principles constructively and comprehensively to postwar industrial problems encouraged the Manchester group to proceed with attempts to win support for an advanced industrial policy from Liberal party leaders, contributors of funds, and rank and file.[2]

Progress among prominent party figures was slow and discouraging. Lord Haldane, for example, "came and spent a week-end with us, talked for seventeen hours, gave us a hearty blessing, and joined the Labour Party."[3] Industrialists associated with the Liberal party tended to be dubious of Ramsay Muir's far-reaching proposals. Approaches to party magnates proving unproductive, alternative methods were considered. A handful of younger Liberal enthusiasts met for a weekend with Muir, Simon, and Edward T. Scott, son of the proprietor of the Manchester Guardian, at Simon's farm in Herefordshire in the spring of 1921. It was during this weekend that the Liberal Summer School was devised. It was concluded that a quasi-academic setting would be more conducive to investigation into and discussion of social and economic problems than ordinary party meetings, and that thoughtful people whose enthusiasm had been aroused by spirited, give-and-take debate would be more successful in educating the apathetic party membership to accept progressive ideas than leaders only half convinced and preoccupied with organizational matters. It was also thought that a movement sponsored by persons unconnected with the official Liberal party organization would be unhampered by the timidity and conservatism associated with the official party since the war and be willing to contemplate more radical policies.[4]

The idea of a political summer school was not new, since both the Fabian Society and the Independent Labour party had sponsored them before the war. However, Ramsay Muir, who apparently suggested the scheme at the Herefordshire meeting, visualized something much more ambitious than the occasional prewar schools convened by the socialists. Muir conceived of an annual conference more on the lines of the British Association for the Advancement of Science, at which all kinds of social and economic problems might be discussed rationally and scientifically from the liberal viewpoint.[5] In Muir's own words,

> it did not seem enough that individuals should write books and articles, or make speeches. The essential thing was discussion and criticism, and the submission of ideas to the judgment of all who were alert and serious enough to take part in the process of discussion. So they worked out the idea of the Summer School, in which papers should be read, on political and social problems, not by politicians, but by men who might be regarded as experts on the side either of scholarship or of practical experience, and in which all who chose to take part in discussion should be free to do so. They knew that many of the best minds engaged in the study of economic and political sciences were in fact Liberals, though not active politicians; and they planned to provide them both a nucleus and a platform.[6]

The next step, in the last week of September 1921, was to invite about one hundred younger Liberals to spend five days at Grasmere, a resort in the Lake District, participating in a trial run of the summer school plan. About seventy of those invited appeared, including a number of Liberal candidates for Parliament but no incumbent M.P.'s or officials of the party organization. The guiding spirits were the leaders of the Manchester group: Muir, Edward Scott of the Guardian, and Simon, now lord mayor of Manchester. To these were added some new figures, several of them associated with Cambridge University, who now joined the enlarged leadership of the Summer School Movement: Walter T. Layton, former economics lecturer at Cambridge, an official of the Munitions Ministry during the war, and subsequently editor of the Economist; Sir William Beveridge, noted for his work in the field of social insurance; and Philip Guedalla, lawyer, businessman, and amateur historian, who had also worked for Lloyd George in the Munitions Ministry and had been adopted as Liberal parliamentary candidate for a London constituency. The participants in the Grasmere conference were deeply interested in an active policy of industrial reconstruction which would provide the British workingman with employment, status, and dignity, and which would be more likely to succeed than the utopian projects of the Labour party intellectuals.

The Grasmere conference, unlike subsequent Liberal

Summer Schools, was completely informal. There were no lectures, each meeting of the whole conference being opened by a short introductory statement by one of the participants and closed with a brief summation by another member. The scheduled meetings were supplemented by spontaneous discussions by small groups. Although sharper differences were revealed at Grasmere than within the Manchester group, there was general agreement that the summer school approach was a good way to stimulate thought and that future meetings, opened to a larger attendance, might influence the mass of Liberal party members.[7]

The Grasmere conferees decided that the Liberal Summer School should be a permanent institution, held each year in a convenient location so that hundreds of Liberals might attend. The Summer School executive committee, selected at Grasmere to plan the next year's and future Summer Schools, later decided to meet in alternating years at Oxford and Cambridge, during Bank Holiday Week. The School was launched with the expressed approval of Liberal party leader H. H. Asquith, who agreed with its founders that it should remain unattached to the party organization if it was to succeed in its purpose not of formulating official party policy but of stimulating inquiry and discussion out of which party programs might gradually develop.[8]

The Grasmere trial summer school had been limited to originators of the plan and a selected group of experts and Liberal activists. The first regular Liberal Summer School at Oxford in August 1922 was open to all comers, though total attendance was limited to 1000 to encourage informality.[9] Actually this maximum figure was not even approached: only about 600 persons were present as enrolled members of the school, though approximately 3000 attended the final rally open to the general public.[10] The Summer School's 1922 program established a basic pattern that was to be followed in most subsequent years. The opening address at the first evening session was given by Asquith, the first of many party chieftains to perform this ritual, in which in characteristic Olympian fashion he praised the Summer School as a movement that might be a significant factor in the Liberal party's revival.[11] The practice was also inaugurated in 1922 of using the last session as a public meeting for party propaganda purposes.[12]

Participants in the nine-day 1922 School (August 1-9) were kept busy attending lectures and the reading of papers by university professors and other experts, but some of the spontaneity of the previous year's trial run seemed to be lacking. The numerous impromptu discussions held at Grasmere were evidently not duplicated at Oxford in 1922. According to observers, interrogating of most speakers was perfunctory, lively audience participation being aroused only by Walter Layton's paper.[13] This lack of enthusiasm may have been partly due to the superficial coverage of a great many domestic and foreign topics rather than concentration in depth on the industrial problem as Muir, Simon, and their Manchester colleagues had originally intended. The speeches and papers dealt with such subjects as the League of Nations, disarmament, international finance, British imperial policy in Egypt and India, and current British foreign policy, in addition to the domestic problems of wages, public versus private ownership, the future of the mining industry, and the economic machinery of the government.[14] However, one young observer praised the 1922 Summer School for debating a variety of subjects never before considered at a Liberal conference, calling it a landmark in the lives of young Liberals whose political views had not crystallized before the war, who wanted to be loyal to the party, but who thought the party was out of touch with their day and generation. A Liberal intellectual of an older generation, C. F. G. Masterman, was also impressed, writing to his wife that "the school was quite admirable. . . . despite gloomy warnings" from party veterans.[15] Whatever the reasons for the shift in emphasis, and the reactions to it, coverage of a broad range of topics was to characterize most of the subsequent Summer Schools.[16] The papers and lectures delivered in 1922 were later published in an inexpensive book, Essays in Liberalism.[17]

Minor innovations were introduced at later Summer Schools held during the twenties. Beginning in 1923, late afternoon discussions were made a regular part of the program, at which the lecturer of the day could be questioned and his ideas criticized.[18] Also in 1923, and for the next four years, the London Liberal newspaper the Daily News published some of the more timely Summer School papers in its New Way Series, several of which achieved circulations exceeding 10,000.[19] An innovation at the 1925 Summer School was the inclusion in the program of some foreign liberals, while the 1928 School saw the first appearance of Conservatives and Labourites as speakers.[20] Attendance at the Schools continued to increase through 1928, reaching the 1000 figure several times. Large attendance was not necessarily an index to a School's success, of course. In the opinion of many friends of the Summer School Movement, its high point was reached at the 1924 School, which had neither a large attendance nor any unusual organizational features, but was marked by intellectual brilliance and high spirits. After the disappointing 1929 election, Summer School attendance dropped off in rough proportion to the decline of the Liberal party's electoral fortunes, so that in the middle thirties hardly more than a hundred participants took part.[21]

Attendance at the Liberal Summer Schools was not restricted to confirmed Liberals, and members of other parties were never turned away. Indeed, young people whose political views were still in flux were encouraged to come in the hope that they would be converted to Liberalism. Perhaps as many as half the attendants at the early Summer Schools were young Liberals and unattached voters who had not yet selected a party, together with some older men and women who either were vaguely drawn to Liberalism for the first time or, having once been Liberals and lost faith, were considering a return to a rejuvenated party. The Summer School "students" were predominantly well-to-do middle class people of above average intelligence and educational background, most of whom paid their own expenses.[22] They came to the school for serious discussion, not for fun. There were no scheduled recreational activities as at the socialist summer schools, and the only entertainment was a skit presented at the end of the session, in which some of the younger "students" caricatured events and personalities of the day.[23]

Except for the opening and closing meetings, speakers and "students" at the Summer School wereexpected to lecture and debate in an academic manner and to avoid emotionalism and extreme partisanship. At least one guest speaker was publicly criticized for violating this rule.[24] This was the one limitation imposed on discussion, which otherwise was allowed and encouraged to become as controversial as the participants wished. The Summer Schools were unquestionably forums for new ideas of interest to all parties. It was at the Oxford Summer School of 1922 that Arnold D. McNair proposed the scheme for nationalizing the royalties of the coal industry that was later elaborated in the Lloyd George-sponsored report Coal and Power and endorsed in its main features by the Samuel Commission of 1926.[25] At the 1924 School Sir William

Beveridge formulated a scheme for establishing widows' and orphans' pensions, and of extending old age pensions, that was later adopted with only minor changes by the Baldwin Conservative government.[26] Proposals for taxing inherited wealth made at the 1926 session were appropriated by the Labour party, eventually appearing in its official program.[27] Most of the Yellow Book recommendations on unemployment and industrial recovery, which became the nucleus of the 1929 Liberal election program, were debated at the 1927 School before being published and adopted as resolutions by a special Liberal Industrial Conference in 1928.[28] Many of the significant papers read at the Summer Schools were the results of long preliminary discussion and research by the Movement's executive committee, following which one expert wrote and delivered the actual lecture.[29]

The organization of the Liberal Summer School was loose and informal. The executive committee elected at Grasmere was enlarged from time to time by cooption as its work load increased. In 1924 a research department was created, to gather data for the executive committee, conduct polls and surveys on current questions, and answer inquiries by patrons of the School. Two years later the research department was discontinued and its staff put to work on the Lloyd George-financed Liberal Industrial Inquiry, from which the Yellow Book emerged. The Summer School always remained formally independent of the official Liberal party organization, and was financially self-sufficient. There were, however, cooperative enterprises, such as the Industrial Inquiry, in which the School and the party organization, or Lloyd George's semi-private headquarters, shared personnel and expenses. There were also interlocking relationships between the School and official party organs through individuals influential in both-- as in the case of Thomas F. Tweed, who between 1921 and 1927 was simultaneously general secretary of the Summer School and organizing secretary of the Manchester Liberal Federation, and also after 1926 director of Lloyd George's land campaign. The most important of the personal connections was that of Ramsay Muir as co-director of the Summer School and officer in the Liberal central office and the National Liberal Federation in the late twenties and early thirties. While Muir was acting in these joint roles the Summer School came closest to being an arm of the official Liberal party structure.[30]

The most important of the cooperative projects in which the Summer School Movement worked with leaders of the Liberal party was the Industrial Inquiry of 1926-8. This was the third policy study sponsored by Lloyd George, and financed by his personal political fund, since his reentry into the Liberal party in 1923. The Summer School Movement had had no formal connection with the previous two, on coal and rural and urban land, though several of its members had participated in these studies as individuals, and both projects--especially the one on coal--had been influenced by previous reports and discussions in the Summer Schools. There were both advantages and disadvantages to the Summer School in working with Lloyd George. Obviously the multimillion-pound political fund at Lloyd George's disposal would enable the School to conduct much more elaborate research into the subject that interested it the most--the condition of British industry--than it could otherwise. On the other hand, the questionable reputation of the Lloyd George Fund might rub off on the highly respectable School. From his viewpoint, Lloyd George was glad to use the talents of the Summer School experts to develop his new ideas, even though he regarded some of them as impractical "professors."[31] The School's executive committee decided to accept Lloyd George's offer of collaboration on condition that the Industrial Inquiry be directed and staffed by persons of its own choice, that it would control the allocation of any funds donated by Lloyd George, and that Lloyd George would not veto its recommendations. Lloyd George accepted these terms, offering the Summer School not only as much money as it needed but whatever assistance it required from the staff of his personal secretariat.[32] Thus the Industrial Inquiry became predominantly a Summer School enterprise, though Lloyd George kept in close touch with it through members of his organization serving on the Inquiry staff, and occasionally took part in deliberations--some of which were held weekends at his country estate.[33]

The directors and principal staff members of the Industrial Inquiry, most of them associated with the Summer School Movement since its inception,[34] supplemented their extensive knowledge and experience of the industrial situation with hearings, to which qualified persons were invited without regard to their politics; investigating teams sent to foreign countries; and great masses of reports and memoranda submitted by their researchers. These data were sifted through a series of committees on such topics as trade unionism, unemployment, state regulation of industry, and industrial wages. The recommendations of the committees were then discussed and synthesized by the directorate of the Inquiry, which was substantially coterminous with the Summer School executive committee. The final product of the Inquiry was the report entitled Britain's Industrial Future, but better known from the color of its cover as the Yellow Book.[35]

The most comprehensive study of British industrial problems up to that time, and described by one writer as "the best available program [for] those desiring a middle way between capitalism and socialism,"[36] the Yellow Book was a realization of the original purpose of the Summer School Movement. Its proposals--including an economic advisory staff to aid the cabinet, a national investment board to plan uses of public capital, public corporations to regulate businesses affecting the public interest, sharing of industrial management by workers, use of the Bank of England's credit powers to fight inflation and deflation, and a vigorous national development program to combat unemployment-- became official Liberal party policy in the 1929 election campaign. After being debated before publication at the Cambridge Summer School of 1927, the proposals were discussed early in 1928 at regional conferences of the National Liberal Federation, and at a special national conference of the Federation. This Liberal Industrial Conference, attended by delegates from all Liberal constituency and regional organizations, endorsed the Yellow Book, which thereby became part of the official Liberal program.[37] The Summer School had reached the peak of its influence within the Liberal party.

The "big five" of the Summer School Movement were Ramsay Muir, Ernest D. (later Lord) Simon, John Maynard (later Lord) Keynes, Walter T. (later Lord) Layton, and Hubert D. (later Sir Hubert) Henderson. The first two belonged to the original Manchester circle, the others to the group of Cambridge economists that merged with it in 1921. Although Simon was probably the person most responsible for launching the Summer School, furnishing not only inspiration but funds,[38] and Layton was at first the most enthusiastic of the Cambridge Liberal dons, they were soon overshadowed by Muir and Keynes.

These two men, both dynamic personalities, were otherwise very distinct types. Muir, though not a really creative thinker, was informed on a great variety of subjects; he had the power as a writer to marshal his facts and arguments effectively, and as a speaker to give them life. Often compared to the Fabians' Sidney Webb, he was a man of great integrity, enthusiastic, tireless--and very dogmatic. "One had the feeling that locked behind his breast was a sacred text in which all the answers to all problems could be found."[39] Keynes, in contrast, was empirical, pragmatic, and somewhat cynical. While Muir was mainly interested in bringing orthodox Liberal principles up to date and applying them to current problems, Keynes believed Liberal doctrines needed a complete refurbishment to meet the demands of wholly changed economic circumstances. Keynes believed Liberals would have to turn their backs on the old idea of laissez-faire and accept government intervention at many points in the economy, while trying to preserve as much private initiative as possible. "There is no reason why [the Liberal party] should continue to exist," Keynes wrote in 1927, "except to contribute . . . to the gradual evolution of a reformed economic society."[40] Muir was not only less of an economic adventurer and innovator than Keynes, but a much more loyal party man. Rejecting Keynes's advocacy of an alliance between the Liberal and Labour parties, Muir also scorned Keynes's suggestion that perhaps Liberalism should try to permeate the two major parties through such media as the Summer School rather than continue to maintain itself as an independent party.

Although Keynes and Muir were intellectually and personally at odds over many things, their disagreements did not split the Summer School Movement because they found different media of expression and avoided head-on conflicts. Muir remained the chief organizer and spokesman of the Summer School and dominated each annual session. Later he was drafted for organizational work in the Liberal party. Keynes devoted his time to research and writing, and to acting as board chairman of the weekly Nation. In 1923, Keynes, Simon, and other members of the Summer School group had raised money to buy control of the Nation from the Rowntree family, intending to use it as the organ of the Movement. Muir was originally slated to be editor, but he agreed to step aside to avoid the strong possibility of clashing with Keynes. Instead, Muir took over the editorship of another small journal, the Weekly Westminster, which before its financial failure a couple of years later acquired a substantial following among younger Liberals impressed by Muir's confident and didactic approach. In the meantime Keynes, assisted by his Cambridge protégé Hubert Henderson as editor, tried to transform the moribund Nation into a profit-making vehicle of the New Liberalism represented by the Summer School. Before it also failed and was forced into merger with the Labour-oriented New Statesman, the Nation became the widely read voice of those in the Summer School Movement and Liberal party who shared Keynesian views on government economic intervention and reformism short of outright state control.[41]

As the Summer School Movement gathered momentum during the twenties, its enthusiasts hoped it would have the same influence on Liberalism as the Fabian Society had had on Labour during the previous generation. To a degree it did. Like the meetings and publications of the Fabians in the 1880s and after, the efforts of the Summer School group helped to give clarity and coherence to the economic and social opinions in which its participants believed. A common body of constructive Liberal thought was developed and defined where there had been a vacuum before. The growing belief that Liberalism was an outworn doctrine useless in solving modern problems was effectively checked. Indeed, in the field of industrial development and reform, its principal interest, the Summer School group gave Britain the only comprehensive policy then in existence. Insofar as this program was dipped into by the official Liberal party, and raided by the opposition parties, the Summer School became, in Ramsay Muir's words, "a sort of university for politicians."[42] There is no question that important parts of the Summer School program were the inspiration for concrete legislative enactments of current and subsequent British governments, and also attracted attention in foreign countries. The Summer School certainly encouraged more scientific thinking and less obtuse partisanship in all British parties, and helped to draw professional politicians and economists closer together.

The Summer School Movement also had a positive, though short-term, effect on the political fortunes of the Liberal party. The drift of young progressives from the Liberal to the Labour party was slowed down. In fact, before the 1929 election there was some evidence that the flow was being reversed. The Summer School Movement was especially influential in arousing interest in Liberalism among university students.[43] By weakening the image of the Liberal party as a staid instrument of middle class orthodoxy, the Summer School helped somewhat to improve relations between the Liberal and Labour parties during the late twenties and early thirties.

On the other hand, the Movement was plagued with weaknesses. It never became the team operation the Fabian Society had been in its heyday. Brilliant and able as the participants were, they were unable to conceal fully their differences behind a common platform. There were too many discordant minds and personalities mingled in the Movement, from municipal socialists like Ernest Simon to fairly traditional capitalists like Walter Layton. Contradictory views were revealed for all to hear at the annual Schools. Another serious weakness was the absence of one or two leaders, comparable to the Webbs in the Fabian Society, who could weld the Movement into a unified fighting force. Ramsay Muir came nearest to filling this role, but he was too much of a doctrinaire Liberal to command the loyalty of the brightest and most flexible thinkers among the New Liberals.

The Summer School Movement also lacked skilled propagandists, like George Bernard Shaw and H. G. Wells among the Fabians, who could write to attract public attention. The Summer School policies, especially the economic ones, were complex, and their proponents did not have the skill to digest and simplify them for popular consumption.[44] Again, Muir was far superior to his colleagues as a pamphleteer and platform lecturer, but he was the least original thinker in the cadre and the one most wedded to orthodox Liberal ideas. The fact that the Summer School Movement was dominated by academic theorists was itself cause for suspicion among many Liberals, both leaders and rank and file.[45] The Fabian intellectuals had been looked up to with awe by the relatively uneducated trade union-based leaders of the early Labour party. The Summer School "professors" inspired less trust among the men of affairs, trained at public school and university, who controlled the purse strings and made policy decisions in the Liberal party of the twenties. Finally, the members of the Summer School cadre seemed to lack complete confidence in their own efforts. Their articles and speeches, even those of zealots like Muir and Simon, exuded an aura of forced optimism, strained enthusiasm, and apology for barely concealed weaknesses. The elan of the Fabians, the belief in ultimate victory for their cause, is missing from the surviving publications of the Liberal Summer School.[46]

Following an acrid policy dispute among its leaders over whether or not to endorse protective tariffs, which exploded at the 1930 Summer School, the Movement gradually petered out during the thirties as public interest in it waned. Its following ultimately was reduced to a handful of Ramsay Muir's friends and disciples. Although annual Summer Schools were held until the Second World War, they ceased to influence British politics significantly. After the 1929 election, and especially after Lloyd George broke with the Liberal party in 1931, the Yellow Book program was given little more than lip service by the party leaders, despite Muir's close relationship with the party organization.[47] The undoubted end of the Liberal party as a political force, which the Summer School had failed to prevent, brought an end to the association of young intellectuals with the Movement.[48] Their identification after 1931 was predominantly with the Labour party. The older leaders of the Summer School, on the other hand, tended to enter the orbit of the National Government. Several became closely connected with it in official or unofficial positions.

As for the ideas generated by the Summer School during the twenties, these were appropriated by both major parties. Some were enacted into concrete legislation or administrative rulings by the National Government, others by postwar Labour and Conservative governments. As Ernest Simon had observed years before, "if the Liberal Summer School does nothing else, it will at least provide ideas for the Labour Party"--and, as it turned out the Conservative party too.

THE LLOYD GEORGE POLICY STUDIES*

During the long anticlimax to his career that followed his wartime premiership, David Lloyd George's most significant contributions to British public affairs undoubtedly were the elaborate policy studies that he sponsored and financed during the twenties and early thirties. Praised by historians and social scientists as the only political tracts of the times to show penetrating insight into the country's economic ailments, these exhaustive reports by committees of outstanding experts were to be deeply mined by successive governments both before and after the Second World War.

Intended by Lloyd George as programs for either a Liberal party revival or a nonpartisan crusade that he himself proposed to lead, the reports were instead appropriated without credit by Conservatives and Labourites who often impugned the reputation of the man who had inspired them. Lloyd George died a disappointed man, forced to see some of the schemes developed by his researchers halfheartedly and incompetently implemented by his enemies of the prewar National Governments, and denied the opportunity to see others enacted with more skill and enthusiasm after the war by moderate Labourites and progressive Conservatives with whom he was more in sympathy.

I

The prototype of Lloyd Geoge's later policy studies was the Land Inquiry of 1912-4. This was a Liberal party enterprise, instigated and encouraged by Lloyd George and fellow progressives in the party but financed by regular party funds. Its object was to launch a new land reform campaign, supplementary to the earlier campaigns for the People's Budget and elimina-

---

*This essay is a revision of "Research Projects of David Lloyd George, 1912-1935," published in Research Studies, XXXVI (December 1968), 279-301. The copyright to the original article is the property of Washington State University.

tion of the House of Lords's veto, that would sweep the Liberals back into office in the prospective general election of 1915.

The idea of appointing a committee of researchers to prepare a land reform scheme to be submitted to the cabinet, and ultimately to the electorate, was derived from the informal research Lloyd George had commissioned under his personal supervision before drafting the National Insurance Bill of 1911. This research had included a trip by Lloyd George himself to Germany, Austria-Hungary, and Belgium to study social legislation; inquiries among physicians made by his friend Dr. Christopher Addison, East London M.P.; and reports submitted by his ministerial colleague Charles Masterman, the trusted civil servant Sir Robert Morant, Thomas Jones of the Welsh National Memorial Foundation, and others. Later, after the Insurance Bill had become law, many of these researchers (the civil servants excluded) had, under the chairmanship of Dr. Addison, constituted a Liberal Insurance Committee to explain the act to the public and combat prejudice against it. Lloyd George hoped in the case of land reform to obviate the need for similar remedial action after the reform had been enacted by conducting a full and open public inquiry in advance, one that would dispel the objections of all but partisan opponents.[1]

The Land Inquiry Committee of the Liberal party was appointed by Prime Minister Asquith as party leader but largely selected by Lloyd George. It was headed by two members of distinguished Liberal landed families—Sir Arthur Dyke Acland, an old friend of Asquith, as chairman and Charles Roden Buxton as secretary—but composed mostly of professional social scientists of advanced Liberal tendencies and Liberal politicians and journalists associated with Lloyd George's progressive wing of the party. A staff of about seventy researchers was employed, including solicitors, architects, and surveyors. The committee began its work in the late summer of 1912; set up numerous subcommittees to investigate such problems as landlord-tenant relations, taxation, land development, and natural resources; and by early 1913 had collected a large mass of evidence showing underutilization of agricultural land, abysmally low wages for farm laborers, progressive depopulation of rural villages, and rent gouging by urban landlords.[2]

Lloyd George began to make use of this material in partisan speeches even before it was published, to the dismay not only of scientists on the committee but of prominent right wing and moderate Liberals such as Lord Crewe, Sir Edward Grey, and John Burns. The influence of these opponents in the party had already prevented the inquiry from receiving the full support, especially financial, of Liberal party headquarters that Lloyd George had been counting on. A substantial part of the financing of the inquiry had to come from donations by wealthy friends of Lloyd George.[3]

Perhaps fortunately for the objectivity of the Land Inquiry, Lloyd George's attention was rather fully occupied during the first half of 1913 in clearing himself of the Marconi wireless scandal charges, so that the committee could complete its studies and publish its reports without further leaks that might have cast doubt on their scholarly validity. Lloyd George seems also to have taken to heart the warnings of confidants such as Lord Beauchamp and Sir George Riddell: the inquiry must have not only the appearance of scholarship but the reality, and he should postpone land campaign oratory until the published reports of the inquiry gave him absolutely accurate facts with which to counter the objections of hostile elements in the Liberal as well as the Conservative party.[4]

The two reports of the Land Inquiry were released in October 1913 and April 1914.[5] Together they furnished a great mine of information on conditions in rural and urban areas that would prove useful to British governments, especially the Asquith Coalition when it enacted its Rent Restrictions Act of 1915, and Lloyd George's own ministry when drafting its ambitious postwar housing acts.[6]

The reports of the Land Inquiry were of considerably more value as permanent reference works than as the temporary political campaign documents for which Lloyd George had primarily intended them. The land campaign never really got off the ground. By the time Lloyd George had set it in motion, public and parliamentary attention was being seized by the home rule and Ulster crises, to be followed soon after by the beginning of the First World War. The anticipated election of 1915, in which the land campaign and the Land Inquiry Report, simplified and popularized by skilled propagandists, were expected to recapture urban working class voters from Labour and win a number of marginal rural constituencies from the Conservatives, never took place. In the 1918 election after the war, the Liberal party was split and the Land Inquiry Report almost forgotten as a political weapon.[7]

II

The Land Inquiry of 1912-4 was created and financed by the Liberal party organization, of which Lloyd George was then a leading member. After he split with Asquith in 1916 and established his Coalition government of Conservatives, Labourites, and dissident Liberals, Lloyd George was never again in good standing with the orthodox Liberals and did not succeed in gaining control of the Liberal Central Association until 1927, although a nominal reunion with the Asquithians was effected in 1923. After his government collapsed in October 1922, Lloyd George maintained, with the resources of the political fund he had accumulated during the Coalition years, an independent political headquarters in Westminster, first at 18 Abingdon Street, three doors from the Liberal Central Association, and after 1925 in much larger quarters at 25 Old Queen Street. It was from these offices that Lloyd George initiated his four great policy studies of the twenties, beginning with the Coal Inquiry of 1924.

Dissatisfied with both the timidity of Ramsay MacDonald's Labour government and Asquith's apathetic leadership of the Liberal party, and urged on by colleagues to assert himself more forcibly in public affairs,[8] Lloyd George decided early in 1924 to use part of his fund to conduct an investigation of what he considered the weakest link in the British economy, the moribund coal industry. The report of the Coal Inquiry would become the nucleus of the next Liberal election program, just as the prewar Land Inquiry Report had been intended to help the Liberal cause in an election that was never held. In March 1924, Lloyd George chose for his Coal Inquiry Committee a few Liberal M.P.'s and a much larger number of industrialists and economists connected only loosely with the Liberal party or not at all. A number of the committee members were associated with the Liberal Summer School Movement, a group of academic Liberals that had been studying the coal industry and other problems of British economic life for several years.

168

After visiting coal fields in Britain, France, and Germany, interviewing hundreds of persons connected with the British coal industry, and reviewing all available literature on the subject, the Coal Inquiry Committee published in July 1924 a thick report entitled Coal and Power.[9] It rejected government operation of the mines, as recommended by the Labour party, and syndicalist control of the mines by the miners, as demanded by the South Wales Miners' Federation, calling instead for a compromise system combining public ownership and regulation with private management. The report recommended the purchase of the mines by the government from their landlord-owners, the leasing of them to private companies for exploitation, the establishment of miners' welfare funds and miners' councils to share in management, and a conversion of coal into electric power, transmitted by government regulated power corporations, to stimulate rural agriculture and industry. It enunciated the progressive Liberal theory that the function of government was to create conditions under which private enterprise could operate effectively in the public interest.[10]

The proposals in Coal and Power attracted considerable attention and praise from disinterested authorities on these questions, but their reception in political circles was less enthusiastic. The Labour government, committed to complete nationalization, rejected them outright.[11] Within the Liberal party, the recommendations received warm support only from the wing of the party that looked to Lloyd George for leadership and ideas. Asquith formally endorsed them, but only after the report had been printed and distributed. The bulk of the Asquithian Liberals, besides resenting their origin with a committee appointed by their enemy, considered them too radical at the time they were published. However, a couple of years later the main parts were adopted in modified form into the official Liberal program. In the meantime the proposals were endorsed in principle by the Royal Commission on the Coal Industry, headed by a prominent Liberal, Sir Herbert Samuel, and aroused the interest of young progressive Conservatives who, as junior ministers in the National Government, finally forced reluctant enactment of the Coal Bill of 1938 expropriating mine sites. As early as 1926, the Baldwin Conservative government created a Central Electricity Board, as suggested by Coal and Power, to regulate distribution of electricity throughout the country.[12]

The Coal Inquiry report was of no help to the Liberals in the snap election of October 1924, and indeed was practically ignored in a campaign dominated by such issues and red herrings as a commercial treaty with the Soviet Union and the Zinoviev Letter. With the Liberals reduced to a small fraction of the House of Commons and thoroughly demoralized, Lloyd George returned to his favorite subjects, agriculture and soil resources, in the continuing hope of evolving a party program that might "dish" Labour.

III

Even before organizing his Coal Inquiry, Lloyd George in June 1923 had appointed two pilot committees on rural and urban land problems to bring up to date the Land Reports of 1913-4.[13]   In the summer of 1924, while their work was overshadowed by the more timely Coal Inquiry, investigators for these committees were visiting continental countries to collect new material on different systems of cultivation, land tenure, and taxation.   After the election, Lloyd George toyed briefly with the idea of concentrating on research for an "Empire Book" that would discuss the relative merits of free trade and imperial preference, but decided instead to complete the land project.[14]   The two pilot committees were combined into a single Land Inquiry Committee with headquarters at 25 Old Queen Street, the Lloyd George "party office."   Several members of the Summer School group were attracted to the enterprise, and for the first time since his return to the Liberal party Lloyd George was able to interest some prominent Asquithians in his plans.[15]   In October and November 1925 the Land Inquiry Committee issued the two parts of its report on rural and urban land issues, which became known as the Green Book and the Brown Book from the colors of their covers.[16]

The Brown Book adhered quite closely to orthodox Liberalism as it had evolved by the twenties.   Building on the earlier Urban Land Report of 1913, it stressed regional planning, attacked city slum conditions, and called for the empowering of local governments to expropriate land for urban renewal and park and highway construction, and to levy "betterment taxes" on land values for public improvements.   This generally noncontroversial report was accepted by nearly all segments of Liberal opinion.[17]

170

The Green Book was quite another matter. Unlike Coal and Power and the Brown Book, it was written to order for Lloyd George, who instructed his researchers to emphasize data supporting his belief that "landlordism had failed." The Green Book was meant to incite readers, emotionally as well as intellectually, against big landowners. The report's bias, and the sensational and provocative language in which it was written, detracted from what was otherwise a carefully prepared work, and naturally antagonized right wing and moderate Liberals who regarded it as a "Lloyd George stunt." The Green Book, which proposed dispossession of landlords, nationalization of agricultural land, and lifetime leases by the government to tenants keeping their holdings in good cultivation, was immediately denounced as "socialistic" by Walter Runciman, Sir Alfred Mond, Edward Hilton Young, W. M. R. Pringle, Sir Charles Hobhouse, and other Liberals of the right.[18]

In order to paper over what was quickly becoming another split in the already dangerously divided party, Asquith--now Lord Oxford--summoned a special Liberal Land Conference in February 1926 to try to work out an agreed party policy.[19] This conference, and the subsequent 1926 annual meeting of the National Liberal Federation in June, accepted the program of the Green Book with considerable modification, notably the restriction of expropriation to "bad" landlords. Lloyd George, realizing that there was formidable opposition to land nationalization even within his own following, and responding to criticisms of the practicality of the original Green Book proposals, was conciliatory in agreeing to amendments.[20]

The rural land policy based on the Green Book had prospects of attracting back to the Liberal party many farmers' and rural laborers' votes lost to the Conservatives in 1924, strength that would more than compensate for the defection, ostensibly over the land policy, of "anti-socialists" such as Mond, Hilton Young, and Lloyd George's former parliamentary private secretary, David Davies.[21] These bright hopes were clouded by the disruption within the party over allocation of the Lloyd George Fund, and an even more serious division--reminiscent of 1916--between Lloyd George and Lord Oxford over the General Strike of May 1926.

Lloyd George had prematurely launched his new land campaign in September 1925--weeks before the Green Book was published and months before the party voted to

171

approve it--at an open air meeting on the country
estate of Francis Dyke Acland, son of the chairman of
the prewar Land Inquiry. At about the same time Lloyd
George--despairing of reaching satisfactory agreement
with the Liberal Central Association over division of
his fund, and doubtful of winning over the Asquithians
to support of the Green Book program--set up at his Old
Queen Street headquarters an independent propaganda
organization, the Land and Nation League, to direct the
land campaign. Thomas F. Tweed, who was also general
secretary of the Liberal Summer School, agreed to act
as chief organizer of the League. For about a year and
a half, the Land and Nation League very actively promoted Lloyd George's land campaign throughout the
country, much of the time independently of the official
Liberal party organization. Following adoption of the
Green Book policy at the Liberal Land Conference of
February 1926, there was nominal--but not very amic-
able--cooperation between the League and the party
machine. During this period the Land and Nation
League, ably staffed and well financed from the Lloyd
George Fund, overshadowed the squabbling Liberal organization. It dropped gradually into the background
after Lloyd George secured control of the Central
Association in the winter of 1926-7, and his mind
turned from agricultural to industrial issues.[22]

IV

    The most elaborate of Lloyd George's postwar
research projects was the Industrial Inquiry of 1926-8,
conducted in cooperation with the Liberal Summer
School. Individual members of the Summer School
Movement had participated in the coal and land studies,
but the School as an organization had remained aloof
from Lloyd George, chiefly because most of the leading
members were affiliated with the Asquithian branch of
the Liberal party. It was not until 1924--three years
after the founding of the Summer School--that the
School's executive committee invited Lloyd George to
speak at the annual summer session. From that time on
Lloyd George and the School drew closer together,
though remaining wary of each other. The leaders of
the School--John Maynard Keynes, Ramsay Muir, and
Ernest D. Simon--questioned Lloyd George's sincerity as
a politician and his dedication to Liberalism, while
Lloyd George was dubious of the practicality of much of
the Summer School's social and economic program.

Nevertheless, it was clear that the School and Lloyd George represented the most intellectually active elements in the Liberal party, and that they could accomplish more in conjunction than separately. The two most significant breaks in the mutual distrust that had separated Lloyd George and the Summer School were the acceptance by Thomas F. Tweed, general secretary of the School, of the post of chief organizer of the Land and Nation League, and speeches by Lloyd George in the House of Commons endorsing Keynes's position condemning the Baldwin government's return to the gold standard. These two events occurred in 1925. By the summer of 1926, Keynes, Tweed, and others in the Summer School Movement sympathetic to Lloyd George had persuaded the executive committee to accept Lloyd George's offer of funds and expert assistance to conduct an Industrial Inquiry, of the kind the School had long wanted to make, but had lacked the means. In spite of his ongoing quarrel with the Asquithian Liberals over the party leadership, Lloyd George was invited to give the keynote speech at the 1926 Summer School.[23]

Part of the agreement between Lloyd George and the Summer School executive committee was that the latter should select the personnel of the Industrial Inquiry, and that Lloyd George should have no veto over its findings. Lloyd George's directed verdict against the landlords in the Green Book was recalled and a repetition feared unless he was specifically restrained. This apprehension may have been groundless, because Lloyd George did not claim to be an expert on industrial conditions as he assumed he was on rural questions. In any event, Lloyd George worked closely with the Industrial Inquiry but did not try to dictate to it. During the eighteen months the study was in progress, its directors and staff were given the use of office quarters at 25 Old Queen Street. Frequently they were invited to spend weekends at Bron-y-de, Lloyd George's country house at Churt, Surrey, where--in the words of John Campbell--"he delighted in feeding them entirely on home-grown produce and refreshing them with cider, buttermilk and mead."[24]

Although most of the principals of the Industrial Inquiry--notably Keynes, Muir, Simon, the economists Walter Layton and Herbert Henderson, and the sociologist Seebohm Rowntree--belonged to the Summer School group, a large portion of the investigatory and clerical staff were on loan from Lloyd George's personal secretariat. W. M. Eager, who had been secretary and principal draftsman of the Land Inquiry of 1923-5, acted in similar capacity for the Industrial Inquiry, assisted by two other Lloyd George lieutenants, Jules Menken and Hubert Phillips. Philip Kerr, later Lord Lothian, a friend and colleague of Lloyd George and frequent speaker at Summer School sessions, was also active in the Inquiry. Besides the interrelationship between Lloyd George's secretariat and the Summer School group, there was also a tie-in between the Industrial Inquiry and the Liberal party organization in the person of Sir Herbert Samuel, newly appointed head of the Central Association, who served on the Inquiry Committee alongside Lloyd George.[25]

The Industrial Inquiry was completed late in 1927 and its report published in a single volume in February 1928.[26] Known popularly as the Yellow Book, it advocated reforms in British industry and finance that would have definitely abandoned laissez-faire but stopped well short of state socialism. Placing special stress on the need to restrict public utilities and monopolies in the public interest, the Yellow Book recommended creation of public regulatory boards and corporations and the establishment of a ministry of industry to coordinate them. The recurrent problems of boom and slump would be fought by a permanent "economic general staff" attached to the prime minister's office, which would make continuous studies similar to the Industrial Inquiry, and by various advisory boards that would offer plans on investment of public funds, exploitation of natural resources, more efficient use of industrial plant, and imperial economic development.

Regarding employer-employee relations, the Yellow Book broke sharply with traditional economic Liberalism and called for national minimum wages for each industry, compulsory profit sharing with workers, and workers' councils that would have a voice in management. The existing national tax system was strongly criticized, especially the heavy local rates, about one-third of which the report suggested should be cancelled and replaced by grants from the central government. Most important of all, the Yellow Book laid out a comprehensive National Development Program for the government to fight steadily worsening unemployment by undertaking vast public works projects--such as highway and waterway construction, urban renewal, electrification, land reclamation, and forestry conservation--that would not merely provide relief for the unemployed but meet long overdue needs and perhaps yield a profit for the exchequer.[27]

The Yellow Book set forth a complete scheme of industrial reorganization aimed at restoring prosperity to depressed Britain, reducing poverty and unemployment, and providing equality of opportunity. Although in its demands for central planning departing considerably from orthodox Liberalism, it was less heretical than the Green Book and fully within the basic Liberal tradition of preserving as much as possible of private initiative and responsibility.

The practical details of the Yellow Book were far in advance of any proposals for industrial reform hitherto formulated by the Labour party, a fact admitted by such left wing journalists as H. N. Brailsford and J. A. Hobson. The rival economic program that the Labour party issued as its 1928 conference manifesto, entitled "Labour and the Nation," bore such a close resemblance to the Yellow Book that critics of the far left denounced it as more capitalist than socialist. The Yellow Book became an inspiration not only for Labour platforms, and eventually government policies, but for the young Conservatives, represented by Harold Macmillan and Robert Boothby, who had already been impressed by Coal and Power and were in process of working out a "Tory democratic" industrial reform program that would begin to see realization during the National Government of the thirties and to a much greater extent after 1951.[28]

The Yellow Book was endorsed with little change by a special Liberal Industrial Conference meeting in London in March 1928. The greater enthusiasm accorded it than the earlier Green Book was accounted for by Lloyd George's having gained control of the party machinery since 1926, by the high prestige the Summer School group--the prinicipal contributors--had acquired, and by the knowledge that a vigorous party platform was essential in the forthcoming parliamentary election, which might be the Liberals' last chance to make a political comeback.[29]

V

Whatever its impact as an economic program, the Yellow Book seemed to have little effect as a campaign document. By-election results during the remainder of 1928 showed that the swing of the pendulum from the

Conservatives was toward Labour and not the Liberals. The poor showing by his party's candidates persuaded Lloyd George that Liberal success in the general election required a single, electrifying theme that would convince marginal voters to risk their ballots on the return of a Liberal government.[30]

This theme, Lloyd George believed, was promise of a war against unemployment. Unemployment was undeniably the most serious social problem of the day, with nearly a million and a half workers out of jobs in 1928. The Yellow Book had offered long-range remedies for the problem but had not focused on it. Therefore Lloyd George appointed another research committee, to work up a concrete set of anti-unemployment policies to set before the voters. Before this committee published the results of its "crash" research early in March 1929, Lloyd George prepared the way by making a categorical pledge at a Liberal party rally on March 1 that if the Liberals formed the next government, it would reduce unemployment to normal proportions within a year without adding a penny to national or local taxes.[31]

The Unemployment Inquiry succinctly described how We Can Conquer Unemployment in a sixpenny, orange-covered pamphlet that was printed in huge quantities and sold at bookstalls throughout the country. This Orange Book elaborated on Lloyd George's St. David's Day pledge and the National Development Program of the Yellow Book by pointing out the great number of public works projects that needed to be done, the unprecedented labor surplus available to build them, and the certain impetus to the economy that would be given by the increased purchasing power of hundreds of thousands of men set to work. Not only would millions of pounds of unemployment insurance payments be saved, but the quickened economy would furnish the government with a huge increase in tax revenue.

The key feature of the Orange Book, and the most controversial, was the Keynesian scheme of deficit financing: keeping taxes steady, raising needed funds through loans, and unbalancing the budget for as long as necessary to complete the "pump priming" of the economy. Only somewhat less controversial was the emphasis put on road building: the construction of expressways that would bypass the large urban centers and reduce traffic congestion, while opening up isolated parts of the country. This massive highway program, the proposed routes for which were illustrated in the

176

Orange Book, was declared capable of alone reducing unemployment by one-fifth to one-third within a year.[32]

In spite of derogatory comments by such varied critics as Winston Churchill, Neville Chamberlain, and Beatrice Webb, We Can Conquer Unemployment impressed both ordinary voters--the Liberals won two parliamentary seats from the Conservatives in by-elections in late March--and fiscal experts, including cautious anti-Lloyd George Liberals like Sir John Simon and Walter Runciman. The respected Economist declared itself satisfied with the plan of the Orange Book to fight unemployment--perhaps not surprisingly, since the editor, Sir Walter Layton, had earlier chaired the Liberal Industrial Inquiry--and a nonpartisan committee of one hundred industrial and financial leaders signed a statement attesting to its prudence and foresight.[33]

To drive home the message of the Orange Book, against Labour party claims that it was pirated from their past manifestos and Conservative jeers at the implausibility of all Lloyd George schemes, the two Summer School economists closest to Lloyd George--John Maynard Keynes and Hubert Henderson--drafted a sparkling little flyer which affirmatively answered the question, Can Lloyd George Do It?[34] This phamphlet, issued on the eve of the general election, so disturbed the Conservative leaders by its wide circulation and stimulation of interest that they tried to counteract its effects by issuance of an official White Paper,[35] in which four cabinet ministers and numerous high civil servants roundly condemned the proposals of Lloyd George's Unemployment Committee as impractical, wasteful, or dangerous. Public works loans--in what became known as the "Treasury view"--allegedly would siphon the limited amount of capital from money markets that otherwise could be used for more productive investment in industry. It was even hinted that Lloyd George might use his make-work program to lay the foundation of a fascist dictatorship.[36] The White Paper, representing the views of the Treasury Establishment toward Lloyd George's proposals, was denounced by the latter as a political hatchet job rather than an objective study, as he contended his inquiry had been.[37]

Although Lloyd George's Unemployment Inquiry and the publications based on it dominated the press for many weeks, made him once again briefly the man of the hour, united the Liberal party to a degree unknown

177

since 1916, and momentarily terrified the leaders of the major parties, they did not spark a Liberal victory in the 1929 general election. The disappointing election results, confirming the status of the Liberals as a weak third party in the House of Commons, ended speculation about a possible Liberal comeback as a governing party.

Nevertheless, the parliamentary Liberal party remained strong enough to hold the balance between the two big parties, neither of which had won an absolute majority of seats. Lloyd George could still try, by throwing the weight of his small party to left or right, to influence governmental policy as the British and world economic crises steadily deepened. He was handicapped by the worsening discord within the Liberal ranks, and the growing hostility toward himself as leader among right wing Liberals who disliked his radical policies but had accepted them earlier only in the hope of winning the election. As Lloyd George sought without success to force the minority Labour government to carry out, if not the plans of the Orange Book, at least their own vague election pledges, segment after segment of the Liberal right defied their leader and went into opposition.

Fearing that Lloyd George might lose control of his followers, who would then turn out the Labour government, Prime Minister MacDonald finally agreed, at Lloyd George's insistence, to a joint conference on unemployment between Labour and Liberal representatives. Between June and October 1930, Lloyd George, Lord Lothian (Philip Kerr), and Seebohm Rowntree met with MacDonald, Chancellor of the Exchequer Philip Snowden, and Vernon Hartshorn, minister for unemployment, in a series of amicable but inconclusive discussions. The Liberals were able to secure agreement in principle on the basic program of the Orange Book, but the ministers refused to be pinned down on details.

The only concrete result of the two party conference was another Liberal economic report, How to Tackle Unemployment,[38] drafted in late October by the three Liberal conferees and their staff assistants, which brought the Orange Book proposals of 1929 up to date and added a new scheme of settling 100,000 unemployed city workers and their dependents on "family farms." Work had begun on the report in August, it was revised as the conference proceeded and agreement was broadened, and approval was somewhat reluctantly bestowed by the annual conference of the National Liberal Federation in October. This report, widely sold to the public as a sixpenny pamphlet, roused new interest in the Liberal unemployment plans as the numbers out of work rose alarmingly, but still the Labour government could not be persuaded to take action.[39]

During the winter and spring of 1930-1 there were signs that the parliamentary Labour party, restive under MacDonald's indecisive leadership, was ready to bypass it and join the Liberals in implementing How to Tackle Unemployment. Such prominent Labourites as George Lansbury, Ernest Bevin, Lloyd George's old colleague Christopher Addison, now Labour minister of agriculture, and even Philip Snowden either approached Lloyd George with offers of cooperation, or demanded that the government adopt the Liberal program to fight unemployment. Working practically behind the prime minister's back, Addison was able, with Lloyd George's help, to round up enough Labour and Liberal votes to put on the statute book in 1931 two bills--the Agricultural Land Utilization Bill and the Agricultural Marketing Bill--which enacted into law limited versions of the Liberal Green Book and resettlement projects.[40]

But at the same time, economizers within the two parties of the left, who believed that spending large sums on development and reconstruction would worsen rather than cure the depression, were gaining the upper hand over the expansionists who followed Lloyd George and Keynes.[41] An ominous portent was the adoption in February 1931, by Conservative and right wing Labour and Liberal votes, of a motion to set up a Committee on National Expenditure, which became the May Committee, influential in the events leading to the fall of the Labour government in August.

By this time Lloyd George really controlled no more than half of the Liberal M.P.'s, and his health was deteriorating. Just as events seemed to be forcing the government, in order to cope with the depression, to take up the plans developed over the years by Lloyd George's research teams, and perhaps even share decision making power with him, political and personal misfortunes were working against him. Forced to undergo a serious operation in late July, and still bedridden during the August-October political crisis, Lloyd George was helpless to prevent the Liberal economizers from grabbing the party leadership, joining with MacDonald and his small following in deposing the

179

Labour ministry, and taking seats in what was actually a Conservative-dominated "National" Government. Following the stacked election of October 27, 1931, Lloyd George resigned as head of the Liberal party, removing his personal office from Liberal headquarters at Abingdon Street—where he had had it since 1927—to a suite in Thames House, Millbank, and took his seat on the front opposition bench with the few Labour ministers who had survived the "National" landslide.

VI

Between 1931 and 1934, Lloyd George was relatively inactive in politics, being principally occupied in writing his War Memoirs. However, he was closely watching the bumbling efforts of the National Government to pull Britain out of the depression, as well as the more dynamic recovery program of Franklin D. Roosevelt and his New Deal in the United States. The activities of Roosevelt's "brains trust" of economic advisers—similar to his own teams of experts of the twenties and to the "economic general staff" recommended in the Yellow Book—especially interested him.[42] In the summer of 1934, with the War Memoirs nearly completed, Lloyd George began to plan a new policy study. In June he discussed with Seebohm Rowntree, Lord Astor (publisher of the Observer), and various university agricultural experts the possibility of a study elaborating on the family farm scheme broached in How to Tackle Unemployment; but they agreed that the National Government would reject out of hand any plan to alter the agricultural status quo, and only Lloyd George had confidence that unemployment could be significantly reduced by resettling urban workers in the country.

Next, following a meeting with Welsh Liberal industrialists at the Eisteddfod festival in August, Lloyd George's mind turned to a Welsh reconstruction program. The possibility of ending his career as he had begun it—as a Welsh reformer—briefly intrigued the aging statesman, but soon the pilot group of Welsh businessmen and academics whom Lloyd George invited to Bron-y-de to discuss the project convinced him that the Welsh economy could not be treated independently of that of England. He therefore decided to alter the basis of the study to take in all of Britain, and to construct a set of proposals that would attempt to do for Britain what Roosevelt was trying to do for the United States.[43]

The Summer School group had scattered since 1931, some following Ramsay Muir, who was now an officer of the Liberal party organization, others offering their services to the National Government, and many going their independent ways. The team of experts whom Lloyd George gathered about him to work out a British "new deal" included a few survivors of the Industrial and Unemployment Inquiries and the earlier policy studies of the twenties, but there were many new participants. Among the newcomers were scholars and theorists like Lionel Curtis, the writer and lecturer on international trade, but most of them were men of affairs like Sir Basil Blackett, a director of the Bank of England, and Sir Edward Grigg, former governor of Kenya and one of Lloyd George's private secretaries when he had been prime minister. The new committee of inquiry was drawn from all parties and from the nonpartisan, and overlapped another group of reformers, the Committee of Liberty and Democratic Leadership, most of whose members belonged to the dissenting Young Conservative faction led by Harold Macmillan and sympathetic to Lloyd George's expansionist views. The regular Liberal party had looked askance at Lloyd George since he had disassociated himself from it in 1931, and now viewed the proposed "new deal" with suspicion, but it had the sympathetic interest of many right wing Labourites who were disturbed by the leftward trend within their party being promoted by Sir Stafford Cripps and his Socialist League.[44]

The "new deal" project passed over much the same ground as the studies that had produced the Yellow and Orange Books, but went on from there to consider new problems. After redrafting the plans for national development and agricultural revival, the researchers turned their attention to unemployment caused by technological displacement and considered the possibility of resettling unemployed workers from the depressed areas in overseas colonies. Opportunities for developing trade within the empire, and with what would today be called the Third World, were thoroughly discussed. The use of tariffs by Britain as weapons to force other countries to lower trade barriers was debated, a subject barred from earlier Lloyd George inquiries by their ties to the Liberal party and its free trade tradition. A major theme of the "new deal" policy study was its attribution of the depression in Britain and other countries to a complete, and possibly permanent, breakdown of the international economic system, and the need for a "new order" to repair the damage and set each country on its feet.[45]

181

As his inquiry proceeded during the autumn of 1934, there was intense speculation in political circles about what the results would be, and for what purposes Lloyd George would use them. He was obviously no longer trying to revive the Liberal party, and was known to be in communication with both leaders and young dissidents in each of the major parties. The belief generally shared by informed persons was that he expected no party to win a majority in the next election, and was hoping for a call to head, or at least direct, a new coalition ministry of Conservatives, Labourites, and Liberals committed to carrying out his "new deal" program. This possibility would be heightened if the election were to return a fair number of M.P.'s from each party pledged to the general terms of the "new deal." These "new deal" members, mostly young men, would contribute the junior ministers upon whom Lloyd George would mainly rely, as Roosevelt relied on his White House "brains trust," to carry out a vigorous national reconstruction. Conceivably the cross-party "new deal" group would form the nucleus for a Center party of the kind Lloyd George had toyed with during the last days of the postwar Coalition.[46]

After a careful preparatory campaign that raised public interest to a high pitch, Lloyd George launched his "new deal" at a large public meeting in Bangor, Wales, on January 17, 1935, the date of his seventy-second birthday. Emphasizing that he was speaking as an elder statesman searching for a nonpartisan solution to national problems and not as a party leader promoting the cause of a single party, he declared that months of careful study had convinced him that only bold measures, like those of the Roosevelt administration in the United States, could pull Britain out of the depression and cure the economic disease of unemployment.

Having denounced the halfhearted recovery program of the National Government, Lloyd George prescribed alternative measures that were essentially the expansionist policies he and his research associates had offered in 1928, 1929, and 1930: the raising of capital loans to spur development, on a massive scale, of housing, roads, railways, electric power, new industries, and agriculture. New features were mostly implemental: establishment of a small inner cabinet whose members would be free of departmental responsibilities, comparable to the war cabinet of 1916-8, to direct the fight for recovery; reorganization of existing ministries and creation of many new ones to deal with specific economic problems, on the model of Roosevelt's "alphabetical agencies"; the division of the annual budget into two parts, one for ordinary expenditures covered largely by taxes, the other for capital expenditures covered by public loans; and creation of a nonpolitical "national development council," comparable to the "economic general staff" and advisory boards proposed in 1929 but with broader powers to make continuous surveys of the national economy and that of the empire, and to lay out plans for industrial and agricultural development. The "national development council" would be a statutory body performing the same work as Lloyd George's private research committees.

In his speech Lloyd George was very critical of the Bank of England, which he claimed had too much influence over government policy and, he implied, had vetoed earlier expansionist policies during the Labour government of 1929-31. This obstacle to reform must be removed, Lloyd George said, and the Bank brought into closer touch with the progressive elements in business and industry, but he was vague on how this should be done and did not call for the nationalization of the Bank.[47]

Lloyd George's Bangor speech, and a subsequent one before the Manchester Reform Club on February 22, impressed observers with their sincerity and vigor, but--in the words of a writer in the New Statesman and Nation--"the cats let out of Mr. Lloyd George's bag were not as impressive as we had been led to expect. They were familiar and rather tame animals."[48] Moderate Labourites were especially disappointed, viewing the "new deal" as little more than a warmed-over Yellow Book, and indeed much less explicit and relevant to the times than the "colored books," which were prepared before the slowdown of the late twenties had turned into a depression. The official Liberals contended that the "new deal" had been part of their own party platform for years; the Young Conservatives welcomed it but promised to improve upon it with their "Next Five Years" program, about to be published; and the government, speaking through Chancellor of the Exchequer Neville Chamberlain, a bitter enemy of Lloyd George, damned the proposals with faint praise, claiming that the better ideas differed little from those already put into effect by the government since 1931, while others --such as the ones dealing with the Bank of England--

183

were too unorthodox to merit consideration.[49]   In
private, Chamberlain was caustic, describing Lloyd
George's schemes as "the poorest stuff imaginable . . .
containing not a single new idea." His only fear was
that "the Daily Mail and the Express will use them
vigorously as a stick to beat the government with."[50]

However, under pressure from discontented junior
ministers and back bench supporters, the triumvirate
directing the National Government--Ramsay MacDonald,
Stanley Baldwin, and Chamberlain--publicly agreed to
examine Lloyd George's plans with an open mind. On
March 1, Prime Minister MacDonald wrote Lloyd George
inviting him to offer detailed recommendations, and the
statistical data on which they were based, in writing
to the cabinet. Lloyd George and his researchers
responded with a hundred-page memorandum which was
submitted to the cabinet on March 14.[51]

After studying the memorandum for a month, a
special cabinet committee met with Lloyd George ten
times during April and May for oral elaboration of the
plans, and cross-examination. Although Baldwin--polit-
ically adroit as usual and a more adventurous economic
thinker than his two colleagues--may have been weighing
the possibility of an entente with Lloyd George, it
seems more probable that the government was marking
time until the king's Silver Jubilee, scheduled for
late May, arrived to distract public attention from the
"new deal." This in fact was what happened. A number
of by-elections held during and shortly after the Jubilee indicated that the public, with its patriotic and
conservative sentiments stimulated by the festival, had
increased its confidence in the National Government and
had not been significantly moved by Lloyd George's
attacks. On June 7, the ailing MacDonald gave way as
prime minister to Baldwin, who reorganized the cabinet
and ministry and gave more representation to the Young
Conservatives. Though his memorandum was still
"under examination," it was clear to Lloyd George, when
he met what he called "the hanging committee" for
another interview after the Jubilee, that--in his own
words--"they knew in their hearts that they were going
to knife me."[52]

Lloyd George was prepared for rebuff by the government and immediately counterattacked with a manifesto, "A Call for Action," published in the press June
13, condemning the cabinet's domestic and international
policies. The manifesto called for formation of a

nonpartisan Council of Action to endorse those candidates in the next election who, regardless of party, were committed to a program of peace through collective security and economic expansionism at home. The linkage of the "new deal" with an international peace/League of Nations theme was intended to draw support from clergymen and laymen of the Anglican and Free Churches who had been critical of the National Government's weak unemployment policy, but were more interested in international affairs and the danger of war.[53] "Yet another . . . far-reaching proposal for putting Utopia into a statute," scoffed a disgruntled Welshman objecting to the identification of the Free Churches with a program of social reconstruction.[54]

A few days after the Council of Action for Peace and Reconstruction[55] was formally organized July 1-2 at a mass meeting presided over by his old colleague, Lord Lothian, Lloyd George published the last of his policy reports under the title Organising Prosperity. This was a revision of the memorandum he had submitted to the cabinet in March, with changes made in response to the criticisms of the special cabinet committee that had studied it for three months. Based on the research conducted during the autumn and winter of 1934, and upon lessons drawn from the successful make-work projects of Germany's Hitler regime, it added little to the "new deal" program enunciated at Bangor in January. Special stress was placed on a huge Prosperity Loan of 250 million pounds which should be raised to finance public works and land reclamation and settlement. As in his earlier reports, Lloyd George was more optimistic about the prospects of agricultural reform as a cure for Britain's economic problems than were most authorities. Dismissed by The Times as owing more to the "realistic" amendments suggested by the cabinet committee than to Lloyd George's own schemes, Organising Prosperity lost some of the usual impact of a Lloyd George gambit because, besides lacking novelty, it was issued on the eve of the summer holiday season.[56]

The government's official statement on Lloyd George's "new deal," a pamphlet entitled A Better Way to Better Times, which was inspired if not actually written by Neville Chamberlain, rejected all of Lloyd George's recommendations as superfluous, inadequate, or likely to exacerbate the conditions they were supposed to correct.[57] Ironically, at about the time this document appeared in late July, a report made by the Board of Trade official who was attempting to induce industries to move into the depressed areas—euphemistically renamed "special areas" by the government—indicated that at least this part of the cabinet's unemployment policy was a dismal failure.[58]

The smug complacency of the government's top ministers and their principal Treasury assistants, in the face of persisting bad conditions, infuriated not only Lloyd George but also the members of the Committee of Liberty and Democratic Leadership, headed by the leading Young Conservative M.P., Harold Macmillan, and a National Labour peer, Lord Allen. Their "plan for Britain," The Next Five Years, had recently been published and showed that expansionist ideas had considerable backing among nominal supporters of the government.[59] The congruency of Lloyd George's economic views with those of the Next Five Years Group was clearly demonstrated at the Liberal Summer School held at Cambridge in early August, where Lloyd George and Lord Allen were the featured speakers. The latter praised the Yellow Book and insisted that the public interest must prevail over the profit motive whether industry remained under private control or was nationalized.[60]

A few days later, on August 12, Lloyd George invited to lunch at Bron-y-de the two spokesmen for the Next Five Years Group, Macmillan and Allen, and the former chairman of the Liberal Industrial Inquiry, Sir Walter Layton, now board chairman of the News Chronicle, last of the London Liberal dailies. After sounding out the possibility of a merger between the Council of Action and the Committee of Liberty and Democratic Leadership, and their respective programs, to fight the pending election campaign, Lloyd George soon showed he was unwilling to make the necessary concession of foregoing heated attacks on the National Government and its Conservative leaders. Lloyd George's stinging criticism of the government in a speech before the Trade Union Club on August 14, a few hours after a second luncheon with Macmillan and Allen, may have been decisive in dooming a collaboration that might possibly have given him some political leverage for promoting his "new deal" after the election.[61]

The long-awaited general election—called by Baldwin at the height of the Italo-Ethiopian crisis to benefit from the customary public fear of changing leadership in an emergency—dealt a crushing blow to Lloyd George's Council of Action and "new deal." Lloyd

186

George had calculated that National Government supporters might be reduced to about 300 seats out of 615 in the new House of Commons. But with only 67 of the 362 candidates endorsed by the Council elected, and the Conservatives alone winning an absolute majority of seats, Lloyd George's hope of holding the balance of power was dashed. Since only 16 of the 67 successful Council of Action candidates were government supporters, and since the government held a very tight whip over its back-benchers, Lloyd George's chances of exerting some influence within the government bloc were virtually nil.[62]

Although the Council of Action remained in being, with headquarters in Horseferry House, a building near Lloyd George's own Thames House office suite, and intervened in selected by-elections up to the outbreak of the Second World War, the "new deal" as a political reality was dead.[63] The 1935 election defeat also signalled the end of Lloyd George's use of his private political fund to finance social and economic policy studies. Resuming the writing of his memoirs and devoting much of his attention and wealth to his experimental farm, Lloyd George made increasingly few incursions into politics, and then usually on foreign and military rather than domestic questions.

VII

Lloyd George's policy studies were all attempts to uncover the defects in the British private enterprise system, with the object of preserving and improving the system by correcting these defects. All the policy reports represented Lloyd George's personal economic views in some degree. If the report was not directly prepared according to its specifications, as were the Green Book and Organising Prosperity, it was indirectly influenced by the selection of the researchers or by participation in the research of Lloyd George himself and persons close to him who thought much as he did. The Yellow Book, almost wholly prepared by the Summer School group, was the most independent, objective, and scholarly of the studies, the one least affected by partisanship and personal bias; but it too was representative of Lloyd George's thinking, because the two principal contributors, John Maynard Keynes and Hubert Henderson, came closest to being Lloyd George's mentors on the industrial and financial problems of the twenties.

None of the policy reports, any more than Lloyd George himself, showed any sympathy for state capitalism--vulgarly known as socialism. Only in <u>Coal and Power</u> and the Green Book was nationalization of an instrument of production proposed, and in both cases private management was to continue. Lloyd George, like Franklin D. Roosevelt in the United States, was never in any real sense a socialist. He was an expansionist capitalist, eager to shake up a stagnant economic system, loosen the hold of unprogressive and unproductive vested interests, and use government action to increase the opportunities for private profit making.

Lloyd George had, in fact, always intensely disliked the idea of a government-managed economy, but he appreciated that the concept had wide currency in Britain, especially as the managed economy of the Soviet Union began to exhibit signs of success in the early thirties. He believed, however, that the free enterprise system could be saved in Britain if private entrepreneurs cooperated with a farsighted government, that people would soon stop wanting to abolish capitalism if they saw that it was recovering, and that in a thriving capitalist nation the "socialist menace"--a phrase he himself sometimes used--would soon cease to exist.[64] Events after the Second World War proved that he was right.

The economic programs set forth in Lloyd George's policy reports were compared by enthusiastic followers to the Soviet Five Year Plans,[65] as well as to the American New Deal upon which the last Lloyd George project was admittedly patterned. These associations hardly inhibited criticism, not only from defenders of classical laissez-faire and from collectivists, but from fellow expansionists. "Men of experience" and "the more responsible economists" who endorsed the economic policies of Neville Chamberlain and Walter Runciman, the Liberal National heading the Board of Trade, had seen their earlier fear of Lloyd George's schemes during the twenties actualized in Roosevelt's "ungentlemanly" treatment of American businessmen. They were not unhappy that Roosevelt's relative failure to conquer the depression seemed to support the British government's policy of caution and to militate against experimenting with a Lloyd George-style "new deal."[66] At the same time the Labour party's left wing was denouncing the Lloyd George "new deal" as small-scale and trivial in relation to the economic crisis, and likely to be as much of a failure as its American counterpart.[67]

While some Liberals condemned Lloyd George's willingness to spend public money with a free hand, and to use tariffs and government subsidies as weapons of economic nationalism,[68] and others, as usual, doubted his trustworthiness,[69] a noted progressive Conservative, sympathetic to the economic viewpoints of both Lloyd George and the Young Conservatives, offered a more balanced criticism. In the reasoned opinion of Leopold Amery, the American New Deal could not be duplicated in Britain because the economic situations in the two countries were quite different. Whereas in the United States there was a basically healthy and self-contained economy suffering only from bad judgment and loss of nerve, in Britain there was a sick economy no longer able, in free competition with other countries, to secure a trade balance in its favor. A massive spending program, by itself, could not cure the sickness, and might worsen it by inflating prices and increasing demand for imported goods.

Not only were Lloyd George's industrial recovery prescriptions of the late twenties unsuited to the problem, Amery believed, but his earlier policies, while in office, had aggravated the situation. By opposing tariff reform, out of loyalty to orthodox Liberalism, Lloyd George had done nothing to correct the growing weakening of Britain's competitive power as an international trader; while his National Insurance Act of 1911--as amended by the Lloyd George Coalition government after the war--had set up the dole system which, by providing the unemployed with a subsistence income at public expense, had obscured the gravity of the depression and discouraged constructive but controversial reforms.

On the other hand, once the National Government had begun using tariffs to regulate selectively the flow of imports, and had ended the drain on the national gold reserve by going off the gold standard-- as Lloyd George had urged--the case for a bold policy of public spending was greatly strengthened. It was especially needed to pump economic life into the nearly derelict "special areas" with which the country was dotted. But the "responsible economists" of the Treasury, strongly supported by Chancellor of the Exchequer Chamberlain, were no more ready to countenance a Lloyd George scheme in the thirties than they had been a decade earlier.[70]

Although bits and pieces of Lloyd George's recovery and reconstruction plans were effected before the Second World War, the more ambitious parts awaited the election of a majority Labour government--more reformist than socialist--after the war, and the accession to the prime ministership twelve years later of Harold Macmillan, Lloyd George's former Young Conservative protégé. The system of managed capitalism that has evolved since 1945--with its limited nationalization, bureaucratic regulation of industry and agriculture, monetary controls, government participation in industrial relations, and (since 1961) National Economic Development Council of expert planners from government, industry, and labor--is to an abundant degree the word of the Colored Books made fact.

LIBERALISM AND THE TWO PARTY SYSTEM*

One of the conventional explanations for the decline of the Liberal party is that it ran afoul of certain features of the British political system, especially the sporting tradition of politics. The British voter, it is said, favors a continuous competition between two party/teams, the Ins and the Outs. One team constitutes the Government of the day, the other the loyal Opposition seeking to outpoint its rival and eventually displace it.[1] The theory is that once the Liberal party ceased to have a clearly defined place in this competition, it rapidly lost ground.

The embryonic British party system was inchoate and factional before the 1867 Reform Act. From that point on, a fairly stable two party system developed both in the House of Commons and in the constituencies as the governing classes responded to the new conditions of emerging political democracy. Although politicians continued to use party labels casually for some time, greater party centralization and discipline increasingly discouraged individual initiative by office holders and candidates. The percentage of divisions in the House of Commons in which nine-tenths of the M.P.'s of each major party who voted went into the same lobby rose from less than 50 percent in 1836 to over 80 percent in 1894.[2]

There were other parties, but normally they were inconsequential. The Irish Nationalist party was electorally insignificant outside Ireland except in a handful of districts, and in Parliament was closely bound to the Liberal party by the home rule question. The Liberal Unionists were similarly united with the Conservatives as a Parliamentary team after 1886, and became virtually one organization with them in most constituencies.

This reliable two party pattern was upset after

---

*This essay is a revision of "British Liberalism and the Two Party System" published in the Duquesne Review, XIV (Fall 1969), 95-111. The copyright to the original article is the property of the Duquesne University Press.

1900 by the appearance of the Labour party. The Labourites, while usually voting with the Liberals in the House of Commons, put up independent candidates against both Conservatives and Liberals in many constituencies. The electoral pacts that the Liberal and Labour organizations entered into between 1900 and 1914, to avoid three-cornered contests that would let in a Conservative, cannot hide the fact that Labour was trying to elect as many M.P.'s as possible at the expense of the major parties. Labour aimed, at the very least, to become a powerful third force in Parliament. Some of its leaders hoped that someday it might become a governing party, one of the competitive teams. Achievement of this latter goal would mean supplanting the Liberals, since the two parties were competing for the same body of voters, the working masses desirous of social reforms. The Conservatives, as the party of resistance to change, had a safe place in British team politics, but after 1900 there was a contest for the role of party of change.

There was another feature of the British political system that forced Liberals and Labourites into rivalry for the privilege of being the second team in the game of politics. Following the Reform Act of 1884-5, most Parliamentary constituencies became single member districts. The plurality—or "first past the post"—system of election was also reverted to after brief experimentation, between 1867 and 1885, with minority representation in certain multi-member urban constituencies.[3] The combination of single member districts with the plurality system of election meant that, in the great majority of constituencies, the Liberal and Labour parties could not divide the "progressive" vote without the risk of giving the Conservative candidate a winning plurality.

In the few two member constituencies that remained after 1885, most of them urban, it was often possible for the "progressive" parties to share the seats without risking loss of one or both of them to the common enemy. The local Liberal Association frequently was agreeable to a pact with the local Labour Representation Committee, especially if pressure was applied by the Liberal whips' office. Hence most of the Liberal-Labour electoral pacts made between 1900 and 1914 were divisions of two member constituencies.

In single member constituencies, either the Liberal Association or the L.R.C. had to forego putting up a candidate if a pact was to be negotiated. This was likely to injure local pride, especially that of long-established Liberal Associations, and usually involved much arm twisting by Liberal headquarters. On the other hand, without a Liberal-Labour pact the chance of Conservative success was greatly enhanced. Once the two parties began competing for the working class vote, it was necessary either to arrange a local pact, which usually was not easy, put up opposing candidates and risk losing the seat to the Conservatives, or destroy the local power of the rival party so that it could no longer attract a significant portion of the electorate. Before 1914, the Labour party was too weak in most constituencies to capture the seat from the Liberals. Although in a few districts Labour had enough leverage to force the Liberals to make a pact, rarely did it have the strength to carry the seat against a Liberal candidate. In the December 1910 general election, for example, the Labour party elected only two M.P.'s over Liberal opposition.[4]

About 37 percent of the adult male population of Britain--largely working class--was legally or technically disfranchised because of the intricate franchise patterns and registration procedures in force before 1918. A governing Labour party was practically impossible until many more workingmen--and women--were able to vote.[5] After the First World War, however, the single member district in combination with plurality election began to work to the advantage of the Labourites in their competition with the Liberals. Not only was the working class proportion of the electorate much increased by the 1918 Representation of the People Act, but the Labour party was considerably stronger after the war in terms of organization, leadership, wealth, and morale. Further, the rival Liberals were split into two feuding sections and discredited by their behavior during the war. From the start of their postwar rivalry, the Labourites had the advantage over the Liberals in most urban working class constituencies.[6]

There now began the process well described by the French political scientists Maurice Duverger and Albert Mabileau. When it became clear to the public after several elections that Labour had drawn ahead of the Liberals in parliamentary strength and was established as the official opposition party, the two party tradition induced anti-Conservative voters to support the Labour party as the one more likely to form a government. Too confident of success to be willing to make local pacts with the Liberals (with a few exceptions), the Labourites first strengthened their hold on the urban seats won from the Liberals right after the war. Then they began to win seats in mixed working class-lower middle class districts that had remained Liberal in the first two or three postwar elections. Finally, having swamped the Liberals except in a very few loyal constituencies, the Labourites went on to compete with the Conservatives in all marginal districts as the surviving party of change. This march to victory over the Liberals was completed by 1935. Seventeen years were needed by the Labourites to vanquish their rivals, if 1918 is taken as the climactic year when Liberal ascendancy ended and the Labour offensive began.[7]

In Duverger's analysis of the fall of the Liberal party, the fate of the Liberals was practically inevitable, given the nature of the political system. While unprepared to endorse the sporting explanation of the two party tradition, which he considered unscientific, Duverger believed unreservedly in the negative effect of the single member district and plurality election system (hereafter referred to as SMP) on a third party that is newly established or has lost ground. This effect, in his view, is both mechanical and psychological. The new or declining party wins fewer seats than its vote throughout the country would seem to entitle it to, because its candidates tend to come in third. This mechanical tendency, besides giving the third party a much weaker voice in the legislature than it has support in the electorate, has a more important, long-term psychological effect. Most third party voters conclude that their votes are being wasted and transfer them to one of the stronger parties, whichever is less objectionable. In due course--considerable time may elapse in the process--the third party fades into insignificance or disappears.[8]

Duverger limited his bipolarization theory to single constituencies, and acknowledged that the same two parties may not be dominant in every constituency. In a federal structure like Canada's the two chief parties may vary from province to province. But in a homogeneous, centralized state like Britain, voters tend, he believed, to see issues from a national standpoint and to behave much the same everywhere. The same party will be frozen out in nearly every constituency.[9] Duverger's argument is strengthened if it is supplemented by the sporting tradition, which Mabileau accepted. Mabileau, indeed, considered the modern

British two party system and the electoral system to be inseparable.[10]

Mabileau's interpretation of the fall of the Liberal party was much more complex than Duverger's, which was limited essentially to the malign effect of electoral politics in hundreds of constituencies. Mabileau agreed that once the electoral system began to take its toll, the Liberals struggled hopelessly. But he gave weight to other adverse factors in the British political system, or "constitutional system" as he called it. These included the sporting tradition, militating against independent third parties unable to form governments; the swing of the pendulum of public opinion from left to right and back again, which gave the Liberals, as a center party, a devastating blow no matter which way it swung; and the weakening (ironically, by the Liberals themselves) of the House of Lords, which put less of a premium on political moderation. Mabileau also went beyond the political system to seek causes for Liberal decline. He concluded that social and economic changes worked to the advantage of Labour, a class party; that the behavior of individual Liberal leaders, particularly Lloyd George, did their party no good at a critical time; and that both the other parties absorbed enough of the Liberal ideology to weaken the need for a party specifically committed to this ideology, once it had completed the great program of political democracy that had been its principal object.[11]

The theory that the British Liberal party was destroyed by the political system, propounded by Duverger and, less dogmatically, by Mabileau, can be tested by examination of the fate of similar parties in other countries. There have been Liberal parties or the equivalents under different names in each of the self-governing "white" dominions of the British Commonwealth. In Canada, a federation of provinces, the Liberal paarty--described by Robert R. Alford as "center-left"--survives as one of two national governing parties, along with the "rightist" Progressive Conservatives. No labor or socialist party has been able to threaten the Liberals nationally. The New Democratic party (formerly known as the Cooperative Commonwealth Federation) elects a number of members to the federal House of Commons and has established itself as one of the major local parties in three provinces. But according to a recent writer, although the New Democratic party, "a genuinely socialist party," has "exhibited increasing political vitality in recent years," it "remains at this writing a 'minor' party with little influence on national policy."[12]

According to Alford, the basic political cleavage in Canada has been between urban-financial and rural-agricultural interests, so that a class-based leftist party becomes "irrelevant politically." Other than the C.C.F./N.D.P., the only third party to seriously challenge the Liberals and Conservatives federally was the short-lived Progressive party of the 1920s, which elected M.P.'s in rural Ontario and the western provinces. After its first election in 1921 it had more seats in the House of Commons than the Conservatives, but at the next poll lost over half of them. Essentially a farmers' special interest group resembling the Australian Country party (discussed below), the Canadian Progressives quickly fell victim to SMP attrition.[13]

The SMP system has operated in all Canadian federal elections and in most provincial contests, but in four of the ten provinces voters select some or all of their legislators from multi-member districts. Except for a few brief experiments with preferential voting and proportional representation, plurality voting has been the rule in provincial elections. Yet the SMP system, and plurality voting in multi-member constituencies, have not prevented the rise of third parties both federally and provincially.[14]

By and large the tendency noted by Duverger of only two parties dominating each constituency has prevailed in Canada. But in spite of James Bryce's observation early in the twentieth century that in Ottawa and the provincial capitals "there was that sort of sporting issue which belongs to a struggle between the Ins and the Outs," this tradition did not establish such deep roots in Canada as in Britain. The two party system did not become sacrosanct. Especially since 1920, there have been frequent national and provincial coalitions and minority governments. Leon D. Epstein described the Canadian federal party system as one of "two-plus parties," and Jean Blondel called it a "two-and-a-half party system." While none of the Canadian third parties has come close to national governing power, they have been strong enough to prevent either major party from winning a majority of seats in nearly half the federal parliaments elected since 1920.[15]

The interweaving of national and provincial politics in Canada has produced a complex mosaic of parties. Strong local parties often have a few representatives in the federal parliament, while remnants of national parties survive in provincial legislatures alongside local governing parties. Douglas W. Rae calculated that locally powerful third parties defeated major party candidates in about 15 percent of the federal parliamentary ridings in one election or more during the 1950s and 1960s. Third parties have been in power or constituted the principal opposition in six of the ten Canadian provinces at various times since 1920. Only in the four "Atlantic provinces" have third parties been noncompetitive with the Liberals and Conservatives.[16]

In a political ethos characterized by "interest" rather than "class," a diluted SMP system that has not discouraged the rise of third parties, and a federative party structure that has now weakened, now protected the two national governing parties, Canada's Liberal party has not only survived but prospered. Although weak provincially outside the Atlantic provinces and French-speaking Quebec, the Liberals have been in power in Ottawa for forty-eight of the last sixty-one years. As a nationwide leftist party has never forced the middle-of-the-road Liberals into a real contest for their share of the Canadian electorate, there is no way of knowing whether they would have lost their national governing status to a leftist rival (perhaps surviving as a governing party in some of the provinces), or become one of three or more major national parties forming governments independently or in coalition.

In federal Australia, the early rise and rapid electoral success of a militant Labour party induced the Liberals and Conservatives to voluntarily merge in 1909. Taking the name National, the new moderate rightist party contended with the leftist Labourites until after the First World War. At that time, a conflict of interests between urban businessmen and the more affluent farmers led to the secession from the National party of rural conservatives who formed the Country party.

To ensure that this division would not split the rightist-moderate vote, the National and Country parties used their federal parliamentary majority to enact a new electoral law. The so-called "Ware formula" retained the single member constituency, but created a system of preferential voting utilizing the

197

single transferable vote. Preferential voting enabled voters of the right and center to make a choice between the National and Country parties, but to pool their votes if neither party's candidates in a constituency had a majority. The preferential voting system was clearly directed against the Labour party, because there was no prospect of its making an electoral alliance with either of the other two parties. The system has benefited the rightist parties both in the national parliament and in state legislatures which have also adopted it. The majority of Australian ministries since 1920 have been coalitions of the Country party (renamed the National Country party in 1975) and the National party or its successors (the United Australia and Liberal parties).[17] The rightist coalitions have been remarkably stable and durable. The federal Liberal-Country ministry of 1949-72 was continuously in office for 264 months, setting a record as the longest uninterrupted coalition government in a democratic state since 1918.[18]

The old Australian Liberal party that merged with the Conservatives into the National party in 1909 was much less a party of change than the contemporary British Liberal party. The radicals of the Lloyd George type who were the dynamic element in British Liberalism before the First World War had, in Australia, mostly thrown in their lot with the Labour party before the two opposition parties merged. Today's Australian Liberal party is a moderate rightist party more analogous to the British Conservative party of Edward Heath and Margaret Thatcher than to the British Liberal party of Jo Grimond and David Steel. L. F. Crisp described the Australian Liberals as the party "of the successful, of the men and women of substance and 'social' consequence . . . [who] are inclined to represent the private accumulation of property and the profit motive as moral factors." Comparing the Australian and Canadian Liberal parties, Henry S. Albinsky noted that while both are business-oriented, the latter caters to a much broader spectrum of interests and therefore is more "liberal." A comparison between Australian and British Liberal parties is not very profitable, since practically all they have in common is the name.[19]

Comparing the Australian Country and the British Liberal parties may be more productive, as both are moderate center parties. But analysis shows that the differences outweigh the similarities. The Country party has always been a minority party representing a a well-established interest group. It has never been a majority governing party contending for the same body of voters with a rival party seeking to supplant it. Nor has the Country party ever been in the same position as the post-First World War British Liberal party, that of a center party fighting for survival, fractured by the swing of the pendulum of public opinion whether it moves from right or left. With its loyal following, and protected by the preferential voting system and its permanent alliance with the Australian Liberal party, the Country party has been in no danger of losing its fixed status. A study of the Australian Country party does not prove to be very helpful in testing the hypothesis that the two party system destroyed the British Liberal party.[20]

Politics in New Zealand, a centralized, unitary state with SMP elections, has resembled British politics more than that of federalist Canada and Australia. Until the 1890s, when political hegemony passed out of the hands of the so-called "oligarchy" of large landholders, there was a factional system in the House of Representatives similar to the one in the British House of Commons before the Second Reform Act of 1867. A strong Liberal party was established throughout the country by 1890, but another decade and a half passed before conservatives united into a single powerful Reform party. Although there had been a well-accepted sporting tradition of government and opposition teams even in the days of factionalism, this tradition did not force the parliamentary parties into a two-party pattern. This may have been due to the long time required to form organized parties outside the House of Representatives, while within the house governing coalitions could be easily constructed from the shifting factions.

In the next stage of party evolution, the overwhelming strength of the Liberals both in the House of Representatives and in the country between 1890 and 1905 inhibited the growth of a strong opposition party. The rise of the Reform party was finally implemented by the breaking away from the Liberal--actually a radical--party of business interests opposing further advanced social legislation. At the same time, the slowing down of the Liberals' social radicalism, in response to this pressure from the right, drove trade unionists to form their own party.

Fearing that the new Labour party, by splitting

the "progressive" vote, would give many Liberal seats to the Reform party, the Liberal government arranged for run-off elections to be held in districts where no majority had been secured in the first balloting. This scheme helped to give the Liberals their greatest electoral victory in 1908, but failed to save them from a severe defeat in 1911 when their percentage of the votes cast fell from 59 percent to 41 percent. In the 1911 election the Liberals lost ground to both opposition parties, but especially to Reform which also benefited from a rural bias in the apportionment of seats. The Reform ministry that took office abolished the run-off system and returned to simple plurality election.

During the First World War, the Reform and Liberal parties of New Zealand joined in a coalition, from which Labour excluded itself because of opposition to conscription. As in Britain, Labour benefited politically from constituting the only true wartime opposition. Despite a vigorous social program designed to challenge the rising strength of Labour, the Liberal party lost heavily in the first postwar election, declining to only 29 percent of the popular vote. The Labour party was the principal beneficiary of this loss in terms of new voters, but the Reform party captured more Liberal seats because of the division of the "progressive" vote.

In the twenties, the political pattern of New Zealand closely resembled that of Britain. The Liberals tried to pursue a radical policy in the House of Representatives, but many individual Liberal Members preferred to vote for the programs of the successive Reform governments. At the polls, the Liberals had lost most of their working class voters to Labour, and were reduced to fighting the Reform party for middle class and rural constituencies. As radical politicians retired or defected to Labour, there was a growing demand from moderate Liberals for fusion with Reform to offset the further rise of Labour, especially after Labour replaced the Liberal party as the official opposition in 1925.

In 1928, led by the veteran radical, ex-Prime Minister Sir Joseph Ward, the Liberals, renaming themselves the United party after admitting some agrarian defectors from Reform, made a vigorous and successful comeback attempt, seeking office on an anti-depression platform something like that of Lloyd George's Liberals in Britain the following year. Although unable to win a majority of parliamentary seats, the United party regained some Liberal seats thought lost to Labour, became the second largest party in the House of Representatives, and formed a ministry with Labour support. This Liberal-United renaissance proved short-lived. Labour party backing ended with the death of Ward and a turn to the right under a new party leader prepared to coalesce with Reform to carry out an economy program similar to that of Britain's National Government. Coalition with the Reform party in the 1931 election was followed by fusion of the two anti-Labour parties under the National label in 1935. Since 1935 the National and Labour parties have alternated in power as the country's two governing parties. There have been no significant third parties.[21]

The decline of the Liberal parties in Britain and New Zealand followed a remarkably uniform pattern between 1905 and 1935, although there were important distinctions. In both countries discontented trade unionists, long allied with the Liberal party, organized a new party to give labor separate parliamentary representation. A wartime coalition between Liberals and Conservatives aided the progress of the Labour party in both countries, so that by 1925 Labour had captured much of the Liberal voting strength. An internal struggle between moderates and radicals weakened both Liberal parties in the twenties, and a radical victory in both parties helped them to a brief electoral upsurge in 1928-9 (much greater in New Zealand than in Britain). In the early thirties moderates regained control of the two Liberal parties and forced them into the orbits of their powerful Conservative rivals. In New Zealand, the entire Liberal (United) party was persuaded to fuse with the Conservative (Reform) party. In Britain, the Liberal party split, with one section (Liberal National) merging with the Conservatives, the other remaining independent as a weak third party.

What role did the electoral system play in the fall of the New Zealand Liberal party? The prewar British Liberals used electoral pacts with Labour, with some success, to prevent the "progressive" vote from being split. The New Zealand Liberals tried run-off elections. This device worked well in one election, was less successful in a second because of drastic loss of popularity by the Liberals, and was then discontinued by the opposition.

Whether, if left in operation, the run-off plan would have helped the Liberals to keep their strength in the House of Representatives cannot be determined. As in Britain, there was a heavy loss of working class votes to Labour, due to dissatisfaction with Liberal war policies, which occurred independently of the electoral system. Run-off elections, moderately effective in reducing the benefits to the Reform party of a split "progressive" vote in the first balloting, might have saved a few Liberal seats in postwar elections, but could not have forestalled a heavy defection to Labour. This defection continued for several elections, as in Britain, with Duverger's polarization pattern evidently at work. As working class voters abandoned the New Zealand Liberal party out of dissatisfaction with its ideology and policies, other voters on the party's left and right also seceded because the party was manifestly declining in strength and effectiveness. However, the weakening of the Liberal party was slower than in Britain, and it did not prevent the party from accomplishing a remarkable revival in 1928. This success is evidence that the polarization effect is not invariably fatal to a party that has lost ground, even though the decline of the New Zealand Liberal (United) party resumed in the next election following the death of its outstanding leader.

South Africa, in spite of its huge black population generally excluded from political participation, was in effect the fourth "white" British dominion before it withdrew from the Commonwealth and became an independent republic in 1960-1. Ethnic issues monopolized the politics of this unitary dominion from its formation in 1910. (A British-type SMP electoral system operated from the beginning.) Starting with three parties--Unionist (pro-British, right of center), Labour (pro-British, left of center), and South African (moderate Afrikaner nationalist favoring cooperation with Britain)--South Africa acquired a fourth in 1913 when elements of the South African party proposing complete independence seceded to form the Nationalist party. During the First World War, the once opposed South African and Unionist parties were driven into alliance against the pro-German policies of the Nationalists. In 1920 the Unionist party was absorbed into the South African party, which tried to unite the two white South African nationalities in support of a broad program of national development and friendship with Britain.

The merging of the larger of the Afrikaner parties
with the conservative British party alienated the
Labourites and induced them to make an electoral pact
with the Nationalists. As a result, the Nationalists
in 1924 replaced the South African party as the largest
in the national parliament and were able to form a
government in coalition with Labour. In 1932, a
National Government similar to that in Britain was
constructed by the two major parties to fight the
depression. A year later, the main parts of the South
African and Nationalist parties merged to create the
United party, leaving behind pro-British and pro-Afri-
kaner rumps that took the names Dominion and Purified
Nationalist. Upon the retirement of General Herzog,
the Nationalist leader who, with General Smuts of the
South African party, had arranged the merger, the old
Nationalist party was gradually reconstructed under the
leadership of Daniel F. Malan. Pursuing a policy of
sympathy to Germany once again during the Second World
War, and after the war advocating militant Afrikaner
nationalism and strict racial segregation, the Nationalists won every South African election between 1948
and the formation of the republic. A weak United party
was the official opposition, and there were several
minor parties.

Ideologically, the South African party and its
successor the United party came closest to occupying in
South Africa the position of the British Liberals as a
center party. However, this centrist position was on
the racial issue rather than on economic questions, and
none of the minor parties that arose after the Second
World War to champion racial equality acquired enough
voting strength to elect more than a handful of M.P.'s.
Not only did these minor parties attract few voters
away from the United party on the racial issue, but
they did little to challenge its increasingly conservative social and economic policies. Hence the United
party did not suffer the bipolarization effect described by Duverger, except for the loss of a very few
adherents to the minor leftist parties and a somewhat
larger number immediately after the war to the resur-
gent Nationalists. The United party kept the support
of the great majority of English-speaking South Afri-
cans, as well as of many Afrikaners friendly to
Britain, together totaling about 40 percent of the
electorate. This proportion of the electorate changed
little despite the party's defeat in successive elections.

Before and after the Second World War, the weakening effect of repeated defeats steadily diminished the influence and parliamentary representation of the once important South African Labour party. An eight-year alliance with the Nationalist party in the twenties and early thirties, which included representation in the dominion cabinet, did not stop this trend, nor did an electoral pact with the United party after the war. The Labour party was also plagued by repeated schisms, in much the same way as was the British Liberal party between the wars. Thus the Labour party in South Africa, though not a center party ideologically, suffered from many of the same effects of an SMP election system as the Liberal party in Britain, effects worsened by the lack of cohesiveness in both parties. A similar decline eliminated the Dominion party, whose representation melted away as its usefulness in the eyes of the voters progressively diminished.[22]

The judgments of Duverger, Mabileau, and other political scientists that the British Liberal party was the victim of Britain's political system are supported by some evidence from the "white" British dominions where similar traditions took root and the electoral systems resemble Britain's. Australia's evidence is least useful for comparative purposes, since no party in recent years has been in a position analogous to that of the British Liberal party. Moreover, the traditional electoral system has been modified by adoption of preferential voting. The federal system is another variable in Australia, although Australian state parties more closely follow the national pattern than do provincial parties in Canada. Canada's heterogeneity has produced a rich variety of national and provincial parties. The negative effect of the SMP system has been diminished by the interlocking of national and provincial politics, which permits parties weak on one level to nevertheless survive on this level because of their viability on the other one. The Canadian Liberal party, displaced as a governing party in a few provinces by the leftist New Democratic party, has by no means disappeared in these provinces. One reason is that the Liberals' status as a national party has protected it while it has been under severe attack in provincial politics.

The politics of New Zealand and pre-republican South Africa gives the most positive support to the adverse political system theory. The fate of the New Zealand Liberal party corresponded very closely to that

204

of its British counterpart, despite a more radical program that presumably enhanced its reputation with working class voters. Yet once the polarization set in, the New Zealand Liberals steadily lost strength. The 1928 election results, and subsequent developments, suggest that weakening of a declining party by the electoral system can be reversed, but that a militant effort, a cohesive organization, brilliant leadership, and a run of luck are required. The New Zealand Liberals were able to recover briefly, but could not sustain their good fortune. The question remains open whether their revival, under the best of conditions, could have become permanent. The same question might be asked about the British Liberal recoveries of 1923 and 1929, both of which turned out to be transitory.

In South Africa, the Labour and Dominion parties both lost votes as the public increasingly questioned their usefulness. As in the case of the British Liberal party, the failure of these parties to justify their existence encouraged defection of voters.

Negative support for the adverse political system hypothesis comes from countries outside the British Commonwealth, where Liberal parties, or their equivalents, have survived as significant parties under different types of political structure than the SMP. A good case is that of Belgium and its Liberal party,[23] still flourishing in the 1980s as a respectable party comprising over ten percent of the Chamber of Deputies of the Belgian parliament. As in Britain, extension of the parliamentary franchise to the working class opened the way for the rise of a Labour-Socialist party at the expense of the older Liberal-Radical party. In the 1894 election, the first after enactment of universal male suffrage, the Socialists rose from no representation to 28 deputies, while the Liberals dropped from 60 to 21. In the next election, polarization evidently occurred. Besides further defections to the Socialists, the Liberals also lost votes to the conservative Catholic party because it seemed a better bulwark against Socialism than their own weakened party. The Liberal representation fell to only 13.

At this point the majority Catholic party, hoping to prevent a Socialist government from eventually coming to power, replaced the traditional SMP election system with proportional representation. Under PR the Liberals, whose deputies under the old election system were disproportionate to their comparatively large popular vote throughout the country, immediately jumped to 33 deputies, roughly proportionate to their national strength. What Duverger called "depolarization" now began. In subsequent elections under PR, voters who had abandoned the Liberals as a declining party, seemingly destined for oblivion or token existence, returned to the fold and brought Liberal strength in the Chamber of Deputies up to a peak of 45, about one-fourth of the membership, in 1908. Liberal deputies have since occupied between 8 percent and 24 percent of the seats in the Chamber, depending on shifts in public opinion. The Belgian Liberal party, thanks to PR, became the kind of "swing party," essential to formation of either rightist or leftist governments, that many British Liberals envisaged as the function of their party after its supercession by Labour as a governing party in the twenties.[24]

The success of the misnamed Radical Socialist party in France during the interwar period is further evidence that Liberal-type parties can survive and prosper in political systems differing from the British. Occupying much the same position between conservatives and leftists as the twentieth century British Liberal party, the French Radical Socialists did not fall victim to polarization and double swings of the pendulum as did their British counterparts. Instead, thanks to the French run-off system, they drew second ballot votes from conservatives who considered them less dangerous than the real Socialists. The electoral system of the Third Republic (reestablished in the Fifth Republic since 1959), which permitted parties to organize whatever local coalitions they wanted for the run-off, made it possible for the Radical Socialists, as the principal center party, to call the tune in scores of constituencies. Either the Socialists were forced to back their candidate to keep out a conservative or, more frequently, if a right-center pact was made against a Socialist, the Radical candidate was assured of rightist votes he could not have hoped to receive in the initial balloting. The run-off system undoubtedly strengthened the Radical Socialist party, which under PR probably would have elected many fewer deputies. During the 1920s the Radical Socialists had the largest single parliamentary delegation. The party declined precipitately following adoption of PR in 1945, although it later picked up strength.[25]

Similar local pacts during the twenties between

the British Liberals and one of their two rivals were, in contrast, embarrassing and unproductive. Although saving the seats of a number of Liberal M.P.'s, these pacts made it very difficult to maintain party discipline when, for example, Liberals elected with local Conservative support were asked to vote for measures introduced by a Labour government. The French Radical Socialists were never expected by their adherents to form a majority government but to participate in, or stand down from, coalition ministries at their leaders' discretion. The British Liberal M.P.'s disappointed their Liberal voters when their party could not form a government, and their Conservative or Labour supporters when party discipline required them to back the very type of government these non-Liberal voters least wanted to see in office. The center party role that Lloyd George and others thought the British Liberals should play in the twenties was wholly alien to the nature of British political traditions and techniques. It was quite natural to the French Radical Socialists schooled in a different tradition.[26]

The loss of governing party status by the British Liberals in the 1920s forced their apologists to try to find a new vocation for them in a suppositious "three party system." The most articulate of these writers was Ramsay Muir, who before the First World War had been a staunch defender of the two party tradition. As late as 1918, Muir argued that multi-party coalition governments encouraged corrupt bargaining. But by 1923, Muir had become convinced that two parties did not adequately represent graduated shades of political opinion. Muir still held to this view in 1930, after Britain had endured over a decade of clumsy three party politics. The former enthusiast for a periodic alternation of Ins and Outs had become a tireless advocate of "true representation of voters" through proportional representation.[27]

Lord Oxford and Asquith, leader of the Liberal party; Lord Grey, former foreign secretary; C. F. G. Masterman, an ex-cabinet minister; and J. Alfred Spender, editor of the <u>Westminster Gazette</u>, were among the prominent Liberals of the day certain that tripartite politics, "despite its manifest and obvious inconveniences," had come to stay.[28] Obviously the loyalty of these Liberals to their party, fighting for its existence, overrode their devotion to the British sporting tradition of politics which would no longer accommodate it. Liberal publicists, of whom Ramsay Muir was the pacemaker, went to the most elaborate lengths to show how British political forms must be altered to conform to a weakened Liberal party. They were not prepared to objectively face the prospect that the political system might well go on as before without the Liberal party.[29]

Despite the belief of some observers--not just British Liberals--in the 1920s that the complexity of social and economic issues was encouraging the rise of several parties in countries where there had been but two,[30] the two party system reasserted itself in Britain and other states retaining the SMP election system. It came back strongest in homogeneous countries like Britain and New Zealand where the sporting tradition of politics ranged a party of farmers, businessmen, and members of professions against a party of industrial workers and lower middle class wage earners. "The division between white and blue collar interests in Britain," wrote K. R. Gladdish, "though not translated 100 percent into electoral behavior, offered in the first half of the twentieth century a clear basis on which to mobilise political support."[31] This revival of the two party system occurred simultaneously with multi-party explosions in countries experimenting with PR and other electoral styles intended to produce more exact election results. It was clearly no accident that the British Liberal party, and parties resembling it, disappeared or were reduced to insignificance in countries retaining the traditional method of choosing legislators, while similar parties kept an effective place in other states practicing the new forms of election.[32]

Although, as Mabileau cautioned, the British political system did not by itself mark the Liberal party for decline, and indeed supported it for many years against its aspiring Labourite rival, it ruthlessly pulled the party down once it had begun to falter. In Belgium, in sharp contrast, PR reinvigorated a faltering Liberal party. However, it did not restore the Belgian Liberal party to major party status. Probably PR or some form of preferential voting would have had much the same effect on the British Liberal party as on the Belgian.[33] In one estimate it was conjectured that use of the single transferable vote, as in Australia, might have changed the 1964 general election results from 317 Labourites, 304 Conservatives, and 9 Liberals to 264 Labourites, 214 Conservatives, and 152 Liberals.[34] Of course, adoption of a new voting scheme would have substantially changed the whole British tradition of contesting political teams, or "adversary politics" as S. E. Finer and other political scientists have recently renamed it.[35]

Could the British Liberal party have survived the adverse political system without a change in the rules of the game, working its way back to governing party status? The resurgence of New Zealand Liberalism, though short-lived, suggests that it might have. The persistence of a governing Liberal party in Canada, and of politically important Liberal parties in Belgium, Denmark, Israel, the Netherlands, Norway, Sweden, and Switzerland, is proof that Liberalism in the twentieth century was not destined for extinction. Lowell G. Noonan wrote in 1954 that "the electoral system was not the fundamental cause of the Liberal decline but it furnished the major parties with a political 'meat axe' with which to finish the job."[36] Evidently the "axe" has been too dull for its work, as the Liberal party not only has survived Noonan's obituary by over a quarter century but drew over six million votes--23.6 percent of the vote for opposed candidates--in the February 1974 parliamentary election. But we must agree with Noonan that the effect of the British political system on the decline of the Liberal party was contributive but secondary. The primary causes of the party's ill fortune must be sought elsewhere.

THE LIBERAL PARTY ALIVE, WELL, AND (MAYBE) RESURGENT*

Can a small, anarchic third party of individual-
ists and do-gooders survive and prosper in a collectivist two party system distinguished by bigness, impersonality, and class rivalry? Arthur Cyr, an American
political scientist who studied under Harvard's Samuel
H. Beer, answered with a qualified "yes." He further
suggested that Britain's politics of collectivism,
functioning for over two generations, may be about to
fall victim to diminishing class consciousness and
blossoming local and regional awareness. Cyr was less
certain that the reviving Liberal party, with its
historic commitment to personal initiative and moral
incentives, will be the principal beneficiary of a new
political ethos. Not only have the major parties been
remarkably adaptive--boldly stealing from the Liber-
als--but now there are the mettlesome Celtic Fringe
"nationalist" parties sometimes outbidding the Liberals
for protest votes.

Cyr built his analysis of post-Second World War
Liberalism upon the paradigm devised by his teacher,
Beer, in the 1950s and today widely accepted as conventional wisdom. In numerous articles and a celebrated
book, British Politics in the Collectivist Age,[1] Beer
demonstrated the rise of a new kind of politics during
the early twentieth century. Apace with the enfran-
chisement of the working class and the growth of the
trade union movement, class lines hardened along an
employer-employee cleavage. Simultaneously, the
mounting complexity of government fostered bureaucratic
centralism, not only in departmental administration but
in party politics. Parliament, once a deliberative
forum, was transformed into a sounding board for a
powerful executive. The latter was served (some would
say mastered) by an authoritative civil service dedicated to efficient planning and management. Elections

---

*This Epilogue is a review of Arthur Cyr, Liberal Party
Politics in Britain, with a Foreward by Michael Steed
(New Brunswick, N.J., 1977). It was written before the
formation in 1981 of the electoral pact between the
Liberals and the schismatic right wing Labourites, the
Social Democrats.

became plebiscitary, utilized to ratify or reject the executive's program, which catered to the aspirations or the anxieties of a universal suffrage electorate. A Labour party of cautious change appealed to the wage earner's desire for psychological respect and material gains, while a Conservative party of moderate resistance spoke for the needs of the propertied and salaried for legitimacy, order, and security. The transition to collectivism was facilitated by the organic social ideologies of both the Conservative and Labour parties, the former emphasizing a hierarchical integration of the whole society, the latter a horizontal division between competing integral classes. Both ideologies were and are in sharp contrast to the individualist and voluntarist foundations of Liberal doctrine.

The Liberal party, Cyr stressed, is a "nineteenth century antique" not only ideologically but in its middle class cadres, flaccid internal structure, and flimsy discipline. (Elsewhere Cyr compared it to the loose-jointed American parties.) The archetypical party of laissez-faire, peaking under Gladstone's inspirational leadership in the middle of Victoria's reign, the Liberals were fated to be squeezed between the two modern collectivist parties that matured between 1900 and 1950. Although some radical Liberals flirted with collectivism during the post-Gladstone years, especially during the last Liberal government of 1905-15, the party as a whole failed to make the transition to the new political world.

Cyr argued that the Liberals were doomed as a major party by their ideology and style, not--as other writers have contended--by external circumstances, internal divisions, or mistaken policies. He disclaimed the respective hypotheses of George Dangerfield, Roy Douglas, Trevor Wilson, and John Glaser that by 1914 Liberalism had become a tired, sluggish movement; that the last Liberal government was foolishly generous to the rising Labour party; that the First World War and its attendant Asquith-Lloyd George feud did in the party; or that the Liberal party deteriorated because the Nonconformist conscience had. Far from being used up, ideological Liberalism has been alive and well throughout the twentieth century, Cyr claimed, and much of the time more radical and innovative than its competitors. Nor has the Nonconformist ethic noticeably flagged, according to Cyr. Although today more secularist than overtly religious, the Free Church element still informs the Liberal party and contributes both activists and electors in disproportionate numbers. The impact of pro-Labour legislation, the Great War, and the party schism are dismissed as "effects of the basic cause of Liberal collapse," which is seen as "a fundamental shift in the forms of representation, and party and governmental power, in British politics."[2] While Conservatives and Labourites adjusted well to the benign new environment, the Liberals could not adapt to its alien modes.

Cyr picked up a theme that John Vincent elaborated in The Formation of the British Liberal Party,[3] his ground breaking study of mid-nineteenth century Liberalism. This is the essentially local orientation of Liberalism, and its dependence upon voluntary participation by highly motivated individuals, mostly from the middle sectors, in a great variety of projects aimed at both community social services and reforms of a wider scope. In a much earlier classic political study, Moisei Y. Ostrogorski traced the beginning of Liberal voluntarism to the anti-slave trade movement of the late eighteenth century, inspired by Nonconformists and Methodist evangelism. Elsewhere in Democracy and the Organization of Political Parties,[4] Ostrogorski accused late nineteenth century radical Liberals of abandoning the "moral power" of town and village Liberalism for "physical force" embodied in the discipline of a centralist party organization. Actually, as Cyr made plain, the radicals never completed the transition to collectivism that Ostrogorski deplored. To this day Liberalism in any part of Britain is only as strong as its local association, and the central organization is weak, factionalized, and uncohesive. The disciplined solidarity, from the top down, of the Conservative and Labour parties at all but a few passing moments in their histories has never been characteristic of the Liberals.

Although Cyr did not fully develop the point, he implied that the principal reason why the Liberal party faltered during the First World War, and was slow to knit afterward, was not the leadership quarrel but the disintegration of morale in local associations across the country. Rank and file Liberals were dismayed and alienated by the atmosphere of the war. As ruinous to the survival of Liberalism as a governing party was the reluctance of local associations before and after the war to welcome working class cadres, essential if the party was to compete successfully with Labour in muni-

213

cipal and parliamentary elections. As H. Stuart Hughes observed, and Cyr reiterated, the British and other European class-based (and biased) Liberal parties were doubly damned: unable to come to terms with the wage earning class, but approving reformist policies bound to turn well-to-do and timid voters against them. Only a powerful central headquarters that could have forced white collared candidates to stand down in scores of constituences, Samuel Beer once suggested, might have saved the Liberal party. This was impossible because the class-biased local associations were autonomous and usually ungovernable. The decline of Liberal representation in local councils before the war, documented in Chris Cook's psephological studies, presaged a general collapse of the party that probably would have happened, Beer and now Cyr have maintained, even if there had been no war.

Cyr agreed with Jorgen Rasmussen--whose The Liberal Party: A Study of Retrenchment and Revival[5] was a searching examination of the fallow years of Liberalism during the thirties, forties, and fifties--that the withdrawal from the Liberals of interest group support, both financial and influential, was crippling to their claims to be a party of government. The impoverished Liberals became dependent on subventions from the Lloyd George Fund and other tainted sources, and were lured into "go for broke" revival schemes launched by rich cranks, like Edward Martell's in the late 1940s. But while Cyr was certain that there was no real hope for Liberal resuscitation as a governing party after 1924 at the latest, he was equally sure that the party was and is in no danger of extinction. Even if some of its leaders had accepted Churchill's 1951 offer of a permanent Conservative-Liberal electoral pact, the party would have undergone one of its idiosyncratic schisms and a body of true believers would have carried on independently.

Cyr credited the survival of an independent national Liberal party during the bleak decade after the Second World War to a London-based party Establishment whose members are linked by ties of family, friendship, and deep commitment to ideological Liberalism. This Establishment is the most central of the "diffuse collection of clubs" that constitutes activist Liberalism in Britain.[6] Less important only because more dispersed and atomized have been the many pockets of provincial Liberalism, often connected with one or more of the Free Churches. Inspired by detestation of collec-

tivism and "special interests," these Liberals are
determined to keep alive the ideals of personal responsibility and voluntary service with which the party has
been historically identified. It was these dedicated
provincial cadres that furnished the shock troops for
the party renaissance that began modestly in the late
1940s, climaxed spectacularly in the early 1960s, and
reached an even higher pinnacle electorally in local
and parliamentary voting in 1972-4.

The core of Cyr's book was a searching analysis of
Liberal politics during the "Grimond revival" of 1956-
67. Although accentuating--perhaps too fervently--the
catalytic role of Jo Grimond, party leader during these
years, Cyr observed that during the earlier period of
the Attlee Labour government and after there had been a
large intake to the party of young people disillusioned
by Labour's shortcomings as an idealistic crusade and
uninspired by Churchill's post-Victorian Conservatism.
Some of these youthful, mostly university-trained
London and provincial Liberals belonged to the Radical
Reform Group that engineered the retirement of veteran
Clem Davies from the party leadership, and the withdrawal to the sidelines of other old campaigners from
the intra-party wars of the twenties and thirties. A
revival was out of the question so long as men and
women initiated to politics during the party's slump,
and instilled with memories of frustration and failure,
still were in charge. Jo Grimond, in his early
forties, symbolized the new wave of activists. As
son-in-law of Lady Violet Bonham Carter, Asquith's
daughter, he was also a charter member of the Liberal
Establishment.

Grimond calculated on a split in the Labour party,
following the passing of the Attlee generation, between
the wild men of the Bevanite left and the rightist
trade union officers and university dons typified by
George Brown and Grimond's personal friend (and biographer of Asquith) Roy Jenkins. When a radical-progres-
sive movement of Liberals and moderate Labourites--
possibly a coalition, perhaps a wholly new party--did
not materialize in the early sixties; when instead
Harold Wilson reunified Labour, revivified it, and
rescued it from the doldrums of three lost general
elections; and when, after the halcyon days of Orpington Man (1962-4), the Liberal revival lost steam and
the party was again beset by internal quarrels and a
generation gap, a disillusioned, bored, and aging
Grimond gave up the leadership. He did not have great
staying power.

215

Cyr maintained--more convincingly than some British pundits--that Grimond left the party a permanent legacy. It was Grimond's dynamic, Kennedyish image, however pop and trendy it sometimes registered, that drew university and media people--frequently the same persons in the TV age--to the Liberal party, inspired these wordsmiths to dress up the party policies to catch the attention of the Sunday newspapers and intellectual weeklies, and induced the general public to take the party seriously for the first time in over thirty years. The marvelous Orpington by-election victory of 1962 was a flash in the-pan. But this exalting moment, when the Liberals momentarily led the two collectivist giants in the opinion polls, gave the party cadres the psychological lift so long wanting. By 1964, partly as the result of dogged canvassing, hundreds of Liberals had been added to local councils throughout Britain, even in places like Liverpool where there had been no Liberal heritage. The three million electors who voted Liberal in 1964, and the six million who did so in February 1974, embraced suburban, white collared Orpington Men disenchanted with class and interest politics and disgusted by what Beer called "pluralist stagnation." These electors, Cyr believed, would have continued to swing disconsolately between Conservatism and Labour, opted for the new Scottish and Welsh regional parties, or abstained but for the new likeness that Grimond and his colleagues gave to Liberalism in the 1960s.

Grimond's successor, Jeremy Thorpe, had little of his former chief's charisma and was crippled by personal eccentricities and resultant misadventures that damaged the Liberal party and forced his resignation in 1976. But Thorpe's record as leader was not without credits. Practicing benign neglect, he allowed the youthful "Red Guard" zealots, disrupters of party assemblies and creators of public nuisances during the late sixties, to talk and act themselves into oblivion. Equally important, Thorpe encouraged more sober young Liberals to implement community action and consumer protection campaigns that enhanced the party's visibility, helping it to elect local councillors and even to win an occasional council majority--something that had not happened since the early 1930s. Cyr, captivated by Grimond, was perhaps less generous to Thorpe than the younger man deserves. If the Liberal party is ever to challenge the present governing parties, it will do so from the respectable grass roots base that took shape during the Thorpe years, although there has

216

been a recession from the level of strength and confidence reached in 1972-4.

This book manifested some of the weaknesses of post-graduate dissertations adapted for book publication. It was too long, it was repetitive, and it was annoyingly equivocal. The prose was bland, often soporific academicese. With its focus on the Grimond era, as in the original thesis completed some years ago, and its more superficial treatment of the Thorpe leadership, the book was obsolescent to a degree only partly corrected by the updating foreward of Liberal publicist Michael Steed. On the other hand, Cyr's study had much more depth, and a lot more to say, than the shallow chapters on recent events in the standard party histories by Roy Douglas and Chris Cook. Although Steed was surely correct when he remarked that there is "as yet no authoritative contemporary work on the Liberal party,"[7] this study by Arthur Cyr was an important if imperfect contribution to the history of the party and of modern British politics generally.

NOTES

THE MURDER OF THE LIBERAL PARTY: A HISTORY LESSON

1. Cf. the analogous judgment of Edwin E. Hargrove, Jr.: "It cannot be contended that Liberalism was murdered by Lloyd George because of defects in his personality. There were far more important factors working. But, Lloyd George helped to give the death blows" ("The Tragic Hero in Politics: Theodore Roosevelt, David Lloyd George, and Fiorello LaGuardia" [unpublished Ph.D. dissertation, Yale University, 1963], p. 691).

ASQUITH: THE LAST BIG WHIG

1. David Lloyd George (Earl Lloyd George of Dwyfor), War Memoirs (Boston, 1935-7), I, 83.

2. Joseph Grimond, "H. H. Asquith," The Prime Ministers, ed. Herbert Van Thal (London, 1975), II, 197. Stephen Koss has made the point that Asquith's mother's family was considerably more affluent and of higher social standing than his father's (Asquith [London, 1976], p. 3).

3. Lloyd George, II, 423. Some of his Yorkshire mill-town background must have shown through to King Edward VII, who told Lord Rosebery that Asquith seemed to him to be "common" and lacking "manners" (Robert Rhodes James, Rosebery: A Biography of Archibald Philip, Fifth Earl of Rosebery [New York, 1963], p. 464).

4. J. Alfred Spender and Cyril Asquith, Life of Herbert Henry Asquith, Lord Oxford and Asquith (London, 1932), I, 73.

5. Stanley Salvidge, Salvidge of Liverpool: Behind the Political Scene, 1890-1928 (London, 1934), p. 160; Cameron Hazlehurst, "Asquith as Prime Minister," English Historical Review, LXXXV (1970), 508.

6. John Maynard Keynes (Baron Keynes), Essays in

219

<u>Biography</u> (New York, 1933), p. 50.

7. Spender and Asquith, I, 214; Baron Beaverbrook
(Sir William Maxwell Aitken), <u>Politicians and the War,
1914-1916</u> (London, 1928-32), I, 222; Roy Jenkins,
<u>Asquith</u> (London, 1964), p. 286.

8. H. N. Brailsford, "The Last of the English
Liberals," <u>Foreign Affairs</u>, XI (1933), 635; H. Wickham
Steed, "Asquith's Place in History," <u>Current History</u>,
XXVIII (1928), 42-3; Alfred M. Gollin, "Asquith: A New
View," <u>A Century of Conflict, 1850-1950: Essays for
A. J. P. Taylor</u>, ed. Martin Gilbert (London, 1966),
p. 108.

9. W. L. Guttsman, "Aristocracy and Middle Class
in the British Political Elite, 1886-1916: A Study of
Formative Influences and of the Attitude to Politics,"
<u>British Journal of Sociology</u>, V (1954), 28-9.

10. Brailsford, p. 634.

11. A. G. Gardiner, "Mr. Asquith," <u>Spectator</u>,
October 22, 1932.

12. Henry W. Nevinson, <u>Last Changes, Last Chances</u>
(London, 1928), p. 303.

13. Scott cited in Ivor Brown, <u>The Way of My World</u>
(London, 1954), p. 190; Hector Bolitho, <u>Alfred Mond,
First Lord Melchett</u> (London, 1933), p. 255; "A Gentle-
man with a Duster" [Harold Begbie], <u>The Mirrors of
Downing Street</u> (London, 1920), p. 41.

14. A. G. Gardiner, <u>Prophets, Priests and Kings</u>
(London, 1914), p. 59.

15. Spender and Asquith, I, 38; Margot Asquith
quoted in <u>ibid.</u>, I, 99; Brailsford, p. 634; Lloyd
George, II, 425; Sir John Marriott, "Asquith's Place in
History," <u>Fortnightly Review</u>, CXXXVIII (1932), 581.

16. Hazlehurst, p. 517; William Verity, "Haldane
and Asquith," <u>History Today</u>, XVIII (1968), 450.

17. Frank P. Chambers, <u>The War Behind the War,
1914-1918: A History of the Political and Civilian
Fronts</u> (New York, 1939), p. 265.

18. Newman Flower, <u>As It Happened</u> (London, 1950),
p. 141.

19. Spender and Asquith, I, 101, 200.

20. Lloyd George, II, 424. Bonar Law, on the other hand had a deep respect for Asquith, both as a statesman and--curiously, considering Law's own far from meager talent--as a crafty politician (Robert Blake, The Unknown Prime Minister: The Life and Times of Andrew Bonar Law [London, 1955], p. 99).

21. Lloyd George, I, 212.

22. Jenkins, p. 265 n.; Grimond, p. 207.

23. Spender and Asquith, I, 213; Jenkins, 102-3.

24. Spender and Asquith, I, 217.

25. Gardiner, "Mr. Asquith."

26. The Mist Procession: The Autobiography of Lord Vansittart (London, 1958), p. 114; Prince Lichnowsky, Heading for the Abyss: Reminiscences (London, 1928), p. 69. Asquith's fondness of the company of young women extended, according to Stephen Koss, to some who were "not quite respectable" (Asquith, p. 93).

27. Cameron Hazlehurst, Politicians at War, July 1914 to May 1915: A Prologue to the Triumph of Lloyd George (London, 1971), p. 169.

28. The Private Papers of Douglas Haig, 1914-1919, ed. Robert Blake (London, 1952), p. 164; Winston to Clementine Churchill, April 22, 1911, quoted in Randolph S. Churchill, Winston S. Churchill: The Young Statesman, 1901-1914 (Boston, 1967), p. 332.

29. Marie Belloc Lowndes, A Passing World (London, 1948), p. 129.

30. Spender and Asquith, I, 67; cf. Verity, pp. 449-50.

31. Beaverbrook, I, 225; Jenkins, p. 299. Asquith's relationship with Venetia Stanley Montague was intimate but probably platonic (Koss, pp. 140-1).

32. Hazlehurst, "Asquith as Prime Minister," p. 512.

33. John Charteris, At G.H.Q. (London, 1931), p. 133. But cf. Gollin, p. 108, where he argues that Asquith, like Gladstone, was reproved by some for "his ability to prevaricate, to act evasively."

34. Sir Lawrence Guillemard, Trivial Fond Records (London, 1937), pp. 34-5.

35. Hazlehurst, "Asquith as Prime Minister," p. 517.

36. Lowndes, p. 117.

37. Sir Alexander Mackintosh, Echoes of Big Ben: A Journalist's Parliamentary Diary, 1881-1940 (London, 1945), p. 111. According to Lord Hankey, he treated such personal attacks "with indifference and even jocularity" (Hankey, The Supreme Command, 1914-1918 [London, 1961], II, 569).

38. A. G. Gardiner, "Asquith," Nineteenth Century, CXII (1932), 616.

39. Lowndes, pp. 116-7.

40. Brailsford, p. 634.

41. Byrum E. Carter, The Office of Prime Minister (Princeton, 1956), p. 212; Roy Jenkins, "From Gladstone to Asquith: The Late Victorian Pattern of Liberal Leadership," History Today, XIV (1964), 450.

42. Guttsman, p. 29; Viscount Cecil of Chelwood, All the Way (London, 1949), p. 135; Sir Winston Churchill, Great Contemporaries (New York, 1937), p. 116.

43. R. MacGregor Dawson, "The Cabinet Minister and Administration: Asquith, Lloyd George, Curzon," Political Science Quarterly, LV (1940), 353, 374.

44. Herbert Asquith, Moments of Memory: Recollections and Impressions (London, 1937), pp. 89-90.

45. Leonard Woolf, "Lord Oxford," New Statesman and Nation, October 22, 1932.

46. Gardiner, "Asquith," p. 614.

47. Ibid., p. 615.

48. An exception is Joseph Grimond, who claimed that most of the "great mistakes and disasters" of the war occurred when Lloyd George was prime minister and firmly concluded that "the evidence shows that Asquith was a competent, steadfast war Prime Minister" (Grimond, p. 206).

49. Dawson, pp. 354-5; A. J. P. Taylor, "Politics in the First World War," Proceedings of the British Academy, XLV (1959), 70.

50. Cecil, p. 135.

51. J. A. Spender, "Lord Oxford and Asquith," Contemporary Review, CXXX (1926), 687; Trevor Wilson, The Downfall of the Liberal Party (London, 1966), p. 39.

52. Gardiner, "Mr. Asquith."

53. Gardiner, "Asquith," p. 608.

54. Chambers, p. 266.

55. J. M. Robertson, Mr. Lloyd George and Liberalism (London, 1923), p. 61; "Lord Haig and Lord Oxford," English Review, XLVI (1928), p. 251.

56. Spender, p. 688; Gardiner, "Mr. Asquith."

57. Carter, pp. 97-8. Cameron Hazlehurst claimed that Asquith "was less contemptuous of the manipulative arts than he pretended to be," but did not make a strong case ("Asquith as Prime Minister," pp. 524-5).

58. Gardiner, "Mr. Asquith."

59. Viscount D'Abernon, An Ambassador of Peace (London, 1929-30), II, 32-3.

60. Carter, pp. 98-9. A "Liberal Journalist," in a letter published in the Nation October 9, 1920, charged that Asquith even tended to give preference to his enemies in the press, especially The Times, and "to give the order of the boot to his journalistic friends." This writer asserted that Asquith remained partial to The Times, though it never had been very friendly to him, had become positively hostile after 1914, and contributed to the overthrow of his government in 1916.

223

61. Brailsford, p. 640.

62. Carter, pp. 269-70; Viscount Samuel, Memoirs (London, 1945), p. 87; David G. Hanes, The First British Workmen's Compensation Act, 1897 (New Haven, 1968), p. 48; Baron Riddell, Diary of the Peace Conference and After, 1918-1923 (New York, 1934), pp. 201-2.

63. James Johnston, Westminster Voices: Studies in Parliamentary Speech (London, 1928), pp. 55, 64; Sir David Low, Autobiography (New York, 1957), p. 101.

64. Johnston, p. 60.

65. Harry Boardman in the Manchester Guardian, September 12, 1952.

66. Leopold S. Amery, "British Government and the War," Quarterly Review, CCXXV (1916), 260-1.

67. Steed, p. 43.

68. Stuart Hodgson, "The Twilight of Parties," Nineteenth Century, CIX (1931), 126.

69. Frank Owen, Tempestuous Journey: Lloyd George, His Life and Times (New York, 1955), p. 68.

70. Koss, pp. 23, 26.

71. Spender and Asquith, I, 350-1; Gardiner, "Asquith," p. 617.

72. "Scrutator" [R. C. K. Ensor] in the Sunday Times, February 19, 1928.

73. Spender and Asquith, I, 201; Baroness Kennet (Kathleen Scott Young), Self-Portrait of an Artist (London, 1949), p. 217.

74. Gardiner, "Asquith," p. 617.

75. Sir Gervais Rentoul, This Is My Case: An Autobiography (London, 1944), p. 96.

76. Baron Percy of Newcastle, Some Memories (London, 1958), P. 78; C. P. Scott's diary, August 9, 1921, quoted in The Political Diaries of C. P. Scott, ed. Trevor Wilson (Ithaca, 1970), p. 400.

77. Spender and Asquith, I, 209.

78. Woolf, "Lord Oxford."

79. Chambers, p. 265.

80. Manchester Guardian, January 16, 1943.

LLOYD GEORGE: "THE GREAT GOD PAN"

1. Frances Lloyd George (Countess Lloyd George of Dwyfor), The Years that are Past (London, 1967), p. 42.

2. Sir Geoffrey Shakespeare, Let Candles Be Brought In (London, 1949), p. 38.

3. Sir Oswald Mosley, My Life (London, 1968), p. 87.

4. Sir Henry Morris-Jones, M.P., quoted in Liverpool Post, January 16, 1934; Shakespeare, p. 39; Lloyd George quoted in Life with Lloyd George: The Diary of A. J. Sylvester, ed. Colin Cross (London, 1975), p. 62.

5. Frances (Lady) Lloyd George, introduction to Malcolm Thomson, David Lloyd George: The Official Biography (London, 1948), pp. 14, 19; Shakespeare, p. 48.

6. Parliamentary Debates, Commons, March 28, 1945, quoted in Lloyd George, ed. Martin Gilbert (Englewood Cliffs, 1968), p. 129; Frances Lloyd George, in Thomson, pp. 19-20.

7. E.g., John Burns, May 14, 1915 diary entry, quoted in William Kent, John Burns: Labour's Lost Leader (London, 1950), p. 243; undated recorded remark of J. C. C. Davidson, quoted in Robert Rhodes James, Memoirs of a Conservative: J. C. C. Davidson's Memoirs and Papers, 1910-1937 (London, 1969), pp. 52-3.

8. G. E. Raine, The Real Lloyd George (London, 1913), p. 9; Amery, "British Government and the War," p. 262.

9. Quotations from Frances Lloyd George, introduction to Thomson, pp. 11-2, 18; cf. Frances Lloyd George, Lloyd George: A Diary by Frances Stevenson, ed. A. J. P. Taylor (New York, 1971), January 17, 1915, entry pp. 21-2.

10. Richard Lloyd George (Earl Lloyd George of Dwyfor), My Father, Lloyd George (New York, 1961), pp. 113-4; Giovanni Costigan, Makers of Modern England: The Force of Individual Genius in History (New York, 1967), p. 241.

11. Raine, p. 157; Shakespeare, pp. 48, 143; Tom Clarke, My Lloyd George Diary (London, 1939), p. 13; Alexander Brady, "The British Governing Class and Democracy," Canadian Journal of Economics and Political Sciences, XX (1954), 318.

12. Wilson, Downfall of the Liberal Party, p. 385; Thomas Jones, Lloyd George (Cambridge, Mass., 1951), pp. 285-6.

13. Leopold S. Amery, My Political Life (London, 1953-5), II, 95.

14. Thomson, p. 48.

15. Sir Colin Coote, Editorial (London, 1965), p. 97; Michael Kinnear, The Fall of Lloyd George: The Political Crisis of 1922 (Toronto, 1973), p. 4; Dawson, "The Cabinet Minister and Administration," p. 374; Wallace quotation from Viscount Castlerosse, Valentine's Days (London, 1934), p. 253.

16. Sir Dingle Foot, "Lloyd George," Observer, November 21, 1954; Frances Lloyd George, introduction to Thomson, pp. 21-2; Lowndes, A Passing World, p. 129; Lord Beaverbrook, The Decline and Fall of Lloyd George (New York, 1963), p. 304; Richard Lloyd George, p. 31; Lloyd George: A Diary by Frances Stevenson, November 30, 1914, entry, p. 14.

17. Thomson, p. 220; Sidney Dark, Not Such a Bad Life (London, 1941), p. 145.

18. Thomson, p. 155.

19. Frances Lloyd George, introduction to Thomson, p. 15.

20.   Harold Macmillan, The Past Masters: Politics and Politicians. 1906-1939 (London, 1975), pp. 55-6; Esmé Wingfield-Stratford, The Victorian Aftermath (New York, 1934), p. 257.

21.   Frances Lloyd George, introduction to Thomson, pp. 13-4; Costigan, pp. 225, 240.

22.   Quotations from Earl of Swinton (Sir Philip Cunliffe-Lister), in collaboration with James D. Margach, Sixty Years of Power: Some Memories of the Men Who Wielded It (London, 1966), pp. 42-3; and Sir Robert Boothby (Baron Boothby), I Fight to Live (London, 1957), p. 32.

23.   See, for example, Lloyd George to Margaret Lloyd George (first wife), June 10, 1890, and September 16, 1911, quoted in Lloyd George Family Letters, 1885-1936, ed. Kenneth O. Morgan (Cardiff, 1973), pp. 28, 159.

24.   Frances Lloyd George, introduction to Thomson, pp. 17-8; Clarke, p. 191; Thomson, p. 166; Haldane quotation from Jones, p. 278.   The "Grey" mentioned was Sir Edward Grey, later Lord Grey of Fallodon, foreign secretary in the Asquith government.   Interestingly, Lloyd George made a special allowance for Asquith.   In the same talk with Clarke, he also remarked, "Of course Asquith was more or less of the same schooling, but . . . . he was a human fellow really and with an understanding of people."

25.   Shakespeare, p. 42.

26.   Sir Stephen Tallents, Man and Boy (London, 1943), p. 226.

27.   Shakespeare, p. 40.

28.   Taylor, "Politics in the First World War," p. 95.

29.   Jones, p. 287; Journals and Letters of Reginald, Viscount Esher, ed. Maurice V. Brett (London, 1934-8), IV, 107.

30.   Carter, The Office of Prime Minister, p. 211.

31.   Jones, p. 281.

32. Dawson, p. 361.

33. Taylor, p. 95.

34. J. A. Spender, The Public Life (London, 1925), I, 120.

35. Carter, p. 100.

36. Tom Clarke, My Northcliffe Diary (London, 1931), p. 98.

37. Carter, pp. 102-3; Beaverbrook, The Decline and Fall of Lloyd George, p. 304; Bolitho, Alfred Mond, p.233.

38. Jones, p. 264.

39. Macmillan, p. 60.

40. George Dangerfield, The Strange Death of Liberal England (New York, 1935), p. 22.

41. Beaverbrook, The Decline and Fall of Lloyd George, p. 304; Shakespeare, p. 39.

42. Johnston, Westminster Voices, pp. 77-8. A veteran reporter wrote that Lloyd George was not impressive as "a disembodied voice" over radio. "He was really built for television" (A. H. Booth, British Hustings, 1924-1950 [London 1956], p. 83).

43. Hargrove, "The Tragic Hero in Politics," p. 201.

44. Jones, pp. 266-7.

45. Owen, Tempestuous Journey, p. 220.

46. St. John Ervine, Bernard Shaw: His Life, Work and Friends (New York, 1956), p. 281.

47. Richard Lloyd George, p. 122; Boothby, p. 28.

48. See, for example, Chris Cook, "A Stranger Death of Liberal England," Lloyd George: Twelve Essays, ed. A. J. P. Taylor (London, 1971), pp. 312-3.

49. Kenneth O. Morgan, "Lloyd George's Stage Army: The Coalition Liberals, 1918-22," Lloyd George:

Twelve Essays, pp. 252-3; John Campbell, Lloyd George: The Goat in the Wilderness, 1922-1931 (London, 1977), p. 313.

50. Amery, My Political Life, II, 230.

51. Beaverbrook, The Decline and Fall of Lloyd George, p. 163.

52. Sylvester, Life with Lloyd George, p. 70; Richard Lloyd George, pp. 18, 26, 29.

53. W. S. Adams, "Lloyd George and the Labour Movement," Past and Present, no. 3 (1953), p. 60; Richard Lloyd George, pp. 26-7; Costigan, pp. 234-5.

54. Adams, p. 59; Churchill quotation from Lucy Masterman, "Recollections of David Lloyd George," History Today, IX (1959), 276.

55. Boothby, p. 28.

56. Adams, pp. 56-7.

57. Sir Arthur Salter (Baron Salter), Personality in Politics: Studies of Contemporary Statesmen (London, 1947), pp. 51-2.

58. Sir Philip Gibbs, "Lloyd George: An Intimate Portrait," Harper's Magazine, CXLIII (1921), 425.

59. Clarke, My Lloyd George Diary, p. 16.

60. Sir James Grigg, Prejudice and Judgment (London, 1948), p. 91.

61. Jones, p. 34.

62. Richard Lloyd George, pp. 49-50; cf. Sir Alfred Davies, The Lloyd George I Knew: Some Side-Lights on a Great Career (London, 1948), p. 20.

63. Raine, p. 5.

64. Davies, p. 87.

65. Richard Lloyd George, pp. 59, 224-5, 228; Lord Beaverbrook, Men and Power, 1917-1918 (New York, 1956), p. 343.

66.   Richard Lloyd George, pp. 221, 223; but cf.
Sylvester, p. 16, and My Darling Pussy: The Letters of
Lloyd George and Frances Stevenson, 1913-41, ed.
A. J. P. Taylor (London, 1975), p. ix.

67.   Richard Lloyd George, p. 211.

68.   Salter, p. 38.

69.   John Montgomery, The Twenties: An Informal
Social History (New York, 1957), p. 81.

70.   Jones, p. 34.

71.   Beaverbrook, The Decline and Fall of Lloyd
George, p. 306.

72.   Jones, pp. 274-5.

73.   Ibid., p. 267; Boothby, p. 31.

74.   Charles L. Mowat, Britain between the Wars,
1918-1940 (Chicago, 1955), p. 10; Thelma Cazalet-Keir,
From the Wings (London, 1967), p. 49; World Within
World: The Autobiography of Stephen Spender (London,
1951), pp. 79-80.

75.   Mowat, p. 10; Milner quotation from A. J.
Sylvester, The Real Lloyd George (London, 1947), p.
12.

76.   W. J. Brown, Brown Studies (London, 1949),
pp. 169-71.

77.   Jones, pp. 282-3.

78.   Boothby, pp. 27-8.   Boothby rated Lloyd
George "a simpleton by comparison" to Baldwin as a
party manager and electioneerer.

79.   Clarke, My Lloyd George Diary, pp. 12-5.

80.   Richard Lloyd George, p. 210.

81.   Statement attributed by Lloyd George to
Joseph Chamberlain, quoted in Frances Lloyd George, The
Years that are Past, p. 246.

LLOYD GEORGE'S LUCRE: THE NATIONAL LIBERAL FUND

1. James K. Pollock, Money and Politics Abroad
(New York, 1932), p. 76. J. L. Garvin, editor of the
Observer, was believed to have originated this gibe.

2. Sir Robert Horne, chancellor of the exchequer
in the Lloyd George Coalition government, speaking
about 1930 and quoted in Brown Studies, p. 172.

3. On Liberal fund raising, see for example Roy
Douglas, The History of the Liberal Party, 1895-1970
(Madison, N.J., 1971), p. 14; William B. Gwyn, Democracy and the Cost of Politics (London, 1962), pp. 112-
5; and Abbott Lawrence Lowell, The Government of
England (London, 1908), II, 1-2. The L. C. A. officially was open to anyone contributing a subscription
of four guineas annually, but comprised mainly past and
present Liberal M.P.'s.

4. Barry McGill, "Francis Schnadhorst and Liberal
Party Organization," Journal of Modern History, XXXIV
(1962), 32-3; H. W. McCready, "Chief Whip and Party
Funds: The Work of Herbert Gladstone in the Edwardian
Liberal Party, 1899 to 1906," Canadian Journal of
History, VI (1971), 289-91.

5. In a conversation with J. C. C. Davidson, a
Conservative party official, in 1927 or 1928, Lloyd
George favorably compared the traffic in honors with
political fund raising in the United States, where
"political parties [were] under the domination of great
financial interests and trusts." In Britain, said
Lloyd George, a rich man who had "bought" a peerage
could be told "to go to the devil" if he demanded
subsequent favors. "It keeps politics far cleaner than
any other method of raising funds," he concluded
(James, Memoirs of a Conservative, p. 279).

6. Harold J. Hanham, "The Sale of Honours in Late
Victorian England," Victorian Studies, III (1960), 286;
James, Rosebery, pp. 380-1; Keith Middlemas, The Life
and Times of Edward VII (London, 1972), p. 202. Lord
Ashton, a Lancaster industrialist and big contributor
to Liberal funds, whose elevation to the peerage was
questioned in 1895, was later to denounce Lloyd George
for "wrecking the historic Liberal party" by using his
fund to promote "socialism." See the Daily News
(London), February 7-11, 1928.

7.   Manchester Guardian, November 18, 1910; Massingham in the Nation, June 14, 1913, quoted in Alfred
F. Havinghurst, Radical Journalist: H. W. Massingham
(Cambridge, Eng., 1974), p. 210; Loreburn interviewed
by C. P. Scott, June 30, 1914, quoted in P. F. Clarke,
Lancashire and the New Liberalism (Cambridge, Eng.,
1971), p. 216.

8.   Sir H. H. Johnston, "Wanted: A New Liberal
Party," English Review, XXIV (1917), 227.

9.   Ponsonby to Gordon Harvie, August 13, 1913,
quoted in J. E. Lindsay, "The Failure of Liberal Opposition to British Entry Into World War I" (unpublished
Ph. D. dissertation, Columbia University, 1969), p.
48.

10.   Roy Jenkins, Mr. Balfour's Poodle: An Account
of the Struggle between the House of Lords and the Government of Mr. Asquith (London, 1954), p. 8.

11.   Trevor O. Lloyd, "The Whip as Paymaster:
Herbert Gladstone and Party Organization," English
Historical Review, LXXXIX (1974), 805-6.   But the generosity of these rich Liberals was insufficient to
allow the Liberal party to employ full-time paid agents
in a majority of constituencies between 1906 and 1910
(Lowell G. Noonan, "The Decline of the Liberal Party in
British Politics," Journal of Politics, XVI [1954],
36-7).

12.   G. T. Garratt, "Money and the Election," New
Statesman and Nation, December 7, 1935.   According to a
study made by Ralph E. Pumphrey, the Liberals began to
create peers at a markedly faster rate than the Conservatives only in 1906, but from 1880 onward had tended
to give more peerages to businessmen than their opponents.   Over one-quarter of the peers created by the
Rosebery, Campbell-Bannerman, and Asquith ministries
were businessmen, compared to 16 percent of the peerages awarded by the Conservatives between 1895 and
1905.   In contrast, only 3 percent of the peers receiving titles from Lord Melbourne's Whig-Liberal government of 1837-41 had been businessmen.   Pumphrey did not
investigate other types of honors ("The Introduction of
Industrialists into the British Peerage: A Study in
Adaptation of a Social Institution," American Historical Review, LXV [1959], 6-9).

13.   Blake, The Unknown Prime Minister, pp. 225-6,

345-6. There had been a similar arrangement between Asquith and Bonar Law during the previous Coalition. Bonar Law's successor, Austen Chamberlain, refused to share responsibility for all honors, approving only those names submitted by the Conservative chief whip. See his letter to Lloyd George, December 3, 1927, Lloyd George Papers, House of Lords Record Office, G/4/3/4.

14. Morgan, "Lloyd George's Stage Army," p. 233.

15. Parliamentary Debates, Lords, August 7, 1917; Lord Selborne's circular letter to Lord Salisbury and other Conservative peers, September 4, 1917, Halsbury Papers, British Library, 56372.

16. For Sutherland's activities, see Thomas Jones, Whitehall Diary, ed. Keith Middlemas (London, 1969-71), July 11, 1922, entry, I, 203; for Gregory's, see Tom Cullen, Maundy Gregory: Purveyor of Honours (London, 1974), esp. pp. 23-5, 97-102, and Gerald Macmillan, Honours for Sale: The Strange Story of Maundy Gregory (London, 1954), esp. pp. 117-22.

17. Guest to Lloyd George, May 16, 1919, May 17, 1920, Lloyd George Papers, F/21/3/23, F/22/1/38; Sir Charles Mallet, Mr. Lloyd George: A Study (London, 1930), p. 251.

18. Pollock, Money and Politics Abroad, pp. 74-5. But it should be noted that Asquith's average annual bestowal of peerages was four higher than the average for the nine preceding governments.

19. Donald McCormick, The Mask of Merlin: A Critical Study of David Lloyd George (London, 1963), p. 237.

20. Harold J. Laski, "The Prime Minister's Honours List," Nation, July 15, 1922. Ralph E. Pumphrey (see note 12, above) showed that 29 percent of the Liberal peers created between 1906 and 1911 were businessmen. Laski's figure of 21 percent evidently applied to the Asquith ministry of 1908-15 and may have been computed differently.

21. Harold Nicolson, King George the Fifth: His Life and Reign (London, 1952), p. 512; Parliamentary Debates, Lords, July 17, 1922; "Government and Press" and "Press Honours," National Review, LXXVIII (1922), 597-600, 763-7. The furore over Beaverbrook's peerage

inspired Arnold Bennett's comic play The Title, which in 1917-8 drew good audiences attracted by the topical subject (Margaret Drabble, Arnold Bennett [New York, 1974], p. 233).

22. Sir George Younger to Bonar Law, January 2, 1921, printed in Beaverbrook, The Decline and Fall of Lloyd George, Appendix 2, pp. 241-3.

23. Parliamentary Debates, Lords, July 17, 1922.

24. Ian Colvin, "What Is Known as the Lloyd George Fund," National Review, XC (1928), 872.

25. The Farquhar scandal, uncovered in January 1923, is discussed in Blake, The Unknown Prime Minister, pp. 496-8, and Beaverbrook, The Decline and Fall of Lloyd George, pp. 127, 203-4, and 298-300 (Appendices 59-61).

26. Kinnear, The Fall of Lloyd George, p. 84.

27. D. D. Cuthbert, "Lloyd George and the Conservative Central Office, 1918-22," Lloyd George: Twelve Essays, pp. 180-1.

28. King George V to Lloyd George, July 3, 1922, Lloyd George Papers, F/29/4/103. The Robinson case is discussed in Fenner (Lord) Brockway, Lloyd George and the Traffic in Honour (London, 1922), pp. 12-3, and Cullen, Maundy Gregory, pp. 112-8.

29. Parliamentary Debates, Lords, June 22, 29, July 17, 1922; Morning Post (London), June 17, 1922. A. J. P. Taylor has contended that the Conservatives did as well, or almost as well, as the Coalition Liberals in making money from these honors: "Something like £3 million went to each partner in the Coalition" (English History, 1914-1945, Oxford History of England, vol. XV [London, 1965], p. 188 n.).

30. For Lord Loreburn's assertion that Asquith's hands were no cleaner than Lloyd George's respecting party funds, see Loreburn to C. P. Scott, August 23, 1919, Scott Papers, British Library, 50909; cf. Wilson, The Downfall of the Liberal Party, p. 112, for the suggestion that Asquith's first objective after removal as prime minister in 1916 was to retain control of Liberal funds.

31. Parliamentary Debates, Commons, July 2, 17, 1922; The Times (London), July 18, 1922. Although the most caustic attacks on Lloyd George during the 1922 honors scandal came from the right, it was not ignored by leftist journals. The Socialist Review, for example, then edited by Ramsay MacDonald, denounced the "auctioneering" of honors and warned that even the Labour party was "guilty of harbouring plutocrats" who might be lured into purchasing titles and ribbons (XX [1922], 57).

32. Letter dated August 14, 1929, Lloyd George Papers, G/16/10/4. It is quoted in Thomson, David Lloyd George, pp. 368-9.

33. Guest to Lloyd George ("Secret"), January 31, 1919, Lloyd George Papers, F/21/3/2.

34. Churchill quoted in The Times, May 10, 1929.

35. Colvin, "What Is Known as the Lloyd George Fund," p. 873. Cf. Lloyd George's letter to Reading, cited above, in which Guest is named as the "chief instrument" in accumulating the fund and the person most likely to initiate legal action for recovery of the capital.

36. H. A. Taylor, Robert Donald (London, 1934), p. 175; W. P. Jolly, Lord Leverhulme: A Biography (London, 1976), p. 167. Peter Rowland has suggested that Beaverbrook was associated with Lever in the early scheme to buy the Chronicle for the Coalition Liberals (Lloyd George [London, 1975], p. 452).

37. Dalziel, a veteran M.P. (since 1892), was a leading member of the anti-Asquith bloc of Liberals that had swung its support behind Lloyd George in the December 1916 government crisis. He was made a peer in 1921, his being one of the "press peerages" denounced by the Duke of Northumberland the following year. See the sketch by R. C. K. Ensor in the Dictionary of National Biography, 1931-1940.

38. Daily Chronicle (London), September 13, 1918.

39. According to Donald's biographer, H. A. Taylor. White in 1918 was given special permission by the Treasury to issue company shares, officially prohibited during the war, possibly in return for his help in buying the Daily Chronicle (Robert Donald, p. 181). For

details of the purchase of the Chronicle, see The Times, October 5, 1918.

40. Owen, Tempestuous Journey, p. 693.

41. Sir Philip Gibbs, Adventures in Journalism (London, 1923), p. 257.

42. [Stanley Morison], The History of "The Times" (London, 1935-52), IV, 1077.

43. Francis Williams (Baron Francis-Williams), Dangerous Estate: The Anatomy of Newspapers (London, 1957), pp. 181-2.

44. Marquess of Bute to Lloyd George, October 18, 1922, quoted in Owen, p. 687.

45. Don M. Cregier, Bounder from Wales: Lloyd George's Career Before the First World War (Columbia, Mo., 1976), pp. 28, 43, 70.

46. Lloyd George to Margaret Lloyd George, September 22, 1926, quoted in Lloyd George Family Letters, pp. 206-7. A later suggestion by Frederick Guest that Sir Robert Donald should be enticed back to the Chronicle either was not acted upon or came to nothing (Guest to Lloyd George, November 29, 1926, Lloyd George Papers, G/8/13/10).

47. Lloyd George to Kellaway, Kellaway to Lloyd George, December 22, 23, 1923, Lloyd George Papers, G/13/1/14,15.

48. Guest to Lloyd George, July 16, 1924, Lloyd George Papers, G/8/13/2; Lloyd George to McCurdy, January 16, 1926, ibid., G/13/1/34; Frances Lloyd George, The Years that are Past, pp. 218-9.

49. The Times, July 21, 1927.

50. Gerald Rufus Isaacs, 2nd Marquess of Reading, Rufus Isaacs, First Marquess of Reading (London, 1939-45), II, 345-6.

51. Colin Seymour-Ure, "The Press and the Party System between the Wars," The Politics of Reappraisal, 1918-1939, ed. Gillian Peele and Chris Cook (New York, 1975), p. 247.

52. Horace Imber to Lloyd George, July 28, 1928, Lloyd George Papers, G/10/10/4.

53. Lloyd George to Margaret Lloyd George, January 3, 1930, quoted in Lloyd George Family Letters, p. 210.

54. See, for example, Lloyd George: A Diary by Frances Stevenson, June 22, 1922, entry, p. 242; Beaverbrook, The Decline and Fall of Lloyd George, pp. 145-6.

55. Sir Almeric Fitzroy, Memoirs (London, 1925), I, 789; cf. "Ephesian" [C. E. Bechhofer Roberts], Lord Birkenhead (London, 1926), p. 147. Roberts, a knowledgeable journalist, denied the existence of a Birkenhead fund, but it was vouched for by Fitzroy, the veteran clerk of the privy council, who had widespread contacts in the political world. See also Lord Gladstone to Lord Beauchamp, January 15, 1923, copy in Sir Donald Maclean Papers, Bodleian Library, Oxford University, 467/4-5.

56. Sir Howard Frank to Lloyd George, September 8, 1922, Lloyd George Papers, F/17/4/9.

57. Reginald Pound and Geoffrey Harmsworth, Northcliffe (New York, 1960), p. 880.

58. Jones, Whitehall Diary, September 21, 1922, entry, I, 208; The History of "The Times," IV, 719-22.

59. See the exchange of letters (November 23-6, 1921) between Churchill, Guest, and Lloyd George regarding the vesting of the Coalition Liberal whips with legal authority to use the fund (Lloyd George Papers, F/22/3/32-5).

60. Younger's expression. See Beaverbrook, The Decline and Fall of Lloyd George, p. 9 n.

61. J. Alfred Spender, Sir Robert Hudson: A Memoir (London, 1930), p. 168.

62. Statement by Lloyd George published in the Daily Express (London), December 3, 1927.

63. Lloyd George to Reading, August 14, 1929, cited above, n. 32.

64. Conversation with C. P. Scott, reported in *The Political Diaries of C. P. Scott*, July 1, 1923, entry, p. 442. Cf. Sir Charles Mallet, *Herbert Gladstone: A Memoir* (London, 1932), p. 287.

65. Ramsay Muir, "The Liberal Party," *Contemporary Review*, CXXX (1926), 7. For the often comic financial negotiations between Liberal and Lloyd George headquarters, see Viscount Gladstone Papers, letters and memoranda of November 13, 28, 30, December 4, 1923, British Library, 46474, 46475. Lloyd George, in his 1929 letter to Reading, claimed that he had given the Liberals £160,000 for the 1923 election. Rowland has suggested that he was adding together the 1923 and 1924 election donations plus a separate £10,000 contribution from the fund to the 1923 Welsh Liberal campaign (*Lloyd George*, p. 631 n.). But at a party meeting in 1925, Lloyd George plainly associated the £160,000 figure with the 1923 election only. He was not challenged (memorandum by Vivian Phillipps of "a meeting of Lord Oxford's colleagues," May 26, 1925, Asquith Papers, Bodleian Library, 34/144).

66. Viscount Gladstone to Sir Donald Maclean, January 13, 1922, Viscount Gladstone Papers, 46474; Guest's memorandum of conversations with L. C. A. officials, December 19, 1923, Lloyd George Papers, G/8/13/1; speech of Sir George Lunn, president, National Liberal Federation, reported in *Proceedings [of the] . . . Annual Meeting of the National Liberal Federation, held at Bradford, November 25th and 26th, 1920* (London, 1921), p. 4.

67. Fewer in any case because of the discrediting of honors by the 1922 scandal. Cf. Wilson, *The Downfall of the Liberal Party*, p. 289.

68. Maclean's memorandum based on notes taken in 1924 but probably drafted and circulated in July 1925, Viscount Gladstone Papers, 46424. For Lloyd George's views on Liberal party organization, see Lloyd George to Asquith, August 20, 1924, enclosing notes by Lloyd George, Asquith Papers, 34/136-43.

69. Quotation from Hudson to Gladstone, January 17, 1924, Viscount Gladstone Papers, 46475. Cf. Gladstone to Maclean, January 1, 1924, *ibid.*, 46474.

70. Gladstone to Asquith, August 1, 1924, Asquith Papers, 34/133; Maclean to Asquith, October 5, 1924,

copy in Viscount Gladstone Papers, 46480; Asquith to Lloyd George, October 3, 1924 (enclosing Maclean to Asquith, same date), Lloyd George Papers, G/16/1/4. Although Gladstone urged Asquith at the beginning of August to put pressure on Lloyd George, he did not do so until two months later.

71. A. J. Sylvester to Lloyd George, late 1924 or early 1925, reporting statement of Geoffrey Howard to the Luton Liberal Association, Lloyd George Papers, G/20/2/10; Lord Gladstone's letter to The Times, June 11, 1926. For Lloyd George's denial of the charge, see his letters to Sir Maurice Levy and Lord Inchcape, November 5, 1924, copies in Lloyd George Papers, G/30/3/33,35. Cf. Jorgen Scott Rasmussen, The Liberal Party: A Study in Retrenchment and Revival (London, 1965), pp. 52-3.

72. The Times, November 12, 1924.

73. Interview published in Yorkshire Observer (Bradford), December 9, 1925; Spender and Asquith, Life of Lord Oxford and Asquith, II, 360.

74. Phillipps to Lloyd George, October 25, 1925, copy in Asquith Papers, 34/152-3; C. P. Scott's notes of talk with Lloyd George, November 13, 1925, The Political Diaries of C. P. Scott, p. 484.

75. Edge to Lloyd George, March 9, June 5, 1925, Lloyd George Papers, G/6/10/8,12. For some fiscal details that may have worried Edge, see "Financial Position [of Liberal party headquarters] on August 4, 1925," unsigned memorandum ("Secret"), Maclean Papers, 468/73.

76. Proceedings [of the] . . . Annual Meeting of the National Liberal Federation, held at Scarborough, May 13th to 16th, 1925 (London, 1925), pp. 23-4. The conception of this kind of fund was shared by, and may have originated with, Lloyd George via Charles McCurdy, who had advised that "nothing but new and democratic methods of raising funds can place the Party in a satisfactory position" (McCurdy to Lloyd George, January 24, 1925, Lloyd George Papers, G/13/1/22).

77. Hudson to Gladstone, February 23, 1925, Viscount Gladstone Papers, 46475; Liberal Magazine, XXXIV (1926), 673.

78. Hudson to Gladstone, July 9, 1925, Viscount Gladstone Papers, 46475; Spender, *Sir Robert Hudson*, pp. 172-3.

79. Composite of citations of Stevenson, Edge, and Thomas in letters exchanged by Lloyd George and Frances Stevenson, August 11, 12, 13, 1925, quoted in *My Darling Pussy: The Letters of Lloyd George and Frances Stevenson*, pp. 84-8. On the other hand, Lord Beauchamp, Liberal leader in the House of Lords, urged Lloyd George to use his fund to compel Liberal headquarters to clean house: "A promise of money on conditions would make you master of the situation" (Beauchamp to Lloyd George, September 23, 1925, Lloyd George Papers, G/3/5/15). For Liberal headquarters's reaction to Lloyd George's "blackmail," see Harold Storey to Sir Donald Maclean, October 22, 1925, Maclean Papers, 468/-88.

80. *Manchester Guardian*, November 21, 1925; cf. Phillipps to Lord Oxford, November 25, 1925, Asquith Papers, 34/147-8.

81. Francis Perrot, a *Nation* columnist, accused Lloyd George of living off the proceeds of his fund. Later the magazine, in a dig at his propaganda machine, asserted that he had become a "street-hawker" for his private policies. Lloyd George struck back by threatening to sue for libel and accusing the *Nation* of being dull, nagging, and "a perpetuator of personal feuds" (exchange of letters between Lloyd George and E. D. Simon, a director of the *Nation*, November 6, 1925, February 23, March 1, 1926, Lloyd George Papers, G/18/3/1,2,3).

82. *Liberal Magazine*, XXXIII (1925), 710-1; Phillipps to Thomas F. Tweed, November 8, 1926, Lloyd George Papers, G/15/5/9. According to Trevor Wilson, this aid took the form of "a grant of between £50 and £200 and the use of a campaign van" after Liberal headquarters had failed to come through with support (*Downfall of the Liberal Party*, p. 342).

83. Campbell, *The Goat in the Wilderness*, pp. 125-6.

84. Memorandum, annotated by Lord Gladstone, of a private conference of Asquithian Liberals, Hotel Victoria, London, December 17, 1925; Maclean to Gladstone, December 24, 1925; Gladstone to Hudson (copies), Decem-

ber 7, 1925, January 16, 1926, Viscount Gladstone Papers, 46474, 46475; Hudson quotation from Spender, Sir Robert Hudson, p. 174.

85. Statement to party officials reported in Manchester Guardian, January 27, 1926.

86. Nation, June 19, 1926.

87. Manchester Guardian, June 12, 1926.

88. Memorandum of Vivian Phillipps, September 22, 1926, Viscount Gladstone Papers, 46475.

89. Earl of Oxford and Asquith, Memories and Reflections (Boston, 1928), II, 287.

90. Tweed to Vivian Phillipps, September 27, 1926, Viscount Gladstone Papers, 46475; memorandum by Phillipps, September 28, 1926, ibid.; "Liberal Party Funds: History of the Recent Negotiations," Liberal Magazine, XXXV (1927), 15.

91. The Times, November 28, 1926, citing the "secret" report of the Hobhouse Committee, leaked to the press probably by Lloyd George's office. According to Lloyd George as paraphrased in the Hobhouse report, any part of his fund's capital drawn upon for Liberal party needs would be credited to the Million Fund. This may account for the £105,000 mentioned by Gwilym Lloyd George in 1939 as having been donated by his father to the Million Fund, but disputed by Liberal party officials (Owen, Tempestuous Journey, p. 692; Rowland, Lloyd George, p. 631).

92. Phillipps to Gladstone, November 11, 1926, Viscount Gladstone Papers, 46475.

93. Manchester Guardian, November 26, 1926. This news story also apparently was leaked "from Old Queen Street" (Vivian Phillipps to Sir Robert Hutchison, November 26, 1926, Lloyd George Papers, G/10/9/5).

94. J. Stuart Hodgson to Lloyd George, November 16, 1926, Lloyd George Papers, G/10/5/2. Lloyd George accused the editors of the Westminster Gazette of harboring the conspirators and even writing their letters to the press. He warned that his "infinitely larger" papers might start a newspaper war if the Gazette did not "play the game" (Lloyd George to Fred

Stern, November 17, 1926, copy in Lloyd George Papers, G/31/1/53).

95. Lord Gladstone to Sir Robert Hudson, December 10, 1926, Viscount Gladstone Papers, 46475.

96. The Times, December 16, 1926; "Liberal Party Funds," pp. 19-20.

97. Nation, November 27, 1926.

98. E.g., Sir Daniel Stevenson's letter to the Westminster Gazette, December 17, 1926.

99. Manchester Guardian, January 20, 1927; "Liberal Party Funds: Further History of the Negotiations," Liberal Magazine, XXXV (1927), 91-2. Lloyd George's remaining stipulations were (1) that his offer was operative only until "three months after the general election," when "the whole situation will have to be studied anew"; and (2) that his contributions must not be used to subsidize local Liberal Associations ("London Letter," Manchester Guardian, January 11, 1927; speech of Sir Charles Hobhouse to the Weymouth Liberal Association, reported in the Observer, January 30, 1927).

100. Hudson had decided to resign after the Administrative Committee's December 15 vote. He absented himself from London during the transition of party headquarters from Asquithian to Lloyd Georgian personnel, December 1926 - January 1927. Lord Gladstone joined him in pinning much of the blame for Lloyd George's victory on Hobhouse and Lord Beauchamp, who had presided over several of the decisive Administrative Committee meetings (Hudson to Gladstone, December 16, 28, 1926; Gladstone to Hudson [copy], January 24, 1927, Viscount Gladstone Papers, 46475).

101. Ramsay Muir, "The Liberals and Party Finance," Nation, October 12, 1929.

102. The Times, January 24, 1927; Ramsay Muir, "The Latest Liberal Split," Nation, January 29, 1927. Council members included Lady Violet Bonham Carter (Lord Oxford's daughter), Sir Godfrey Collins (last Asquithian chief whip), Lord Cowdray (oil millionaire and proprietor of the Westminster Gazette), A. G. Gardiner, Lord Gladstone, Hudson, Maclean, Phillipps, Pringle, Runciman, and J. Alfred Spender (editor of the

Westminster Gazette).

103. Gladstone to Sir Herbert Samuel, April 30, 1927, quoted in Campbell, The Goat in the Wilderness, p. 159.

104. Gladstone to Maclean (draft), February 21, 1927, Viscount Gladstone Papers, 46474.

105. Hudson to Gladstone, June 17, 1927; Phillipps to Gladstone, May 17, July 25, 1928, May 6, 1929, Viscount Gladstone Papers, 46475; quotation from Phillipps to Gladstone, June 24, 1929, ibid.

106. Gladstone to Hudson, April 22, 1927, Viscount Gladstone Papers, 46475; Maclean to Gladstone, August 1, 1928, ibid., 46474.

107. Phillipps to Gladstone, June 5, July 19, November 4, 1929, Viscount Gladstone Papers, 46475.

108. See, for example, the exchange of letters by J. Alfred Spender and W. L. Mackenzie King (Canadian Liberal party leader), November 4 - December 15, 1931, Spender Papers, British Library, 46385.

109. Douglas, The History of the Liberal Party, p. 198.

110. The Times, February 16, 1927. Lloyd George, in a letter to Sir Robert Perks--a former Rosebery associate--absolving him of responsibility for "that foolish ebullition of Rosebery's," added that "I have a fair conjecture as to who persuaded him to rush into a controversy, from which a mere perusal of his own Honours List would have induced him to refrain" (Lloyd George to Perks, March 29, 1927, Lloyd George Papers, G/31/2/20).

111. E.g., Daily News, August 7, 1927.

112. "Lord Rosebery's Question," National Review, XC (1928), 676. According to Frances Stevenson, Lord Beaverbrook may have fed some material on the Lloyd George Fund to the Morning Post. She recorded on August 18, 1927, that Lloyd George "had words on the telephone" with Beaverbrook and was "furious with him" (Lloyd George: A Diary, p. 251). In a letter to Austen Chamberlain Lloyd George intimated that several Conservative ministers were "[taking] a hand in circulating

this slander" (Lloyd George to Chamberlain, December 14, 1927, Lloyd George Papers, G/4/3/6).

113. See James, _Memoirs of a Conservative_, pp. 293-4.

114. _The Times_, December 3, 1927; Victor A. Cazalet, "Peeps into a War Chest: Britain's Liberal Party and Campaign Funds," _Independent_ (New York), October 22, 1927; Colvin, "What Is Known as the Lloyd George Fund," pp. 874-7.

115. "A Political Correspondent," "The Mystery Fund," _Outlook_ (London), February 26, 1927; "The Lloyd George Millions," _National Review_, XC (1927), 36-7. Similar language is used, and the same points made, in a pamphlet also entitled _The Lloyd George Millions_, published by the _Morning Post_ in the fall of 1927 and widely circulated.

116. Exchange of letters between Samuel and St. Davids, quoted in John Bowle, _Viscount Samuel: A Biography_ (London, 1957), p. 263; Hobhouse's Weymouth speech, reported in the _Observer_, January 30, 1927.

117. Colvin, "What Is Known as the Lloyd George Fund," p. 875.

118. Gwyn, _Democracy and the Cost of Politics_, p. 239: St. Davids to Samuel, July 9, 1929, cited in Douglas, _The History of the Liberal Party_, p. 200. According to St. Davids, the Chronicle Corporation shares were no longer paying dividends due to the slump in newspaper stock. Besides the outgo from his fund for political expenses, Lloyd George before 1930 reportedly drew £240,000 from it for the work of the Land and Nation League and £650,000 for his policy studies (1939 statement of Gwilym Lloyd George, cited in Owen, _Tempestuous Journey_, p. 692; cf. Sir Ivor Jennings, _Party Politics_ [Cambridge, Eng., 1960-2], II, 265).

119. Sinclair to Lloyd George, February 2, 1927, Lloyd George Papers, G/18/4/3; Gwilym Lloyd George's statement, 1939 cited above. Trevor Wilson's assertion that "in June 1930 all financial assistance from [Lloyd George] ceased" (_The Downfall of the Liberal Party_, p. 353) is in error.

120. Muir to Lloyd George, July 23, December 1,

1929, Lloyd George Papers, G/15/6/12, 16; Kerr to Lloyd George, December 12, 1929, *ibid*., G/5/14/5.

121. Sir Donald Maclean to Lord Gladstone, July 21, 1929, Viscount Gladstone Papers, 46474; Vivian Phillipps to Gladstone, July 23, 1929, *ibid*., 46475; Lord Reading to Lloyd George, August 21, 1929, Lloyd George Papers, G/16/10/5. In a letter from Lord Grey to Gladstone, August 3, 1929, is the curious remark that Sir Herbert Samuel had "admitted that [Liberal headquarters] did not think there was any present need of Ll. G.'s funds" (Viscount Gladstone Papers, 45992). Cf. Ramsay Muir to Gladstone, January 6, 1930: "There is a real danger that we may be wiped out. . . . The chest is practically empty" (quoted in Wilson, The Downfall of the Liberal Party, p. 353).

122. The Times, January 15, 16, 19, 1930; Douglas, The History of the Liberal Party, pp. 209, 229.

123. Sylvester, Life with Lloyd George, December 30, 1931, August 27, December 16, 1932, entries, pp. 68, 75, 87.

124. Ibid., September 18, October 1, 1931, entries, pp. 39, 40; The Times, October 9, 1931. According to Trevor Wilson, seven Liberal candidates opposed the National Government and presumably were aided by the Lloyd George Fund (The Downfall of the Liberal Party, p. 371); Roy Douglas has suggested that there were "a few more" (The History of the Liberal Party, p. 221).

125. Owen, Tempestuous Journey, pp. 691-2.

126. A. J. Sylvester memorandum, April 25, 1934, attached to letter from Sir James Marchant, Lloyd George Papers, G/21/1/40.

127. According to A. J. Sylvester, Lloyd George's private secretary, his employer drew upon the fund for private, nonpolitical expenses at least once. In March 1938, he requested a check from the trustees to pay travel bills and to cover expenses incurred for his country estate in Surrey. Lloyd George may have been temporarily short of cash--his income from journalism fell sharply in 1938--and possibly intended to repay the fund. See Life with Lloyd George, entries of March 16, July 8, 1938, and March 16, 1943, pp. 202, 213, 313.

128. Sir Percy Harris to Lloyd George, March 5, 1936, Lloyd George Papers, G/9/2/1. Harris, newly elected Liberal chief whip, was nominally chairman of the Liberal Central Association, but the central office was managed by Johnstone, treasurer of the L. C. A., an old adversary of Lloyd George.

129. Sir John Davies to Lloyd George, December 9, 1936, printed in Beaverbrook, The Decline and Fall of Lloyd George, Appendix 37, p. 280. The possibility of objection to a Labour trustee by surviving donors to an anti-Labour fund strangely was not mentioned by Davies.

130. Sylvester, Life with Lloyd George, July 22, 1938, entry, pp. 213-4; Richard Lloyd George, My Father, Lloyd George, p. 216.

131. Sylvester, Life with Lloyd George, April 4, 1934, June 28, 1935, April 14, 1938, entries, pp. 106, 125, 206.

132. Ibid., November 21, 1938, entry, pp. 221-2; Walter Belcher to Lloyd George, and Lloyd George's draft reply to Belcher, February 14, 16, 1939, Lloyd George Papers, G/3/7/1,2; Owen, Tempestuous Journey, pp. 691-2.

133. Sylvester to Lloyd George, May 2, 1941, July 30, 1943, Lloyd George papers, G/25/2/79, 121; Sir Percy Harris to Lloyd George, June 11, 1942, ibid., G/9/2/6.

134. Sylvester, Life with Lloyd George, April 22, 1943, entry, p. 314; Frances Lloyd George to W. J. Williams, secretary, Ffestiniog Liberal Association, July 13, 1944, Lloyd George Papers, G/23/6/6; Cregier, Bounder from Wales, p. 27. As late as 1943, a member of Lloyd George's office staff had no other duty but servicing the Lloyd George Fund.

135. Sylvester, Life with Lloyd George, June 11, 1938, entry, p. 211; Thomas Jones, A Diary with Letters, 1931-1950 (London, 1954), June 27, 1945, entry, p. 535.

136. Jones, Lloyd George, p. 224.

LIBERAL THINK TANK: THE SUMMER SCHOOL MOVEMENT

1. D. H. Robertson, "Sir Hubert Henderson, 1890-1952," Economic Journal, LXIII (1953), 925.

2. "The New Manchesterism," Nation, January 1, 1921; Ramsay Muir, Politics and Progress: A Survey of the Problems of To-day (London, 1923), pp. 2-4. Liberalism and Industry was published in London by Constable.

3. Sir Ernest D. Simon (Baron Simon of Wythenshawe), "The Manchester Meetings," in Stuart Hodgson, ed., Ramsay Muir: An Autobiography and Some Essays (London, 1943), p. 182.

4. Sir Ernest D. Simon, "The Liberal Summer School," Contemporary Review, CXXXVI (1929), 274; Mary Stocks, Ernest Simon of Manchester (Manchester, 1963), p. 69.

5. Sir Walter Layton (Baron Layton), "A Liberal Philosopher," Ramsay Muir, ed. Stuart Hodgson, p. 148.

6. Ramsay Muir, "The Liberal Summer School and the Problems of Industry," Contemporary Review, CXXXII (1927), 285.

7. The Times, September 28, 1921; "A Lake School of Liberals," Nation, October 8, 1921. For the Cambridge recruits, see Sir Henry Clay, ed., The Inter-War Years and Other Papers: A Selection from the Writings of Hubert Douglas Henderson (Oxford, 1955), pp. xv-xvi; Robert Lekachman, The Age of Keynes (New York, 1966), pp. 43, 69-70; and André Siegfried, Post-War Britain (London, 1924), p. 262. Keynes and Henderson joined the Movement after Grasmere. J. A. Hobson, New Liberal journalist and "outcast" economist, was an active participant at Grasmere but did not affiliate with the Summer School.

8. Manchester Guardian, October 1, 1921. Muir and Layton were chosen as joint directors of the School, Simon as treasurer, and Thomas F. Tweed, a Manchester Liberal politician, as general secretary. The plan to meet in the university towns may have been suggested by the university extension summer sessions held by Oxford and Cambridge.

9. Circular letter to Liberal Associations from Thomas F. Tweed, general secretary of the Liberal Summer School, reproduced in the Liberal Magazine, XXX (April 1922), 230-1.

10. The Times, August 2, 10, 1922.

11. Complete text in the Liberal Flashlight, No. 20 (August 1922), a Liberal party pamphlet.

12. The propaganda rally was sometimes omitted in years of political disappointment for Liberals, as after the 1929 election debacle.

13. The Times, August 3, 5, 1922.

14. Liberal Magazine, XXX (September 1922), 577-616.

15. Sydney Brown, "At the Summer School," Ramsay Muir, p. 204; Masterman quoted in C. F. G. Masterman, p. 323.

16. The 1927 School's program was restricted to industrial policy only.

17. London: Collins, 1922.

18. Manchester Guardian, August 3, 1923; Liberal Magazine, XXXI (September 1923), 534-5.

19. Joseph R. Starr, "The Summer Schools and Other Educational Activities of the British Liberal Party," American Political Science Review, XXXI (1937), 707, n. 11.

20. Liberal Magazine, XXXIII (September 1925), 540; Manchester Guardian," August 10, 1928; "The Liberal Summer School," Nation, August 11, 1928. One of the speakers at the 1922 School had been Lord Robert Cecil, an Independent Tory, who sat with the Asquith Liberals in the House of Commons.

21. Nation, August 9, 1924; Starr, p. 708.

22. There were a few "scholarships" for interested persons of limited means awarded by local Liberal associations and, competitively, by the Liberal newspapers the Daily News and Weekly Westminster. Probably most of the Liberal association grants went to deserv-

ing Liberals.

23. See, for example, the Liberal Magazine, XXXVII (July 1929), 480.

24. C. F. G. Masterman at the 1924 School. See the Weekly Westminster, August 9, 1924.

25. Nation, July 17, 1926. McNair had been secretary to the 1919 Sankey Commission on the Coal Industry.

26. Weekly Westminster, August 2, 1924; Sir Ernest D. Simon, "The Liberal Summer School," Contemporary Review, CXXX (1926), 301.

27. Muir, "The Liberal Summer School and the Problems of Industry," p. 282. Although never hesitant to borrow what they wanted from successive Liberal Summer Schools, Labour party spokesmen publicly disparaged them. "Very wordy, very academic, and very feeble" was Ramsay MacDonald's summation of the Cambridge Summer School of 1923 (Socialist Review, XXII [September 1923], 108).

28. Simon, "The Liberal Summer School [1929]," p. 275.

29. Essays in Liberalism, v.

30. Joseph R. Starr, "Research Activities of British Political Parties," Public Opinion Quarterly, I (1937), 105. For details about Tweed, see the Nation, August 11, 1923, The Times, March 29, 1927, and Manchester Guardian, August 2, 1928; about Muir, see the Westminster Newsletter [of the Liberal Central Association], May 1930, the article by J. S. Meston in Ramsay Muir, ed. Stuart Hodgson, and the sketch by Ernest Barker in the Dictionary of National Biography, 1941-1950.

31. Lloyd George to Margaret Lloyd George, September 22, 1926, quoted in Lloyd George Family Letters, p. 207.

32. Lloyd George's contributions exceeded £10,000.

33. G. P. Gooch, Under Six Reigns (London, 1958), p. 198; Roy F. Harrod, The Life of John Maynard Keynes

(New York, 1951), p. 375. Keynes seems to have been most influential in persuading the Summer School executive committee to accept Lloyd George's offer. While distrusting Lloyd George as a politician, Keynes admired his energy and progressive outlook. The two men also shared common views on the use of public works to relieve unemployment and the undesirability of returning to the gold standard. Both were contemptuous of--and themselves disliked by--the Labour party's Ramsay MacDonald.

34. Notably Layton (chairman), Muir, Keynes, Simon, Henderson, and Seebohm Rowntree, the sociologist.

35. London: Benn, 1928. The paperback edition had a large circulation, including use as a university textbook.

36. Harrod, p. 392.

37. "The Reception of the Industrial Report," Nation, February 11, 1928; Ramsay Muir, "Liberalism and Industry," Contemporary Review, CXXXIII (1928), 555-6.

38. A. P. Nicholson, The Real Men in Public Life: Forces and Factors in the State (London, 1928), p. 264.

39. Harrod, p. 336.

40. Speech to a meeting of the London Liberal Candidates' Association, published in H. L. Nathan and H. Heathcote Williams, eds., Liberal Points of View (London, 1927), p. 219.

41. For the acquisition of the Nation by the Summer School group and its publishing history under Keynes and Henderson, see Michael Bentley, The Liberal Mind, 1914-1929 (Cambridge, Eng., 1977), p. 185; Havighurst, Radical Journalist, pp. 294-302; and Robertson, "Sir Hubert Henderson," p. 924.

42. Muir, "The Liberal Summer School and the Problems of Industry," p. 286.

43. A late, temporary recruit was the future Labour prime minister, Sir Harold Wilson, active in the Oxford University Liberal Club between 1934 and 1937. See Paul Foot, The Politics of Harold Wilson (Harmondsworth, Eng., 1968), pp. 23-39.

44. A weakness noted as early as 1922 by Stuart Hodgson in "The Opportunity of Liberalism," Nineteenth Century, XCII, 187.

45. Bentley, pp. 212, 218.

46. Liberal Magazine, XXXVIII (August 1930), 347; Stocks, Ernest Simon of Manchester, pp. 93-4.

47. See New Statesman and Nation, July 2, August 6, 1932.

48. A. L. Rowse, Politics and the Younger Generation (London, 1931), p. 85. According to Thomas F. Tweed, former general secretary of the Movement, the hundred or so Liberals present at the 1934 Oxford Summer School were mostly elderly people with an anti-Labour bias. "The whole School was definitely illiberal" (memorandum by A. J. Sylvester, Lloyd George's principal private secretary, August 6, 1934, Lloyd George Papers, G/21/3/58).

49. Quotation from Simon, "The Liberal Summer School [1926]," p. 303. In 1936 Harold W. Stoke wrote that "the service of the Liberal party to Great Britain has taken a new channel: providing programs for non-Liberal governments" ("Propaganda Activities of British Political Parties," American Political Science Review, XXX, 124).

THE LLOYD GEORGE POLICY STUDIES

1. Christopher Addison (Viscount Addison), Politics from Within, 1911-1918 (London, 1924), I, 20-2; Beatrice Webb, Our Partnership, ed. Barbara Drake and Margaret I. Cole (London, 1948), pp. 473-7. According to the biographer of the sociologist-philanthropist Seebohm Rowntree, the original suggestion for an investigation of land, housing, and rating reform came from a self-appointed committee of provincial Liberals interested in drafting a new Liberal party program. Seebohm Rowntree and his father, Joseph Rowntree the chocolate manufacturer, were members of this committee, and the former was appointed to the Land Inquiry Committee (Asa Briggs, Social Thought and Social Action: A Study of the Work of Seebohm Rowntree, 1871-1954 [London, 1961], p. 64).

2. C. P. Scott's diary, January 16, 1913, The Political Diaries of C. P. Scott, pp. 68-70; C. Roden Buxton to Lloyd George, March 8, 1913, Lloyd George Papers, C/2/2/4. For details of the Land Inquiry Committee see H. V. Emy, "The Land Campaign: Lloyd George as a Social Reformer, 1909-14," Lloyd George: Twelve Essays, p. 49, and Simon Maccoby, English Radicalism: The End? (London, 1961), pp. 87-93.

3. Seebohm Rowntree to Lloyd George, June 26, 1913, Lloyd George Papers, C/2/2/23; John Burns to Lloyd George, October 9, 1913, ibid., C/3/9/1; Lloyd George to William H. Lever, and reply, October 5, 22, 1913, ibid., C/2/3/14, C/10/1/58; Manchester Guardian, November 10, 1913; Wilson, The Downfall of the Liberal Party, p. 323.

4. Beauchamp to Lloyd George, April 13, 1913. Lloyd George Papers, C/3/5/1; Owen, Tempestuous Journey p. 241.

5. The Land: The Report of the Land Enquiry Committee. Volume I: Rural. Volume II: Urban (London, 1913-4).

6. Simon Maccoby, English Radicalism, 1886-1914 (London, 1953), p. 511; Gillian Sutherland, "Social Policy in the Inter-War Years," Historical Journal, XVI (1973), 430.

7. For the use of the land reports in campaign propaganda, see Cecil Beck to Lloyd George, October 4, 1913, Lloyd George Papers, C/4/1/4; Lloyd George to Percy H. Illingworth, October 24, 1913, ibid., C/5/4/7; Emy, pp. 58-9; A. G. Gardiner, Life of George Cadbury (London, 1923), p. 165; and J. A. Spender, Life, Journalism and Politics (London, 1927), I, 159. Bentley B. Gilbert has suggested that Lloyd George may have been dissuaded only by political tactics from launching a "rural revival" campaign during the 1918 "coupon election" ("David Lloyd George: Land, the Budget, and Social Reform," American Historical Review, LXXXI [1976], 1066).

8. Philip Kerr to Lloyd George, February 4, March 1, 1924, Lloyd George Papers, G/12/5/2,3; Vivian Phillipps to Lloyd George, March 19, 1924, ibid., G/16/5/3.

9. Coal and Power: The Report of an Enquiry Pre-

sided over by the Right Hon. David Lloyd George (London, 1924).

10. Coal and Power, passim; C. F. G. Masterman [a member of the Coal Inquiry Committee], "Coal and Power," Contemporary Review, CXXVI (1924), 433-42. The key feature of Coal and Power--nationalization of mine property--was adapted from a scheme advanced at the 1922 Liberal Summer School. See Nation, July 17, 1926.

11. The Times, July 14, 1924.

12. Wilson, p. 285; Proceedings [of the] . . . Annual Meeting of the National Liberal Federation, held at Weston-super-Mare, June 15th to 18th, 1926 (London, 1926), pp. 14-5; Bowle, Viscount Samuel, pp. 242-3; Mowat, Britain between the Wars, pp. 342, 448.

13. W. M. Eager to Sir Geoffrey Shakespeare, April 15, 1948, Eager Papers, Reform Club (London), "Sundry Papers."

14. Jones, Lloyd George, p. 212.

15. W. M. Eager (secretary, Land Inquiry Committee), diary entry, n.d. [about November 7, 1924], Eager Papers.

16. The Land and the Nation: Rural Report of the Liberal Land Committee, and Towns and the Land: Urban Report of the Liberal Land Committee (both London, 1925).

17. E. D. Simon, "The Liberal Urban Land Report," Contemporary Review, CXXIX (1926), 1-9; Roy Douglas, Land, People and Politics: A History of the Land Question in the United Kingdom (London, 1976), p. 192.

18. Hilton Young to Lloyd George, August 26, 1925, Lloyd George Papers, G/10/14/18; Hobhouse to Asquith, September 3, 1925, Asquith Papers, 34/226-8; Michael Bentley, "The Liberal Response to Socialism, 1918-29," Essays in Anti-Labour History: Responses to the Rise of Labour in Britain (London, 1974), p. 64. Genuine socialists reacted variously to the Green Book. While George Lansbury approvingly declared that "such a policy can[not] be applied without tearing up the capitalist system root and branch," F. W. Jowett saw it

only as "brazen effrontery" that was "not intended to work" but only to "catch votes." Christopher Turnor thought that the Rural Report might "prove the first step toward the complete nationalisation of the land and the agricultural industry" (Landsbury's Labour Weekly, October 17, 1925; Daily Herald, November 17, 1925; Socialist Review, XXVI (1926), 329.

19. Oxford to Lloyd George, November 21, 1925, Asquith Papers, 34/245-9; "Political Correspondent," Daily Herald, December 9, 1925.

20. Proceedings [of the] . . . National Liberal Federation . . . 1926, pp. 11-2, 43-7; Hubert Henderson to Lloyd George, November 9, 1925, Lloyd George Papers, G/10/2/2; Stuart Hodgson to Lloyd George, January 5, 1926, ibid., G/10/5/1; Lloyd George to C. P. Scott, February 10, 1926, ibid., G/17/11/19.

21. Daily Herald editorial, November 25, 1925; A. H. Henderson-Livesey to Lloyd George, July 6, 1938, Lloyd George Papers, G/12/3/11.

22. Lord Oxford to Sir Donald Maclean, September 12, 1925, Maclean Papers, 468/76-7; C. P. Scott's notes of talk with Lloyd George, November 13, 1925, The Political Diaries of C. P. Scott, p. 483; "Minute of Conversation between Col. T. F. Tweed and W. M. Eager, at Midland Hotel, Manchester," March 19, 1926, Eager Papers; Eager to Sir William Edge, July 21, 1926, ibid., "Sundry Papers."

23. Muir, "The Liberal Summer School and the Problems of Industry," p. 287; Harrod, The Life of John Maynard Keynes, p. 375.

24. John Campbell, "The Renewal of Liberalism: Liberalism without Liberals," The Politics of Reappraisal, p. 102.

25. W. M. Eager to Thomas Jones, May 1, 1945, Eager Papers, "Sundry Papers."

26. Britain's Industrial Future: The Report of the Liberal Industrial Inquiry (London, 1928). Note that Inquiry was spelled with an "I" instead of the customary British "E" so that the name would not be abbreviated by its enemies to "LIE."

27. Britain's Industrial Future, passim; The

Times, February 10, 1928; *Nation,* February 11, April 7, 1928.

28. J. B. Hobman, "The Liberal Report: A Friendly Note of Criticism," *Daily News,* February 6, 1928; J. A. Hobson, "The Liberal Revival in England," *Nation* (New York), June 20, 1928; Harold Macmillan, *Winds of Change, 1914- 1939* (London, 1966), pp. 165-6.

29. *Liberal Magazine,* XXXVI (1928), 183; *Nation,* April 7, 1928.

30. Lloyd George to Philip Kerr, August 11, 1928, Lloyd George Papers, G/12/5/14; Sir Herbert Samuel to Lloyd George, October 6, 1928, *ibid.,* G/17/9/2.

31. Seebohm Rowntree to Lloyd George, February 8, 1929, quoted in Briggs, *Social Thought and Social Action,* p. 206; *The Times,* March 2, 1929.

32. *We Can Conquer Unemployment: Mr. Lloyd George's Pledge* (London, 1929), pp. 12-21.

33. *The Times,* March 13, 1929; *Evening Standard,* March 19, 1929; *Economist,* March 23, 1929; *Beatrice Webb's Diaries, 1924-1932,* ed. Margaret I. Cole (London, 1956), p. 191.

34. John Maynard Keynes and Hubert D. Henderson, *Can Lloyd George Do It? An Examination of the Liberal Pledge* (London, 1929). It was published by the *Nation.*

35. *Memoranda on Certain Proposals Relating to Unemployment, Prepared under the Direction of the Chancellor of the Exchequer,* Cmd. 3331 (London, 1929).

36. *Ibid.,* p. 23.

37. *Manchester Guardian,* May 29, 1929.

38. David Lloyd George, Marquess of Lothian, and B. Seebohm Rowntree, *How to Tackle Unemployment: The Liberal Plans as Laid Before the Government and the Nation* (London, 1930).

39. A. J. Sylvester (principal private secretary to Lloyd George) to Sir Robert Hutchison (Liberal chief whip), September 10, 1930, Lloyd George Papers, G/10/9/11; *The Times,* October 18, 1930.

40. "Political Correspondent," Manchester Guardian, September 18, 19, 1930; Lord Lothian to Lloyd
George, January 4, 1931, Lloyd George Papers,
G/12/5/26; Douglas, Land, People and Politics, pp.
198-200.

41. Ross McKibbin, "The Economic Policy of the
Second Labour Government, 1929-1931," Past and Present,
no. 68 (1975), pp. 112-7; Robert Skidelsky, Politicians
and the Slump: The Labour Government of 1929-1931 (London, 1967), p. 388.

42. Robert Boothby to Lloyd George, and reply,
November 29, 30, 1933, Lloyd George Papers, G/3/12/1,2;
"Janus" [Wilson Harris], "A Spectator's Notebook,"
Spectator, February 16, 1934; Clarke, My Lloyd George
Diary, pp. 241-5; Henry Pelling, America and the Brit-
ish Left: From Bright to Bevan (London, 1956),
pp. 133-5.

43. A. J. Sylvester to Lloyd George, April 4,
1934, Lloyd George Papers, G/21/1/33; Lloyd George to
Sir Walter Layton, and reply, August 29, 31, 1934,
ibid., G/141/26/1,3; Lloyd George: A Diary by Frances
Stevenson, October 15, 1934, entry, p. 283.

44. Lord Astor to Lloyd George, December 22,
1934, Lloyd George Papers, G/141/3/1; A. L. Rowse to
Megan Lloyd George, n.d. [about December 28, 1934],
ibid., G/21/4/77; Lloyd George to Sir Edward Grigg,
January 1, 1935, ibid., G/141/20/2; Jones, A Diary with
Letters, p. 84.

45. Sylvester, Life with Lloyd George, October
15, 1934, entry, p. 112; Annual Register, 1934 (London,
1935), part I, pp. 102-3; Annual Register, 1935 (London
1936), part I, pp. 2-3.

46. The Times, December 4, 1934; Spectator,
December 21, 1934; New Statesman and Nation, December
22, 1934; New English Weekly, December 27, 1934.

47. Sylvester, Life with Lloyd George, January
11, 16, 17, 18, 1935, entries, pp. 115-6; Manchester
Guardian, January 18, 1935.

48. New Statesman and Nation, January 26, 1935.

49. "Stimulus from Bangor," Spectator, January
25, 1935; "New Deal or Three Card Trick?" National

Review, CIV (February 1935), 163; New Statesman and
Nation, February 9, March 2, 1935; Round Table, XXV
(March 1935), 360-1; Manchester Guardian, March 27, 28,
1935; Political Quarterly, VI (April 1935), 68-9; Keith
Feiling, The Life of Neville Chamberlain (London,
1947), pp. 241-2.

50. Chamberlain to Ida Chamberlain, January 30,
1935, quoted in Maurice Cowling, The Impact of Hitler:
British Politics and Foreign Policy, 1933-1940 (Cambridge, Eng., 1975), p. 55.

51. Lloyd George to Thomas Jones, March 16, 1935,
Lloyd George Papers, G/141/24/2; Jones, A Diary with
Letters, pp. 143-4. According to Kingsley Martin, the
government agreed to examine the "new deal" proposals
only after ascertaining that none of the "big name"
economists--Keynes, Henderson, and Layton--who had been
behind the Yellow Book had helped to draft the new
plan. The ministers had access to a preliminary draft
of the memorandum circulated among Lloyd George's Young
Conservative friends, and knew that it was easily
vulnerable to criticism by Treasury experts ("A London
Diary," New Statesman and Nation, March 16, 1935).

52. Ramsay MacDonald's diary, March 21, 1935,
quoted in David Marquand, Ramsay MacDonald (London,
1977), pp. 768-9; Sylvester, Life with Lloyd George,
April 18, May 25, 1935, entries, pp. 120, 122; Sylvester to Lloyd George, May 21, 1935, Lloyd George Papers,
G/22/1/10; Lloyd George: A Diary by Frances Stevenson,
May 23, July 1, 1935, entries, p. 310.

53. Daily Herald, June 13, 1935; John Rowland to
Frances Stevenson, June 18, 1935, Lloyd George Papers,
G/141/41/6; Lloyd George to Robert Wilson, August 20,
1935, ibid., G/37/2/29; Stephen E. Koss, "Lloyd George
and Nonconformity: The Last Rally," English Historical
Review, LXXXIX (1974), 88-93.

54. Sir Alfred Davies to The Times, June 19,
1935, quoted in Davies, The Lloyd George I Knew,
p. 107.

55. A. J. P. Taylor portrayed Lloyd George's
"thread-bare" 1935 Council as a "bizarre echo" of the
1920 "councils of action" used successfully by the
labor movement to oppose British intervention against
Bolshevik Russia (English History, 1914-1945, p. 357).
But according to a letter of March 12, 1920, from

A. J. Balfour to Bonar Law, Lloyd George was himself
thinking of calling his projected Center party "The
Council of Action" (Kenneth Young, Arthur James Balfour
[London, 1963], p. 427).

56. The Times, July 2, 3, 1935; "Mr. Lloyd
George's Programme," Spectator, July 19, 1935; Lloyd
George to John Morgan, July 31, 1935, Lloyd George
Papers, G/37/1/23. Leslie Hore-Belisha, the Liberal
National transport minister in the National Government,
claimed to W. P. Crozier of the Manchester Guardian
that Lloyd George had "lifted pretty completely" into
his report Hore-Belisha's own scheme of nationalizing
the country's main roads (Crozier, Off the Record:
Political Interviews, 1933-43, ed. A. J. P. Taylor
[London, 1973], July 19, 1935, interview, p. 49).

57. The Times, July 23, 1935.

58. Report of the Commissioner for the Special
Areas (England and Wales), Cmd. 4951, cited in Mowat,
Britain between the Wars, p. 466. When the bill establishing this program was being debated in November
1934, Lloyd George had compared it unfavorably to the
Public Works Administration and other recovery programs
of the American New Deal (Fredric M. Miller, "The
Unemployment Policy of the National Government, 1931-
1936," Historical Journal, XIX [1976], 468).

59. The Next Five Years: An Essay in Political
Agreement (London, 1935). The Committee, better known
as the Next Five Years Group, is discussed at length in
Arthur Marwick, "Middle Opinion in the Thirties: Planning, Progress, and Political Agreement," English
Historical Review, LXXIX (1964), 285-98; Thomas C.
Kennedy, "The Next Five Years Group and the Failure of
the Politics of Agreement in Britain," Canadian Journal
of History, IX (1974), 45-68; and L. C. Carpenter,
"Corporatism in Britain, 1930-1945," Journal of Contemporary History, XI (1976), 3-25.

60. New Statesman and Nation, August 10, 1935.
The proposals in The Next Five Years to subsidize agricultural industries and to impose uniform tariffs on
all imports, including foods and raw materials, did not
please orthodox Liberals (Sir Herbert Samuel, "The
Present Situation," Contemporary Review, CXLVIII [Sep-
tember 1935], 262).

61. "Janus" [Wilson Harris], "A Spectator's

Notebook," Spectator, August 16, 1935; Plough My Own Furrow: The Story of Lord Allen of Hurtwood as Told Through His Writings and Correspondence, ed., Martin Gilbert (London, 1965), p. 206; Macmillan, Winds of Change, p. 377.

62. Lloyd George: A Diary by Frances Stevenson, July 17, 1935, entry, p. 312; Harold Macmillan to Lloyd George, November 22, 1935, Lloyd George Papers, G/141/30/4; The Times, November 26, 1935,; Robert Hield, "A New Parliament," Fortnightly Review, CXLIV (December 1935), 643. Even before the election, Baldwin had issued a clear warning of reprisals for those "who hunt with packs other than their own" (Swinton, Sixty Years of Power, p. 178).

63. The Times, June 13, October 19, 23, 1936, March 31, 1938; Lloyd George to Mrs. Philip Noel-Baker, June 20, 1936, Lloyd George Papers, G/1/14/2; W. J. Brown to Lloyd George, and reply, July 7, 13, 1937, ibid., G/39/3/154, 155; Duchess of Atholl to Lloyd George, December 26, 1938, ibid., G/43/2/97; Richard Acland to Lloyd George, April 17, 1939, ibid., G/1/3/1; Sylvester, Life with Lloyd George, January 12, 1938, entry, p. 187. The treasurer of the Council of Action was signing checks in its name as late as 1943 (Sylvester to Lloyd George, February 5, 1943, Lloyd George Papers, G/25/2/19).

64. Lloyd George to Professor Irving Fisher, September 27, 1935, Lloyd George Papers, G/37/2/25.

65. Basil Murray, L. G. (London, 1932), p. 125.

66. Duchess of Atholl, "Planning," National Review, CV (September 1935), 323; Maccoby, English Radicalism: The End? p. 542.

67. Daily Herald, February 23, 1935; Lord Strabolgi, "The Political Scene," Nineteenth Century, CXVIII (October 1935), 469-70.

68. Samuel, "The Present Situation," pp. 262-3.

69. Sir Percy Alden, "The Government and the National Programmes," Contemporary Review, CXLVIII (September 1935), 287-8.

70. Amery, My Political Life, III, 93-4; cf. James Meade, "The Keynesian Revolution," Essays on John

<u>Maynard Keynes</u>, ed. Milo Keynes (Cambridge, Eng., 1975), p. 83.

LIBERALISM AND THE TWO PARTY SYSTEM

1. John A. Hawgood developed this argument fully in "The Evolution of Parties and the Party System: The Nineteenth Century," <u>Political Parties and the Party System in Britain: A Symposium</u>, ed. Sydney D. Bailey (New York, 1952), pp. 38-9. Variations are found in Alan Beattie, <u>English Party Politics</u> (London, 1970), I, 136-8; David Butler and Donald Stokes, <u>Political Change in Britain</u>, 2nd ed. (New York, 1976), p. 109; and Anthony Downs, <u>An Economic Theory of Democracy</u> (New York, 1957), pp. 25-6.

2. Allen Potter, "Great Britain: Opposition with a Capital 'O'," <u>Political Oppositions in Western Democracies</u>, ed. Robert A. Dahl (New Haven, 1966), pp. 5-13; cf. J. P. D. Dunbabin, "Parliamentary Elections in Great Britain, 1868-1900: A Psephological Note," <u>English Historical Review</u>, LXXXI (1966), 85.

3. See Charles Seymour, <u>Electoral Reform in England and Wales, 1832-1885</u> (New Haven, 1915), pp. 341-2. Under the "minority provision" of the 1867 Reform Act, in four boroughs given a third seat each elector was to have only two votes, enabling a well-organized minority to elect one M. P. It proved to be possible, as in Birmingham, for a better-organized majority to defeat the act's intent and elect all three Members.

4. P. F. Clarke, "The Electoral Position of the Liberal and Labour Parties, 1910-1914," <u>English Historical Review</u>, XC (1975), 829; James Cornford, "Aggregate Election Data and British Party Alignments, 1885-1919," <u>Mass Politics: Studies in Political Sociology</u>, ed. Erik Allardt and Stein Rokkan (New York, 1970), p. 116.

5. See Neal Blewett, "The Franchise in the United Kingdom, 1885-1918," <u>Past and Present</u>, no. 32 (1965), pp. 32-8; and Grace A. Jones, "Further Thoughts on the Franchise, 1885-1918," <u>Past and Present</u>, no. 34 (1966), pp. 135-8.

6. Cf. P. F. Clarke, "Electoral Sociology of

Modern Britain," History, LVII (1972), 54. Not taken into account here is the simultaneous deterioration of Liberalism in British municipal government, which began before the war. For a recent discussion, see Chris Cook, "Liberals, Labour and Local Elections," The Politics of Reappraisal, pp. 166-88.

7. Cf. the analyses by D. E. Butler, The Electoral System in Britain, 1918-1951 (Oxford, 1953), pp. 173-80; Thomas W. Casstevens, "The Decline of the British Liberal Party: A Comparative and Theoretical Analysis" (unpublished Ph.D. dissertation, Michigan State University, 1966), pp. 166-72; Michael Kinnear, The British Voter: An Atlas and Survey (London, 1968), p. 129; and J. F. S. Ross, Elections and Electors: Studies in Democratic Representation (London, 1955), pp. 462-4. Ross divided the period 1918-35 into two parts, with 1924 as the decisive year for the Liberals. Between 1918 and 1924 there was a neck and neck race between the two "progressive" parties, but after 1924 it became evident that Labour had won. Ross thought that if the Liberals had contested more constituencies in 1924, their nationwide vote might have been much more impressive and might have discouraged defection. Many voters, he believed, having had to vote for a non-Liberal candidate in 1924, did not choose to return to their old party when a Liberal candidate was again on the ballot in 1929. "It is interesting to speculate whether, had the Liberals fought in 1924 as many seats as did Labour, the subsequent story might not have been different" (p. 464). The choice of 1935 as the terminal year of the Liberal-Labour rivalry was disputed by Frank Bealey and Michael Dyer, who argued that Labour did not prove its claim to win a parliamentary majority and become a true governing party until 1945, and that the Labour vote did not reach "a gently undulating plateau of electoral fortune" before the postwar election ("Size of Place and the Labour Vote in Britain, 1918-1966," Western Political Quarterly, XXIV [1971], 104-5).

8. Duverger believed that the Labour party in Britain, and its equivalents in other countries, were permitted to survive during infancy by financial and electoral support from well-established trade unions. Otherwise such parties, making little or no progress in the face of strong opposition from liberal and radical parties, would have been destroyed by loss of votes to their rivals and abstentions (Political Parties: Their Organization and Activity in the Modern State [London,

1955], p. 227). This explanation has not been entirely accepted by critics of Duverger, such as Leslie Lipson ("Party Systems in the United Kingdom and the Older Commonwealth: Causes, Resemblances, and Differences," Political Studies, VII [1959], 21-2). For other challenges to Duverger's bipolarization theory, see David J. Elkins, "The Measurement of Party Competition," American Political Science Review, LXVIII (1974), 683-4; John G. Grumm, "Theories of Electoral Systems," Midwest Journal of Political Science, II (1958), 357-76; John D. May, "Democracy, Party 'Evolution,' Duverger," Comparative Political Studies, II (1969), 227-8; and W. Phillips Shively, "The Elusive 'Psychological Factor': A Test for the Impact of Electoral Systems on Voting Behavior," Comparative Politics, III (1970), 115-25.

9. Maurice Duverger, "The Influence of the Electoral System on Political Life," International Social Science Bulletin, III (1951), 315. Duverger was of course writing before the rise of regional parties in the "Celtic fringe" during the 1960s and 1970s. S. E. Finer agreed with Duverger that the SMP system has militated against the Liberal party during and since its decline, as its thinly spread vote has not enabled it to win a proportionate share of seats. But the same system has aided the Scottish and Welsh nationalist parties because their votes are regionally concentrated (cited in Eric Moonman, "Electoral Reform," Parliamentarian, LVII [1976], 246).

10. Albert Mabileau, Le parti libéral dans le systeme constitutionnel britannique (Paris, 1953), pp. 78-9. But Lipson pointed out that historically the British two party tradition long antedated single member districts, which were not the rule until after 1885 ("The Two-Party System in British Politics," American Political Science Review, XLVII [1953], 347. Leon D. Epstein asserted that "ways of conducting elections are more the results than the cause of party systems" (Political Parties in Western Democracies [New York, 1967], p. 37).

11. Mabileau, pp. 201-3, 311-3.

12. Robert R. Alford, Party and Society: The Anglo-American Democracies (Chicago, 1963), pp. 15, 46; Douglas A. Hibbs, Jr., "Political Parties and Macroeconomic Policy," American Political Science Review, LXXI (1977), 1472 n. 14.

13. Robert R. Alford, "Class Voting in the Anglo-American Political Systems," Party Systems and Voter Alignments: Cross-National Perspectives, ed. Seymour M. Lipset and Stein Rokkan (New York, 1967), pp. 79-80; Alan C. Cairns, "The Electoral System and the Party System in Canada, 1921-1965," Canadian Journal of Political Science, I (1968), 59. The Progressive party was an exception to Duverger's rule that upstart third parties tend to fade because of chronic parliamentary underrepresentation; its popular vote fell faster than its seats. Cairns attributed the brief success of the Progressives against the SMP system to their votes being regionally concentrated.

14. Duff Spafford, "The Electoral System of Canada," American Political Science Review, LXIV (1970), 168-9.

15. James Bryce (Viscount Bryce), ModernDemoc-racies (Toronto, 1921), I, 473, quoted in Donald V. Smiley, "The Two-Party System and One-Party Dominance in the Liberal Democratic State," Canadian Journal of Economics and Political Science, XXIV (1958), 313; Leon D. Epstein, "A Comparative Study of Canadian Parties," American Political Science Review, LVIII (1964), 49; Jean Blondel, "Party Systems and Patterns of Government in Western Democracies," Canadian Journal of Political Science, I (1968), 184-5.

16. Douglas W. Rae, The Political Consequences of Electoral Laws, rev. ed. (New Haven, 1971), p. 94; Edmond F. Ricketts and Herbert Waltzer, "Electoral Arrangements and Party Systems: The Case of Canada," Western Political Quarterly, XXIII (1970), 703-7.

17. James Jupp, Australian Party Politics (Melbourne, 1964), chs. 1, 6, 7; Joan Rydon, "Electoral Methods and the Australian Party System, 1910-1951," Australian Journal of Politics and History, II (1956), 73-81; L. C. Webb, "The Australian Party System," in S. R. Davis et al., The Australian Political Party System (Sydney, 1954), pp. 94-104.

18. Lawrence C. Dodd, Coalitions in Parliamentary Government (Princeton, 1976), p. 153. The long survival of the Liberal-Country ministry of 1949-72 was aided by the secession from Labour of an anti-Communist splinter party, Democratic Labour, which was endorsed by several Roman Catholic bishops.

19. L. F. Crisp, Australian National Government (Croydon, Austral., 1965), p. 192; Henry S. Albinsky, Canadian and Australian Politics in Comparative Perspective (New York, 1973), ch. 5.

20. The Country party has a role in Australian politics similar to that of the British Liberal Unionist party after 1886 and the Liberal National ("Simonite") party after 1931. Unlike the Country party, however, both these satellites of the British Conservative party eventually merged with their more powerful ally. The Country party has been useful to the Australian Liberals as the two Liberal splinter groups were useful to the British Conservatives: all three have attracted moderate voters who might otherwise have voted for a left-of-center party or abstained.

21. Leslie Lipson, The Politics of Equality (Chicago, 1948), pp. 190-1; R. S. Milne, Political Parties in New Zealand (Oxford, 1966), chs. 2, 3,; Alan D. Robinson, "Class Voting in New Zealand," Party Systems and Voter Alignments, p. 100, 111; Keith Sinclair, A History of New Zealand (Harmondsworth, Eng., 1959), pp. 166-7, 197, 202-4, 242-7. A Social Credit party, appealing to farmers and small businessmen, elected a Member to the House of Representatives in 1963 and 1966, collapsed after the 1969 election, but came to life again in the late 1970s. Two of its candidates were successful in the 1981 election.

22. Jan H. Hofmeyr, South Africa, 2nd ed., edited by J. P. Cope (New York, 1952), pp. 113-9; Leo Marquand, The People and Politics of South Africa, 4th ed. (London, 1969), pp. 145-58; Stanton Peele and Stanley J. Morse, "Ethnic Voting and Political Change in South Africa," American Political Science Review, LXVIII (1974), 1520-1; A. W. Stadler, "The Afrikaner in Opposition, 1910-1948," Journal of Commonwealth Political Studies, VII (1969), 204-15. The United party (renamed the New Republic party in 1977) was the official opposition party in the Republic of South Africa from 1961 to 1978, when it was superseded by the Progressive Reform party, itself a merger of two small preexisting parties. After the 1978 parliamentary election the Nationalist party had 134 seats, Progressive Reform 17, and the New Republic party 10.

23. Called the Party of Liberty and Progress since 1961.

24. Val R. Lorwin, "Belgium: Religion, Class, and Language in National Politics," <u>Political Oppositions in Western Democracies</u>, pp. 156-8. PR has not always "protected" or "rescued" Liberal parties, as it did in Belgium. In some other European countries, e.g. Norway and Switzerland, adoption of PR brought about the division of once-powerful Liberal parties into two or more weaker parties. In Sweden, the Liberal party held together but lost its homogeneity and weakened in parliamentary discipline and morale (Gunnar Gyllander, "The Three-Party System in Sweden," <u>Contemporary Review</u>, CXXVI [1924], 625).

25. Duverger, "The Influence of the Electoral System on Political Life," pp. 341-2; W. L. Midleton, <u>The French Political System</u> (London, 1932), pp. 73-6, 93-102.

26. See Midleton, pp. 117-23, for illustrations of the Radical Socialists' role as a swing party in the Chamber of Deputies in the 1920s. Alan H. Taylor claimed that the pacts were the major reason for Liberal collapse in the twenties and thirties ("The Effect of Electoral Pacts on the Decline of the Liberal Party," <u>British Journal of Political Science</u>, III [1973], 243-8). The difficulty of forming viable coalitions or minority governments when party leaders are constrained in bargaining negotiations, as the British Liberals were in the 1920s, was discussed by Lawrence C. Dodd in "Party Coalitions in Multiparty Parliaments: A Game-Theoretic Analysis," <u>American Political Science Review</u>, LXVIII (1974), 1094-9, 1104, 1114.

27. Muir, <u>Politics and Progress</u>, p. 144, and <u>How Britain Is Governed</u> (London, 1930), chs. 4, 5. Donald V. Smiley in 1958 stated that Muir was "the only modern writer I have found who gives a forthright dissent from [the] point of view" that "the two-party system [is] the norm of the liberal-democratic polity" ("The Two-Party System and One-Party Dominance in the Liberal Democratic State," p. 312 and n.). More recently, Alan J. Beattie, writing after the formation of Harold Wilson's minority Labour government in February 1974, and questioning "the tendency to elevate thirty years of two-party politics into a law of nature," recalled some of Muir's arguments ("The Two-Party Legend," <u>Political Quarterly</u>, XLV [1974], 288-99). Muir's pre-First World War views are summarized in F. J. C. Hearnshaw, "Liberalism," <u>National Review</u>, CIII (1934), 588.

28. Quotation from Earl of Oxford and Asquith, Fifty Years of Parliament (Boston, 1926), II, 191. Cf. C. F. G. Masterman, The New Liberalism (London, 1920), pp. 23-4; Wilson Harris, J. A. Spender (London, 1946), p. 179; and, for Lord Grey's position, S. R. Daniels, "The Three-Party System," Contemporary Review, CXXXVIII (1930), 308.

29. This lack of candor was deplored by some Liberals: e.g., Gilbert Murray, "The Parliamentary System," Contemporary Review, CXLI (1932), 296.

30. See, for example, the letter of John H. Humphreys to the Nation, December 15, 1923.

31. K. R. Gladdish, "Two-Party Versus Multi-Party: The Netherlands and Britain," Parliamentary Affairs, XXVI (1973), 468. But note Jean Blondel's observation of a few years ago that "two-party partisanship [in Britain] reached a high point in 1950 and 1951; it has decreased fairly regularly ever since." From about three-quarters of the registered electorate in 1950, the combined vote of the two major parties declined to about 55 percent in the October 1974 general election. (It rose again to 61 percent in 1979.) "A marked increase of this trend," Blondel wrote, "would begin to threaten the position of the main parties--which can no longer be said to be wholly beyond attack" (Voters, Parties, and Leaders: The Social Fabric of British Politics [Harmondsworth, Eng., 1975], p. 73).

32. In multi-party coalition governments, participating Liberal parties have tended to obtain a disproportionately large number of ministerial portfolios because of their strategic ideological position (Eric C. Browne and Mark N. Franklin, "Aspects of Coalition Payoffs in European Parliamentary Democracies," American Political Science Review, LXVII [1973], 465, 469).

33. Cf. Arthur Cyr, Liberal Party Politics in Britain, with a Foreward by Michael Steed (New Brunswick, N.J., 1977), p. 220, and Leon D. Epstein, "What Happened to the British Party Model?" American Political Science Review, LXXIV (1980), 18.

34. David Butler, Arthur Stevens, and Donald Stokes, "The Strength of the Liberals Under Different Electoral Systems," Parliamentary Affairs, XXII (1969), 10-5.

35. Max Beloff and Gillian Peele, The Government of the United Kingdom: Political Authority in a Changing Society (New York, 1980), p. 103.

36. Noonan, "The Decline of the Liberal Party in British Politics," p. 38.

EPILOGUE

1. New York, 1966.

2. Cyr, p. 65.

3. London, 1966.

4. 2 vols., London, 1902.

5. London, 1965.

6. Cyr, p. 185.

7. Steed, Foreward to Cyr, p. 11.

SUGGESTIONS FOR FURTHER READING

I

Someone has yet to write a general history of the
Liberal party that is up to date, scholarly, and read-
able. There is neither a brief survey comparable to
Henry Pelling's Short History of the Labour Party, nor
a detailed, multi-volume series along the lines of A
History of the Conservative Party, published by
Longmans.

Chris Cook, A Short History of the Liberal Party,
1900-1976 (London, 1976), is the most recent survey.
According to its blurb it incorporates new research,
but its author seems to have relied heavily upon scis-
sors and paste. The best chapters are the introductory
ones about the nineteenth century party. Roy Douglas,
The History of the Liberal Party, 1895-1970 (Madison,
N.J., 1971), is a better book than Cook's, but it too
is more of a chronicle than an interpretation of the
Liberal saga. Douglas's argument that early twentieth
century Liberal magnates were too generous to the embryonic Labour party has been rejected by subsequent
writers.

Although intended simply to introduce a collection
of documentary extracts for undergraduate seminars,
Kenneth O. Morgan's ninety-seven page essay in The Age
of Lloyd George: The Liberal Party and British Politics, 1890-1929 (London, 1971), may well be the best
place to begin a study of modern British Liberalism.
The documents themselves, many of them reproduced from
the private papers of Lloyd George and other Liberal
politicians, prove that whatever else may be said about
these men, they were a contentious lot. Morgan teamed
up with Cameron Hazlehurst in 1971 to record The Liberals in the Twentieth Century for Sussex Tapes International. Part of their taped discussion makes better
use than Cook of monographic research into the party's
decline, while the rest focuses upon Lloyd George as "a
rural Welsh outsider" variously regarded as "folk hero
or monster," but in either case "the most creative
politician of the inter-war period."

There are five older surveys, dated and flawed but

worthy of note: W. Lyon Blease, A Short History of English Liberalism (New York, 1913); Hamilton Fyfe, The British Liberal Party: An Historical Sketch (London, 1928); Sir Henry Slesser, A History of the Liberal Party (London, 1944); R. J. Cruikshank, The Liberal Party (London, 1948); and R. B. McCallum, The Liberal Party from Grey to Asquith (London, 1963). Blease's work combines an obsolescent narrative history with an intelligent discourse upon Liberal ideology in the Edwardian era; Fyfe, a Labour journalist, attacked the Liberals for being stodgy and reactionary when in fact they were at least as dynamic and "progressive" as their leftist opponents; Cruikshank's pedestrian factual account is accompanied by some colorful illustrations; the Slesser and McCallum studies, both well-written and sound enough when published, have been outmoded by research during the past generation.

The ideological content of British Liberalism was treated seventy years ago by Blease, and more recently and objectively in the editors' introduction to Alan Bullock and Maurice Shock, eds., The Liberal Tradition from Fox to Keynes (London, 1956), a collection of excerpts from the writings of Liberal thinkers and statesmen. British radicalism, which must be distinguished from Liberalism which it overlaps, was canvassed thoroughly by Simon Maccoby in his six volume study going back to 1762, which includes copious quotations from source material. His final two volumes are English Radicalism, 1886-1914 (London, 1953), and English Radicalism: The End? (London, 1961), the latter stopping just short of the Liberal revival of the late 1950s. Moccoby also edited The English Radical Tradition, 1763-1914 (London, 1952), another anthology of documentary extracts. John W. Derry, The Radical Tradition: Tom Paine to Lloyd George (London, 1967), contains well-balanced interpretive essays on Joseph Chamberlain and Lloyd George.

For British Liberalism's relationship to that of Europe and North America, the following works should be consulted: Guido de Ruggiero, The History of European Liberalism, trans. R. G. Collingwood (London, 1927), which compares the British, French, German, and Italian varieties; Harold J. Laski, The Rise of European Liberalism: An Essay in Interpretation (London,1936); David Harris, "European Liberalism in the Nineteenth Century," American Historical Review, LX (1955), 501-26; and Robert Kelley, The Transatlantic Persuasion: The Liberal-Democratic Mind in the Age of Gladstone (New

York, 1969), a comparative study of British Liberalism and its equivalents in Canada and the United States.

There is a rich assortment of works about Liberalism's expanding and then diminishing role in the British party system. Ivor Bulmer-Thomas, The Party System in Great Britain (London, 1953), is a rather oversimplified, popular historical account. The same author's Growth of the British Party System, 2 vols. (London, 1965), is more sophisticated but similarly unanalytical. In the first volume there is a good description of Victorian party organizations, including that of the Liberals. Comparable treatment of politics and parties is found in Sir Ivor Jennings, Party Politics, 3 vols. (Cambridge, Eng., 1960-2), criticized by some reviewers as lacking scholarly rigor. Jennings, an authority on British constitutional law, stressed the evolution of parties in response to changing public opinion. A fourth work that does not substantially depart from conventional narrative history is Robert Rhodes James, The British Revolution: British Politics, 1880-1939, 2 vols. (London, 1976-7). As one reviewer remarked, the "subtle political and social revolution" that James claimed to be discussing was evidently so subtle that nothing more was heard of it.

Samuel H. Beer, British Politics in the Collectivist Age (New York, 1966), has much more analytical depth than the Bulmer-Thomas, Jennings, and James books. He contended that about the turn of the century British society and politics entered a collectivist stage, for which the Liberal party with its individualist and voluntarist traditions was less well equipped than its Conservative and Labour competitors. It was the unreadiness of the early twentieth century Liberals for collectivism, not subsequent party quarrels, that reduced them to minor party status. Writing sixty-five years before Beer, the Russian political scientist Mosei Y. Ostrogorski had argued in Democracy and the Organization of Political Parties, 2 vols., trans. Frederick Clarke (London, 1902), that the Liberals, inspired by Joseph Chamberlain, were adapting their party machinery to the politics of mass democracy; but, Beer explained, this transformation had been incomplete because of the reluctance of Liberal cadres to admit representatives of the working class.

Ostrogorski lucidly dissected the apparatus of the Liberal party as it functioned in the early 1890s. The structure and operation of the party about a decade later was examined, more prosaically, by Abbott Lawrence Lowell in The Government of England, 2 vols. (London, 1908). With the advantages of historical perspective and archival research, Harold J. Hanham produced Elections and Party Management: Politics in the Time of Disraeli and Gladstone (London, 1959), a book described by John Vincent as the "essential starting point for all work in Victorian party history." Robert T. McKenzie, British Political Parties: The Distribution of Power within the Conservative and Labour Parties (London, 1955), "Ostrogorski brought up to date," virtually ignores the Liberals except for a three page appendix describing the skeleton of party machinery in the early 1950s.

The micropolitics, as distinguished from the macropolitics, of the late Victorian and Edwardian periods was the focus of Henry Pelling in Social Geography of British Elections, 1885-1910 (London, 1967). In what his publisher called a "political Baedeker," Pelling after prodigious exploration of contemporary sources laid bare the grass roots rivalries of the two (sometimes three) parties in every British parliamentary constituency. In his concluding chapter, Pelling generalized from his constituency probes to indicate some possible explanations for the collapse of the Liberals after the First World War. The failure of the Liberal party to successfully appeal to the voters newly enfranchised in 1918 is displayed graphically in Michael Kinnear, The British Voter: An Atlas and Survey since 1885 (London, 1968). Kinnear's psephological maps depict the results of each general election, as well as illustrating special topics such as the relationship of Nonconformism to the Liberal vote and the competition between the Asquith and Lloyd George Liberals between 1918 and 1923.

Two quite recent studies employed complex psephological techniques--survey research and regression analysis--to examine and explain British voting behavior. Both David E. Butler and Donald E. Stokes, Political Change in Britain, 2nd ed. (New York, 1976), and William L. Miller, Electoral Dynamics in Britain since 1918 (London, 1977), suggested that Beer's collectivization paradigm may have to be modified to take into account a shift from religious to class politics after the First World War. Comparison by Butler and Stokes of the political attitudes of generational cohorts coming of age before and after the war showed a marked swing away from Liberalism in the younger cohorts, among whom religious identification was relatively weak but class identification relatively strong. Using a different methodology Miller reached similar conclusions.

The standard works on British electoral institutions and reforms are still Charles Seymour, Electoral Reform in England and Wales, 1832-1885 (New Haven, 1915), and David E. Butler, The Electoral System in Britain, 1918-1951 (Oxford, 1953). Supplementing them are Neal Blewett, "The Franchise in the United Kingdom, 1885-1918," Past and Present, no. 32 (1965), pp. 27-56, and Peter F. Clarke, "Electoral Sociology of Modern Britain," History, LV (1972), 31-55. All these works make it clear that the Liberal party had little to fear from Labour before the democratization of the franchise in 1918, and much to fear afterward. Butler traced the futile efforts of the Liberals to stabilize their deteriorating position during the twenties by procuring some form of preferential voting instead of "first past the post." In "The Strength of the Liberals under Different Electoral Systems," Parliamentary Affairs, XXII (1969), 10-5, David E. Butler, Arthur Stevens, and Donald E. Stokes demonstrated that proportional representation or the alternative vote would indeed have significantly benefited the Liberals, the former more than the latter. Earlier, Maurice Duverger in "The Influence of the Electoral System on Political Life," International Social Science Bulletin, III (1951), 314-52, and Political Parties: Their Origin and Activity in the Modern State (London, 1955), had argued persuasively that the centrist Liberals after 1918 were doomed as a governing party by a bipolarization tendency benefiting their leftist and rightist opponents whichever way the political pendulum swung.

II

The Liberal party did not formally begin at any one point but mutated from Whiggery, Radicalism, and liberal Toryism between 1832 and 1868. This piecemeal development is traced historically in Donald Southgate, The Passing of the Whigs, 1832-1886 (New York, 1962), and analyzed in John Vincent, The Formation of the British Liberal Party, 1857-1868 (London, 1966). Vincent identified the Liberals with the Nonconformist

and Evangelical upper middle class, with its strong
voluntarist bent and urban leadership function. Liberalism, according to Vincent, was rooted in the manufac-
turing towns of the Midlands and the North of England,
and prospered so long as the working people of these
communities faithfully accepted the stewardship of the
Liberal elite. A much older monograph by Frances E.
Gillespie, Labor and Politics in England, 1850-1867
(Durham, N.C., 1927), describes but fails to explain
the inability of John Bright and other mid-nineteenth
century Liberals to forge a permanent alliance with the
trade union movement. W. E. Williams, The Rise of
Gladstone to the Leadership of the Liberal Party,
1859-1868 (Cambridge, Eng., 1934), shows how an Evangelical Tory was able to establish a moral ascendancy
over Britain's lower middle and working class voters
for over a generation. Gladstone, by E. J. Feucht-
wanger (New York, 1975), is the best political biography of the statesman, strongest for the years after
1868; but John L. Hammond and M. R. D. Foot, Gladstone
and Liberalism (London, 1952), should also be perused.

Ostrogorski is still unsurpassed in his assessment
of the Liberals' endeavors to come to terms with
emerging mass democracy. Peter Fraser, Joseph Chamberlain: Radicalism and Empire (London, 1966), evaluates
the Birmingham politician's aborted attempt to transform the Liberals into a radical imperialist party,
although--in the words of one reviewer--the author did
a bit of "special pleading." Fraser's book should be
compared with the most recent appraisal of the controversial statesman, Joseph Chamberlain: A Political
Study, by Richard Jay (New York, 1981). The Liberal
Unionist defection is the theme of Gordon L. Goodman,
"Liberal Unionism: The Revolt of the Whigs," Victorian
Studies, III (1959), 173-89, and is also dealt with at
length in Southgate, The Passing of the Whigs. Barry
McGill, "Francis Schnadhorst and Liberal Party Organization," Journal of Modern History, XXXIV (1962), 19-
39, explains this strange man's singular role in the
party machine, both before and after the Chamberlainite
schism. Chamberlain's principal legacy to the Liberal
party needs a new evaluation based on archival research, but the fundamental details are set forth in
Robert Spence Watson, The National Liberal Federation
from Its Commencement to the General Election of 1906
(London, 1907). Roy Jenkins, Sir Charles Dilke: A
Victorian Tragedy (London, 1958), is a sprightly biography of Liberalism's "lost leader," but has little to
say about Kilke's influence as a radical back-bencher

in the two decades after his disgrace.

The "faddism"--Celtic Fringe regionalism, disestablishment and other Nonconformist enthusiasms, temperance zealotry, Lib-Labism, Liberal imperialism, and the rest--that almost tore the party apart during Gladstone's later years--is the subject of D. A. Hamer, Liberal Politics in the Age of Gladstone and Rosebery (Oxford, 1972). In a revisionist interpretation, Gladstone and Radicalism: The Reconstruction of Liberal Policy in Britain, 1885-1894 (Brighton, 1975), Michael Barker claimed that the old statesman was not obsessed with Irish home rule but was also a committed social reformer of Great Britain as well as Ireland--was, indeed, the true founder of the New Liberalism. Peter Stansky, Ambitions and Strategies: The Struggle for the Leadership of the Liberal Party in the 1890s (Oxford, 1964), minutely records the squabbling and intrigue that racked the party just before and after the Grand Old Man's retirement. Stansky was less successful in reevaluating the place of the Newcastle Program in the development of post-Gladstonian Liberal policy.

A scholarly political biography of that enigmatic politician, Lord Rosebery, has not yet appeared. The facts of his life are recounted urbanely in Robert Rhodes James, Rosebery: A Biography of Archibald Philip, Fifth Earl of Rosebery (New York, 1963). In The Quest for National Efficiency, 1899-1914 (Oxford, 1971), G. R. Searle attempted with only moderate success to prove that Rosebery's ideas and example inspired such disparate reformers as Haldane, Lloyd George, and the Webbs, all concerned about Britain's faltering world mission. That Rosebery was seen as a possible regenerator of the fractured post-Gladstonian Liberal party is illustrated by a contemporary article of Sidney Webb, "Lord Rosebery's Escape from Houndsditch," Nineteenth Century, CCXCV (1901), 366-86. Webb called upon Rosebery to disavow the "faddists" and Little Englanders and convert Liberalism into a party of social reform and enlightened imperialism. Rosebery's tepid and vacillating leadership of the Liberal imperialist faction of the party, which included Asquith, Grey, and Haldane, is thoroughly scrutinized in H. C. W. Matthew, The Liberal Imperialists: The Ideas and Politics of a Post-Gladstonian Elite (London, 1973), and Peter D. Jacobson, "Rosebery and Liberal Imperialism, 1899-1903," Journal of British Studies, XIII, no. 1 (1973), 83-107. Roy Jenkins, "From Gladstone to Asquith: The Late Victorian Pattern of Liberal

Leadership," History Today, XIV (1964), 445-52, compares and contrasts the political syles of the G.O.M. and his two successors as party chief.

Many authors have chronicled and analyzed the stormy relationship between Liberalism and Labour at the turn of the century. For Labour's debut, there are standard works by G. D. H. Cole, Ross I. McKibbin, Henry Pelling, Philip P. Poirier, and J. H. Stewart Reid, among others. Royden J. Harrison, Before the Socialists: Studies in Labour and Politics, 1861-1881 (Toronto, 1965), takes up the story of labour and radical dissonance about where Frances E. Gillespie's older work leaves off. An unpublished dissertation for the London School of Economics by A. D. W. Crowley (1952) focuses upon "The Origins of the Revolt of the British Labour Movement Against Liberalism, 1875-1906." The outset of the long decline of municipal radicalism in Greater London is traced, with much informative detail, in two works by Paul Thompson: "Liberals, Radicals and Labour in London, 1880-1900," Past and Present, no. 27 (1964), pp. 73-101, and Socialists, Liberals and Labour: The Struggle for London, 1885-1914 (London, 1967). Several essays in Henry Pelling, Popular Politics and Society in Late Victorian Britain (London, 1968), suggest that disillusionment of trade union leaders with the Liberal party began early and was repressed only because they had nowhere else to go politically.

The skill of the post-Rosebery generation of National Liberal politicians in coming to terms, at least temporarily, with their pluralist clientele has not been sufficiently appreciated or explained. One such adept wire-puller was Herbert Gladstone, whose last biographer was his friend Sir Charles Mallet in 1932. There have been two monographic studies of Gladstone: H. W. McCready, "Chief Whip and Party Funds: The Work of Herbert Gladstone in the Edwardian Liberal Party, 1899 to 1906," Canadian Journal of History, VI (1971), 285-303, and Trevor Lloyd, "The Whip as Paymaster: Herbert Gladstone and Party Organization," English Historical Review, LXXXIX (1974), 785-813. In addition, two articles by Frank Bealey discuss the notorious Lib-Lab pact--negotiated by Gladstone and Ramsay MacDonald--in effect until the First World War: "Negotiations between the Liberal Party and the Labour Representation Committee before the General Election of 1906," Bulletin of the Institute of Historical Research, XXIX (1956), 261-74, and "The Electoral

Arrangement between the Labour Representation Committee and the Liberal Party," Journal of Modern History, XXVIII (1956), 353-73. The chief whips of the last Liberal governments--George Whiteley, J. A. Pease, the Master of Elibank, Percy Illingworth, and John Gulland--all await scholoarly treatment. Some of Elibank's letters are quoted in Arthur C. Murray, Master and Brother: Murray of Elibank (London, 1945).

Commensurate with the expanding impact of labor upon Liberal politics was the relative decline of Nonconformist power, although this slump was forcefully defied by many Free Church Liberals. The most extensive and rounded treatise is Stephen E. Koss, Nonconformity in Modern British Politics (London, 1975), but John F. Glaser, "English Nonconformity and the Decline of Liberalism," American Historical Review, LXIII (1958), 352-63, is both more insightful and more debatable.

III

There is a crisply written survey of The Great Liberal Revival, 1903-6, by Michael Craton and H. W. McCready (London, 1966). A. K. Russell, Liberal Landslide: The General Election of 1906 (Newton Abbot, Eng., 1973), contains a thorough but superficial account of Liberal electioneering. The busy record of the successive Campbell-Bannerman and Asquith ministries is recounted briskly and noncommittally in Colin Cross, The Liberals in Power, 1905-1914 (London, 1963), and at greater length--to the point of tedium--by Peter Rowland in his two volumes about The Last Liberal Governments (London, 1968-71). A useful feature of Rowland's work is the full-length quotation of prominent Liberals' significant letters and memoranda. The well-researched biography of Sir Henry Campbell-Bannerman by John Wilson (London, 1973), has been summed up by reviewers as rather too admiring. Much more penetrating is the interpretive monograph by José Harris and Cameron Hazlehurst, "Campbell-Bannerman as Prime Minister," History, LV (1970), 360-83.

Herbert Henry Asquith and his fellow Liberal ministers have been dealt with voluminously by historians and biographers. Stephen E. Koss, Asquith

(London, 1976), has upstaged all previous lives; but Roy Jenkins's smoothly written biography (London, 1964) remains valuable for its many quotations from the prime minister's letters to Venetia Stanley Montagu, while the authorized Life of Lord Oxford and Asquith, 2 vols. (London, 1932), by J. A. Spender and Cyril Asquith, is still indispensable for its detail. Among other studies of merit are R. B. McCallum, Asquith (London, 1936), and Cameron Hazlehurst, "Asquith as Prime Minister, 1908-1916," English Historical Review, LXXXV (1970), 502-31. Lord Oxford and Asquith's own Fifty Years of Parliament, 2 vols. (Boston, 1926), and Memories and Reflections, 2 vols. (Boston, 1928), although hurriedly turned out in old age, contain scattered passages of interest from memoranda and letters. Margot Asquith, surely the most eccentric hostess of No. 10 Downing Street but not without political clout, does not yet have a biographer but was characteristically revealing about herself in her Autobiography, 4 vols. (New York, 1922).

So much has been written about Lloyd George that the output has been called an industry. A lot of this material is redundant, but the reader wishing to cull it himself may consult the comprehensive bibliographies in the works by Kinnear (1973), Cregier (1976), Campbell (1977), and Fry (1977) described below. The less patient reader will be aided by two historiographical essays both entitled "Lloyd George and the Historians": Kenneth O. Morgan, Transactions of the Honourable Society of Cymmrodorion, 1971, part I, pp. 65-85, and Bentley B. Gilbert, Albion, XI (1979), 74-86. Also helpful, for recent literature, is the review article by David Brooks, "Lloyd George, For and Against," Historical Journal, XXIV (1981), 223-30.

The best life in a single volume is Peter Rowland, Lloyd George (London, 1975), although as one reviewer noted the author failed to see the wood for the trees. Much less monotonous is Frank Owen, Tempestuous Journey: Lloyd George, His Life and Times (New York, 1965), but this journalistic biography--while its writer dipped into the Lloyd George archive collected by Lord Beaverbrook--is too slapdash to be reliable. For the Welshman's youth and early days in politics, there are Donald McCormick's spiteful but provocative Mask of Merlin (London, 1963); John Grigg, The Young Lloyd George (London, 1973); and W. R. P. George, The Making of Lloyd George (London, 1976), based upon family papers. His prewar career as a Nonconformist

spokesman and Liberal minister is recapitualted in
W. Watkin Davies, Lloyd George (London, 1939), and Don
M. Cregier, Bounder from Wales (Columbia, Mo., 1976).
John Grigg, Lloyd George: The People's Champion, 1902-
1911 (Berkley, Calif., 1978), is heavily padded with
long quotations from other books but has a few new
anecdotes about its hero's philandering.

Specialized studies of aspects of Lloyd George's
multifarious activities before the First World War
include Dorothy J. Ernst, "The Social Policies of David
Lloyd George" (1942), a dissertation for the University
of Wisconsin; William J. Braithwaite, Lloyd George's
Ambulance Wagon, ed. Sir Henry Bunbury (London, 1957),
a civil servant's memoir of the fight for national
insurance; Bentley B. Gilbert, "David Lloyd George:
Land, the Budget, and Social Reform," American Historical Review, LXXXI (1976), 1058-66; Chris J. Wrigley,
David Lloyd George and the British Labour Movement
(Hassocks, Eng., 1976); and Michael G. Fry, Lloyd
George and Foreign Policy: The Education of a Statesman, 1890-1916 (Montreal, 1977). Kenneth O. Morgan
wrote two brief and thoughtful appreciations, David
Lloyd George: Welsh Radical as World Statesman (Cardiff, 1963), and Lloyd George (London, 1974), the
latter enhanced by many well-chosen photographs and
cartoons. "The Tragic Hero in Politics," Edwin C.
Hargrove's 1963 dissertation for Yale University,
treats Lloyd George as well as the Americans Theodore
Roosevelt and Fiorello LaGuardia as well-intentioned
reformers flawed by the exigencies of democratic
politics.

Published letters and speeches of Lloyd George
himself and contemporary observations about him have
become almost as numerous as secondary sources. For
the years before 1914, Lloyd George Family Letters,
1885-1936, ed. Kenneth O. Morgan (Cardiff, 1973), are
very revealing, as are Lloyd George: A Diary by Frances
Stevenson, ed. A. J. P. Taylor (New York, 1971), for
the war-time era, and My Darling Pussy: The Letters of
Lloyd George and Frances Stevenson, 1913-41, ed. A. J.
P. Taylor (London, 1975), for the postwar period.
Lloyd George's best oratory, sometimes emended, was
published in several collections listed in the previously cited bibliographies. There is a good cross
section in Martin Gilbert, ed., Lloyd George (Englewood
Cliffs, N.J., 1968). Two other great treasure troves
of Lloyd Georgiana are the diary of Lord Riddell,
selectively published in three volumes (London, 1933-

4), and The Political Diaries of C. P. Scott, 1911-
1928, ed. Trevor Wilson (Ithaca, N.Y., 1970). Both
diarists were powerful newspapermen whose goodwill the
Welshman cultivated for many years. The contemporary
journalism about Lloyd George was abundant, and may be
represented by two books: Frank Dilnot, Lloyd George:
The Man and His Story (New York, 1917), sympathetic;
and G. E. Raine, The Real Lloyd George (London, 1913),
hostile.

A number of Lloyd George's relatives, friends, and
enemies recalled his earlier political career in
memoirs published many years after the events. Important examples of this memorabilia, which the historians
must use cautiously, are Sir Alfred Davies, The Lloyd
George I Knew (London, 1948); William George, My
Brother and I (London, 1958); Lucy Masterman, "Recollections of David Lloyd George," History Today, IX
(1959), 274-81; Richard Lloyd George, My Father, Lloyd
George (New York, 1961); and Frances (Stevenson) Lloyd
George, The Years That Are Past (London, 1967). Dame
Margaret: The Life Story of His Mother, by Richard
Lloyd George (London, 1947), recollects the statesman's
gusty marriage from his wife's standpoint, in counter-
point to the books by "the other woman," Frances Stevenson.

Newspaper proprietors and journalists gravitated
to Lloyd George, so it is not surprising that memoirs
and biographies of the leading Edwardian newspapermen
tell us almost as much about the Welshman as the
personages being commemorated. In addition to the
Riddell and Scott diaries already mentioned, there is
much about Lloyd George, and also about his Liberal
colleagues and party politics, in T. D. Darlow, William
Robertson Nicoll (London, 1925); J. Alfred Spender, The
Public Life, 2 vols. (London, 1925), and Life, Journalism and Politics, 2 vols. (London, 1927); Harold
Spender, The Fire of Life: A Book of Memories (London,
1926); H. A. Taylor, Robert Donald (London, 1934);
Reginald Pound and Geoffrey Harmsworth, Northcliffe
(New York, 1960); Stephen E. Koss, Fleet Street
Radical: A. G. Gardiner and the Daily News (London,
1973); and Alfred F. Havighurst, Radical Journalist:
H. W. Massingham (Cambridge, Eng., 1974).

The biographical material about Asquith's other
ministerial colleagues is also abundant and uneven in
quality. The following selection is arranged by subject, the more perceptive or informative items being

starred: *Winston S. Churchill, 5 vols. to date (London, 1966-77), begun by Randolph S. Churchill and continued by Martin Gilbert, together with "companion volumes" containing thousands of letters by, to, or about Winston Churchill; *Lady Violet Bonham Carter (Lady Asquith), Winston Churchill as I Knew Him (London, 1965), by Asquith's politically-savvy daughter; Henry Pelling, Winston Churchill (London, 1974), a rather pedestrian tome; James Pope-Hennessy, Lord Crewe, 1858-1945; The Likeness of a Liberal (London, 1955); Viscount Grey of Falloden, Twenty-Five Years, 1892-1916, 2 vols. (London, 1925), almost entirely about foreign affairs; *Keith Robbins, Sir Edward Grey (London, 1971), which show that "the amiable bird-watcher" was not without interest or influence in domestic politics; *Viscount Haldane, An Autobiography (Garden City, N.Y., 1929); Dudley Sommer, Haldane of Cloan (London, 1960); *Stephen E. Koss, Lord Haldane: Scapegoat for Liberalism (New York, 1969), mostly about wartime politics; H. Montgomery Hyde, Lord Reading: The Life of Rufus Isaacs, First Marquess of Reading (London, 1967); Stephen McKenna, Reginald McKenna, 1863-1943 (London, 1948); *Lucy Masterman, C. F. G. Masterman (London, 1939), essentially a diary with many passages about Lloyd George; Sir David Waley, Edwin Montagu (London, 1964); *D. A. Hamer, John Morley: Liberal Intellectual in Politics (Oxford, 1968); *A. J. A. Morris, C. P. Trevelyan, 1870-1958: Portrait of a Radical (Belfast, 1977); Viscount Samuel, Memoirs (London, 1945); John Bowle, Viscount Samuel (London, 1957).

To the foregoing biographical works should be added several contemporaneous records of the world of Liberal high politics before the First World War. These include, in addition to the Riddell and Scott diaries, Beatrice Webb's Diaries, 1912-1924, ed. Margaret I. Cole (London, 1952); Letters of Sidney and Beatrice Webb, 3 vols., ed. Norman Mackenzie (Cambridge, Eng., 1978); and Inside Asquith's Cabinet: From the Diaries of Charles Hobhouse, ed. Edward David (London, 1977), a junior minister's prickly, not to say paranoid, account of cabinet infighting. A. G. Gardiner's polished essays in Prophets, Priests and Kings, The War Lords, and Pillars of Society (London, 1914, 1915, 1916), capture the tone if not the substance of Liberal politics as peace merged into war. The distaff side of Edwardian Liberal politics is etched in Margot Asquith's Autobiography and, more lightly, in the works of Marie Belloc Lowndes: The Merry Wives of Westminster, A Passing World, and Diaries and Letters, 1911-1947, ed. Susan Lowndes (London, 1946, 1948, 1971).

IV

There is an amplitude of material, primary and secondary, on the development of the fabianist New Liberal ideology and its contribution to the early welfare state. A good introduction is Harold J. Schultz, ed., English Liberalism and the State: Individualism or Collectivism? (Lexington, Mass., 1972), which traces the ideology of New Liberalism back to Bentham, J. S. Mill, and T. H. Green. Schultz's anthology contains extracts from the works of such early twentieth century New Liberal theorists as Leonard T. Hobhouse, John A. Hobson, and Herbert Samuel. Their ideas are set forth more fully in Samuel, Liberalism: An Attempt to State the Principles and Proposals of Contemporary Liberalism in England (London, 1902), which has an introduction by Asquith; Hobson, The Crisis of Liberalism: New Issues of Democracy (London, 1909); and Hobhouse, Liberalism (London, 1911). Other important works in this genre are Leo Chiozza Money, Riches and Poverty (London, 1905), and two tracts by Charles F. G. Masterman, The Condition of England (London, 1909), and The New Liberalism (London, 1920), the latter an attempt to justify the continued existence of the Liberal party. Winston Churchill got into the New Liberal act, possibly with mixed motives, in a controversial letter to the Nation, March 7, 1908, which the editor entitled "The Untrodden Field of Politics" (extracts in Morgan, The Age of Lloyd George, pp. 144-8). His subsequent speeches on social reform were published in Liberalism and the Social Problem (London, 1909).

Michael Freeden, The New Liberalism: An Ideology of Social Reform (New York, 1978), is the best interpretive study of the ideas and the movement. Also helpful are Francis H. Herrick, "British Liberalism and the Idea of Social Justice," American Journal of Economics and Sociology, IV (1944), 67-79, and J. Roy Hay, The Origins of the Liberal Welfare Reforms, 1906-1914 (London, 1975); the latter concisely demonstrates the interaction of ideology, pressure group politics, and party strategy. In Liberals and Social Democrats (Cambridge, Eng., 1978), Peter F. Clarke examined the ideas

282

of the New Liberal intellectuals Hobhouse, Hobson, and John L. Hammond, as well as the Fabian Graham Wallas. A prosopographical approach to the New Liberals is taken in David Hopkinson, "Vintage Liberals," History Today, XXVIII (1978), 364-71.

The actual legislative yield of the New Liberal movement concerned Bentley B. Gilbert in The Evolution of National Insurance in Great Britain: The Origins of the Welfare State (London, 1966); José Harris in Unemployment and Politics: A Study of English Social Policy, 1886-1914 (Oxford, 1972); and H. V. Emy in Liberals, Radicals and Social Politics, 1892-1914 (Cambridge, Eng., 1973). In addition, there are good summaries in two essays: Samuel J. Hurwitz, "The Development of the Social Welfare State in Prewar Britain, 1906-1914," The Making of English History, ed. Robert L. Schuyler and Herman Ausubel (New York, 1952); and Ronald V. Sires, "Liberal Reform Legislation, 1906-14: An Interpretation," Southwestern Social Science Quarterly, XXXV (1954), 107-15. A salutary corrective to the enthusiasm shown in most of these works is the disenchanted view of Sr. John Francis Berry, S. S. J., in her 1966 dissertation for St. Louis University, "Exposition of British Welfare Liberalism." Peter F. Clarke microscopically scanned the political impact of the movement on one English region in Lancashire and the New Liberalism (Cambridge, Eng., 1971). Clarke's thesis--that the ideologically revived Liberal party was in excellent health in 1914--was vehemently disputed by Joseph White in his review, "A Panegyric on Edwardian Progressivism," Journal of British Studies, XVI, no. 2 (1977), 143-52. White went so far as to declare that Clarke was writing "unacknowledged counterfactual history."

Neal Blewett, The Peers, the Parties and the People: The British General Elections of 1910 (London, 1972), thoroughly if repetitiously scrutinizes the two elections, which deprived the Liberals of their last parliamentary majority and returned Irish home rule to politics's front burner. The efforts of some Liberal publicists to draw working class voters' attention to issues other than Ireland and the House of Lords are exemplified by Thomas J. Macnamara, The Political Situation: Letters to a Working Man (London, 1909), the same author's Tariff Reform and the Working Man (London, 1910), and Aneurin Williams, Unemployment and Land Nationalisation (London, 1909). Lloyd George's controversial and clandestine 1910 scheme for a national coalition government is discussed in G. R. Searle, The Quest for National Efficiency, and as a step toward the eventual wartime coalition in Robert J. Scally, The Origins of the Lloyd George Coalition: The Politics of Social-Imperialism, 1900-1918 (Princeton, 1975). Scally's book is very stimulating, although marred by hasty draftsmanship. Another Lloyd George demarche, the land inquiry and campaign, was treated in a rather humdrum way by Roy Douglas in Land, People and Politics: A History of the Land Question in the United Kingdom, 1878-1952 (London, 1976), and more critically in H. V. Emy, "The Land Campaign: Lloyd George as a Social Reformer, 1909-14," Lloyd George: Twelve Essays, ed. A. J. P. Taylor (London, 1971).

Votes for women as an issue in Liberal party politics is related dispassionately in David Morgan, Suffragists and Liberals: The Politics of Women's Suffrage in England (Oxford, 1975). The frenzy of the suffragette movement as one phase of a crisis in consensual Liberalism, together with labor violence and the threat of Irish civil war, is the subject of George Dangerfield's impressionistic but suggestive Strange Death of Liberal England (New York, 1935). Dangerfield argued that the leadership of the Liberal party had become either frivolous, like Asquith, or opportunistic, like Lloyd George. Other historians have contended that the Liberal establishment was beginning to split between the principled and the expedient, and the flurry over the Marconi affair highlighted this dichotomy. The standard work is Frances Donaldson, The Marconi Scandal (London, 1962). Yet another widening division in the party, between moderates and radicals, is dealt with in several of the essays in A. J. A. Morris, ed., Edwardian Radicalism, 1900-1914 (London, 1974), and Alan O'Day, ed., The Edwardian Age: Conflict and Stability (Hamden, Conn., 1979). Morris's own book, Radicalism against War, 1906-1914: The Advocacy of Peace and Retrenchment (Totowa, N.J., 1972), and an article by Howard S. Weinroth, "The British Radicals and the Balance of Power, 1902-1914," Historical Journal, XIII (1970), 653-82, testify to the growing distrust toward ministers over foreign policy formation by many Liberal back-benchers and rank and file. Lively sketches of several of the radical critics of Liberal foreign policy are found in A. J. P. Taylor, The Trouble Makers: Dissent over Foreign Policy, 1792-1939 (London, 1957). Max Beloff, Britain's Liberal Empire, 1897-1921 (London, 1969), analyzes the contributions of the last Liberal governments to imperial devolution and the development of the Commonwealth. The unending Irish problem has been evaluated afresh in Patricia Jalland, The Liberals and Ireland: The Ulster Question in British Politics to 1914 (Brighton, Eng., 1980). Jalland suggested that inability to settle this vexing matter may have damaged the Liberal party almost as much as the effects of the First World War.

A few years ago there was a sharp controversy over whether the Liberal party's goodwill toward its emerging rival, Labour, threatened the older party's existence. Roy Douglas in his 1971 history of the Liberal party claimed that it did. Jeremy Thorpe, the current Liberal leader, made the same charge more acidly in his introduction to Douglas's book. But in the second volume of The Last Liberal Governments (pp. 350-5), Peter Rowland countered that the alliance with Labour had done Liberalism little harm, and that Labour might have emerged greatly weakened from a normal peacetime election in 1915. Trevor Lloyd went even further than Rowland in "Lib-Labs and 'Unforgivable Electoral Generosity,'" Bulletin of the Institute of Historical Research, XLVIII (1975), 255-9. Far from "letting the cuckoo into the nest," Lloyd argued, Herbert Gladstone's pact enabled the two "progressive" parties to win more seats between them than the Liberals could have won alone.

Another recent academic dispute has been over working class support for the Liberal party, and the effects of franchise reform on the party's fate. In Lancashire and the New Liberalism and an article, "The Electoral Position of the Liberal and Labour Parties, 1910-1914," English Historical Review, XC (1975), 828-36, Peter F. Clarke claimed that before the war the Liberal party had a solid electoral position with the workers. On the other hand, Ross I. McKibbin's Evolution of the Labour Party, 1910-1924 (London, 1976), advances the thesis that the 1918 Representation of the People Act, by enabling workmen disfranchised before 1914 to exhibit their class loyalty to Labour, changed the relative position of the "progressive" parties. In his review of McKibbin's book (English Historical Review, XCI [1976], 157-63) and in his own article, "Liberals, Labour and the Franchise," English Historical Review, XCII (1977), 582-90, Clarke reasserted his position that before the war the Liberals were winning, and holding, new working class votes. A slightly different tack was taken by McKibbin and his co-authors, H. C. G. Matthew and J. A. McKay, in their 1976 monograph, "The Franchise Factor in the Rise of the Labour Party," _English Historical Review_, XCI, 723-52. They contended that the 1918 franchise reform not only trebled the electorate but changed its character to Labour's benefit, swamping informed voters by those lacking political awareness. All these authors have something to say about the falling off of sectarian voting, a matter discussed more fully in the psephological studies of Butler and Stokes (1976), Miller (1977), and Cook (various dates). Chris Cook, in two essays--"Liberals, Labour and Local Elections," _The Politics of Reappraisal, 1918-1939_, ed. Gillian Peale and Chris Cook (London, 1975), and "Labour and the Downfall of the Liberal Party," _Crisis and Controversy: Essays in Honour of A. J. P. Taylor_, ed. Alan Sked and Chris Cook (London, 1976)--not only analyzed the swing from Liberalism to Labour after the expansion of the local government franchise in 1918, but also argued that deterioration of Liberal strength in municipal politics had begun years before the war.

Monographs on Liberal politics in the various British regions both before and after the First World War have not been numerous. In addition to Henry Pelling's impressive but necessarily cursory survey of each British parliamentary constituency in _Social Geography of British Elections_, there is Kenneth O. Morgan's ground-breaking _Wales in British Politics, 1868-1922_ (Cardiff, 1963). The latter is supplemented by the same author's "Twilight of Welsh Liberalism: Lloyd George and the Wee Frees, 1918-1935," _Bulletin of the Board of Celtic Studies_, XXII, pt. 4 (1968). Scotland has been less well served than Wales, but readers may profitably study a 1951 dissertation for Harvard University by David C. Elliot, "The Liberal Party in Scotland from the Midlothian Election to the First World War," as well as the eight page survey in James G. Kellas, _Modern Scotland: The Nation since 1870_ (New York, 1968).

V

Liberal resentment--not only among radicals--toward cabinet ministers for leading the country and party into the First World War is documented in Maccoby, _English Radicalism_; Morris, _Radicalism against_

War; Taylor, The Trouble Makers; and J. E. Lindsay, "The Failure of Liberal Opposition to British Entry into World War I" (Columbia University dissertation, 1969). Stephen E. Koss, Sir John Brunner: Radical Plutocrat, 1842-1919 (Cambridge, Eng., 1970), recounts the president of the National Liberal Federation's crusade to check the armaments race and the drift toward Armageddon. The soul-searching of Liberal ministers in July-August 1914 is particularized in Cameron Hazlehurst, Politicians at War, July 1914 to May 1915: A Prologue to the Triumph of Lloyd George (London, 1971), which is also the fullest scholarly account of wartime politics until the fall of the last Liberal government. Hazlehurst and A. J. P. Taylor were the progenitors of the revisionist school which in the 1960s and '70s sought to reclaim Lloyd George's reputation from his Asquithian detractors. Other works by Taylor in this genre, all provocative, are "Politics in the First World War," Proceedings of the British Academy, XL (1959), 67-95, which reappeared as one of the essays in his Politics in Wartime (New York, 1965); Lloyd George: Rise and Fall (Cambridge, Eng., 1961); and chapters 1, 2, and 3 of his English History, 1914-1945 (Oxford, 1965). In "Asquith's Predicament, 1914-1918," Journal of Modern History, XXXIX (1967), 283-303, Barry McGill analyzed the pressures upon the Liberal leader in his uncomfortable dual role of party politician and head of a war government.

The classic report of the rise and fall of the Asquith coalition government of 1915-6 is Lord Beaverbrook, Politicians and the War, 1914-1916, 2 vols. (London, 1928-32); as a participant in both governmental crises Beaverbrook wrote with understandable self-interest, so that his narrative--though generally excellent in detail--must be refracted by academic works such as Hazlehurst's and Martin D. Pugh, "Asquith, Bonar Law and the First Coalition," Historical Journal, XVII (1974), 813-36. Hazlehurst took pains to rebut the charge in Stephen E. Koss, "The Destruction of Britain's Last Liberal Government," Journal of Modern History, XL (1968), 257-77, that Lloyd George and Churchill conspired to bring down the Liberal government, but he may have protested too much. In Lord Haldane: Scapegoat for Liberalism, Koss was on firmer ground in his treatment of Asquith's jettisoning of his friend, the lord chancellor. The Haldane dismissal is related more circumspectly in William Verity, "Haldane and Asquith," History Today, XVIII (1968), 447-55.

Lloyd George's careering as the "man of push and go" is depicted approvingly in Ralph J. Q. Adams, Arms and the Wizard: Lloyd George and the Ministry of Munitions, 1915-1916 (London, 1978). R. MacGregor Dawson, "The Cabinet Minister and Administration," Political Science Quarterly, LV (1940), 348-77, contrasts his modus operandi with that of Asquith and Curzon. The deteriorating relationship between prime minister and wayward colleague was chronicled by Lloyd George's Aspasia, Frances Stevenson, in the journal published two generations later as Lloyd George: A Diary. There is much information about the Asquith-Lloyd George split and the subsequent politics of the 1916-22 Coalition in Robert Blake, The Unknown Prime Minister: The Life and Times of Andrew Bonar Law (London, 1955). Readers should compare the contemporary account of the fall of Asquith by his supporter Lord Crewe in Lord Oxford, Memories and Reflections, vol. II, with "The Conspiracy Myth," by Lloyd George's apologist Cameron Hazlehurst in Lloyd George, ed. Martin Gilbert. The background and blossoming of the December 1916 coup are analyzed in J. M. McEwen, "The Struggle for Mastery in Britain: Lloyd George versus Asquith," Journal of British Studies, XVIII (1978), 131-56. Edward David, "The Liberal Party Divided, 1916-1918," Historical Journal, XIII (1970), 509-33, dismisses explanations of the party schism on grounds other than the leaders' personal rivalry and disagreement over war policy. Lord Beaverbrook, Men and Power, 1917-1918 (London, 1956), continues its author's inside story of wartime politics. The Maurice Debate in the House of Commons, which allegedly formalized the breach in the Liberal party, is argued from its instigator's standpoint in Sir Frederick Maurice, Intrigues of the War (London, 1922), and in his diary published fifty years later as The Maurice Case: From the Papers of Major-General Sir Frederick Maurice, ed. Nancy Maurice (London, 1972). The affair is discussed objectively in John Gooch, "The Maurice Debate," Journal of Contemporary History, III, no. 4 (1968), 211-28, and disputed heatedly in an exchange by Lloyd George's widow and Maurice's daughter in the Spectator, November 16, 23, and December 7, 1956.

The importance of the Representation of the People Act of 1918 in creating a brand-new electoral game between the contending parties is spelled out in Martin Pugh, Electoral Reform in War and Peace, 1906-1918 (London, 1978). Several authors have written monographs on the fateful postwar general election, including J. M. McEwen, "The Coupon Election of 1918 and Unionist Members of Parliament," Journal of Modern History, XXXIV (1962), 294-306; Trevor Wilson, "The Coupon and the British General Election of 1918," Journal of Modern History, XXXVI (1964), 28-42; and Roy Douglas, "The Background to the 'Coupon' Election Arrangements," English Historical Review, LXXXVI (1971), 318-32. Long before the Coupon Election the Liberal party had begun to disintegrate as anti-war radicals gravitated toward Labour. The course of this secession, as important to the party as the Asquith-Lloyd George schism, may be reconstructed with the aid of apologia such as Sir Charles Trevelyan, From Liberalism to Labour (London, 1921), and the following studies: Laurence W. Martin, Peace without Victory: Woodrow Wilson and the British Liberals (New Haven, 1958); Robert E. Dowse, "The Entry of Liberals into the Labour Party, 1910-1930," Yorkshire Bulletin of Economic and Social Research, XIII, no. 2 (1961), 78-87; Catherine Ann Cline, Recruits to Labour: The British Labour Party, 1914-1931 (Syracuse, N.Y., 1963); and Marvin Swartz, The Union of Democratic Control in British Politics during the First World War (Oxford, 1971).

Written matter on Lloyd George's prime ministership in war and peace is abundant, even superfluous. The best introduction is Kenneth O. Morgan, "Lloyd George's Premiership: A Study in Prime Ministerial Government," Historical Journal, XIII (1970), 130-57. Morgan discussed the postwar premiership in considerably more detail in Consensus and Disunity: The Lloyd George Coalition Government, 1918-1922 (New York, 1979). Other important treatises on "prime ministerial" as contrasted with "cabinet" government are Byrum E. Carter, The Office of Prime Minister (Princeton, 1956); and the essays on Lloyd George (by Kenneth O. Morgan) and Asquith (by Cameron Hazlehurst) in John P. Mackintosh, ed., British Prime Ministers in the Twentieth Century, 2 vols. (London, 1977-8). Sir Harold Wilson proffered some acute observations about Lloyd George, a prime minister to whom he has been likened, in A Prime Minister on Prime Ministers (London, 1977). Lloyd George's own War Memoirs, 6 vols. (London, 1934-6), and Memoirs of the Peace Conference, 2 vols. (New Haven, 1939), indispensable for their profuse detail and documentary extracts, are vindicatory rather than objective. Some, but not all, of their bias is corrected in Thomas Jones, Whitehall Diary, 1916-1930, 3 vols. (London, 1969-71), and Jones's biographical study, Lloyd George (Cambridge, Mass., 1951). Jones, assistant secretary to the cabinet after December 1916, was partisan to Lloyd George. More disinterested was his superior, Sir Maurice Hankey, who published selections from his diaries in The Supreme Command, 1914-1918, 2 vols. (London, 1961). The Downing Street "garden suburb" created by Lloyd George was viewed from the inside by Sir Joseph Davies in The Prime Minister's Secretariat, 1916-1920 (Newport, Eng., 1951); by a gossipy Tory historian, Sir Charles Petrie, in The Powers Behind the Prime Ministers (London, 1958); and in a scholarly study by John Turner, Lloyd George's Secretariat (Cambridge, Eng., 1980).

The legion of contemporary "instant books" praising and defending Lloyd George as warlord and statesman is equalled in quantity and ardor by those censuring and assailing him; there are good lists in the biographies by Jones (1951) and McCormick (1963). Outstanding among these books in perception, characterization, and impartiality is "E. T. Raymond" [E. R. Thompson], Mr. Lloyd George (New York, 1922). More acerbic is "Lloyd George: An Intimate Portrait," an article by Sir Philip Gibbs in Harper's Magazine, CXLIII (1921), 423-8, and Arnold Bennett's fictionalized portrayal of the Welshman in Lord Raingo (London, 1926). The impressions of caricaturists are registered in David Low, Lloyd George and Co. (London, 1921), and Editors of Punch, Lloyd George Cartoons, intro. by W. Algernon Locker (London, 1922). There is forthright commentary about Lloyd George's press relations during these years in James D. Margach, The Abuse of Power: The War Between Downing Street and the Media from Lloyd George to James Callaghan (London, 1978).

That curious mutation of First World War politics, Coalition Liberalism, is surveyed in Kenneth O. Morgan, "Lloyd George's Stage Army: The Coalition Liberals, 1918-1922," Lloyd George: Twelve Essays. Among the biographies, memoirs, and published diaries of "Coalies," arranged by subject with the more enlightening ones starred, are: *Viscount Addison, Politics from Within, 1911-1918, 2 vols. (London, 1924), and *Four and a Half Years: A Personal Diary from June 1914 to January 1919, 2 vols. (London, 1934); *Kenneth O. Morgan and Jane Morgan, Portrait of a Progressive: The Political Career of Christopher, Viscount Addison (London, 1980); *Sir Winston Churchill, The World Crisis, 1911-1918, 2 vols. (London, 1938); *Robert Rhodes James, Churchill: A Study in Failure, 1900-1939 (London, 1970); Sir Colin Coote, Editorial (London, 1965);

R. C. K. Ensor, "James Henry Dalziel, Baron Dalziel of Kirkcaldy," Dictionary of National Biography, 1931-1940 (1949); H. A. L. Fisher, An Unfinished Autobiography (London, 1940); David Ogg, Herbert Fisher, 1865-1940: A Short Biography (London, 1947); Alfred Cochrane, "Frederick Edward Guest," DNB, 1931-1940; *Robert Jackson, The Chief: The Biography of Gordon Hewart, Lord Chief Justice of England (London, 1959); J. R. M. Butler, Lord Lothian (Philip Kerr), 1882-1940 (New York, 1960); Hector Bolitho, Alfred Mond, First Lord Melchett (London, 1933); *G. M. Bayliss, "The Outsider: Aspects of the Political Career of Sir Alfred Mond, First Lord Melchett" (University of Wales thesis, 1969); Sir Tudor Rees, Reserved Judgment: Some Reflections and Recollections (London, 1956); *Sir Geoffrey Shakespeare, Let Candles Be Brought In (London, 1949).

Readers should offset the usually self-congratulatory reminiscences of former Coalitionists with these Asquithian diatribes against Coalition politics: Harold Storey, The Case Against the Lloyd George Coalition (London, 1920), a good source, despite its acrimony, for the abortive Centre party scheme; J. M. Robertson, Mr. Lloyd George and Liberalism (London, 1923); Sir Charles Mallet, Mr. Lloyd George (London, 1930); and Sir Llewellyn Woodward, Short Journey (London, 1942), recollections of an orthodox Liberal historian replete with such adjectives about Lloyd George, his premiership, and his breakaway party as "sly," "malignant," and "catastrophic." Not only Asquithian Liberals but "die-hard" Conservatives and public spirited or sensation-seeking journalists zeroed in on the most notorious practice of the Lloyd George Coalition: abuse of the honors list. Contemporary exposés include A. Fenner Brockway, Lloyd George and the Traffic in Honour (London, 1922), and Harold J. Laski, "The Prime Minister's Honours List," Nation, July 15, 1922. Gerald Macmillan, Honours for Sale: The Strange Story of Maundy Gregory (London, 1954), and Tom Cullen, Maundy Gregory: Purveyor of Honours (London, 1974), are two readable and fairly accurate popular accounts of the brisk trade in ribbons and titles. That Lloyd George did not initiate the business, although he flooded the market, is proven in William B. Gwyn, Democracy and the Cost of Politics in Britain (London, 1962), and in two articles by Harold J. Hanham: "Political Patronage at the Treasury, 1870-1912," Historical Journal, III (1960), 75-84, and "The Sale of Honours in Late Victorian England," Victorian Studies, III (1960), 277-89.

Kenneth O. Morgan testified to the constructive work of the Coalition as well as its delinquencies in Consensus and Disunity, cited above. The frustrations of Liberal reformers stalemated by Conservative economizers are documented in Paul Barton Johnson, Land Fit for Heroes: The Planning of British Reconstruction, 1916-1919 (Chicago, 1968), and Laurence Orbach, Homes for Heroes: The Evolution of British Public Housing, 1915-1921 (London, 1977). Lloyd George's successes and failures in postwar foreign policy are examined from various angles and distances in John Maynard Keynes, The Economic Consequences of the Peace (London, 1919), and Essays in Biography (London, 1933); Sir Valentine Chirol, "Four Years of Lloyd Georgian Foreign Policy," Edinburgh Review, CCXXXVII (1923), 1-20; H. A. L. Fisher, "Mr. Lloyd George's Foreign Policy, 1918-1922," Foreign Affairs, I (1923), 69-84; W. Watkin Davies, "The Foreign Policy of Lloyd George," Fortnightly Review, CLVIII (1945), 268-75; and Gordon A. Craig, "The British Foreign Office from Grey to Austen Chamberlain," The Diplomats, 1919-1939, ed. Gordon A. Craig and Felix Gilbert (Princeton, 1953). The two standard works on the final months of the Coalition are Lord Beaverbrook, The Decline and Fall of Lloyd George (New York, 1963), and Michael Kinnear, The Fall of Lloyd George: The Political Crisis of 1922 (Toronto, 1973). Some of Beaverbrook's tall stories in the former were rectified by A. J. P. Taylor in his biography of the press baron (London, 1922).

VI

The decline of the postwar Liberal party from its prewar eminence has tantalized many authors to propound explanations. Two early attempts are Albert Mabileau, Le parti libéral dans le systeme constitutionnel britannique (Paris, 1953), and Lowell G. Noonan, "The Decline of the Liberal Party in British Politics," Journal of Politics, XVI (1954), 24-38. The burden of Mabileau's argument is that the Liberals had completed their reformist task--introduction of political democracy--and were duly supplanted by a more up-to-date "party of movement." Noonan emphasized the weakening of the Liberal party by poor leadership, factional quarrels, loss of interest group support, and an electoral system detrimental to minority representation. During the 1950s and early 1960s a number of postgraduate students at British and American universities investigated the problem of Liberal collapse. Their dissertations include J. M. McEwen, "The Decline of the Liberal Party in Great Britain, 1914-1926" (University of Manchester, 1952); Trevor Wilson, "The Parliamentary Liberal Party in Britain, 1918-1924" (Oxford University, 1959); Thomas C. Howard, "The Liberal Party in British Politics, 1922-1924" (Florida State University, 1965); and Thomas W. Casstevens, "The Decline of the British Liberal Party: A Comparative and Theoretical Analysis" (Michigan State University, 1966). Wilson's dissertation, revised, expanded and published as The Downfall of the Liberal Party, 1914-1935 (London, 1966), inaugurated a heated debate in British academia that did not subside for over a decade.

Wilson contended that the decision to go to war and the ruthless conduct of military operations by Liberal ministers struck Liberalism a paralyzing blow, and that the destructive behavior of Lloyd George after the war completed the party's ruin. Vigorous exception to this argument was taken by many scholars, including the Lloyd George-ophils Taylor, Hazlehurst, and Morgan and their disciples, as well as several--such as Chris Cook and Roy Douglas--who claimed that the party was making a powerful comeback in the twenties but was the victim of ill luck or bad strategy. Other participants in the disputation were historians of the Labour party like Beer, Pelling, and McKibbin, who believed that Liberalism was decadent and that the war did not matter, or that the huge enlargement of the franchise in 1918 created new electoral rules in which the Liberals were sidelined and both their schisms and their policies became irrelevant. J. A. Thompson, ed., The Collapse of the British Liberal Party: Fate or Self-Destruction? (Lexington, Mass., 1969), is a serviceable anthology of these competing views. A monograph by Don M. Cregier, The Decline of the British Liberal Party: Why and How? (Brattleboro, Vt., 1966), analyzes the party's slump as seen by contemporary politicians, journalists, and academics.

The studies of "high politics" in the early 1920s highlight the disinclination of many orthodox Liberal politicians to come to terms with harsh electoral realities: Maurice Cowling, The Impact of Labour, 1920-1924: The Beginning of Modern British Politics (Cambridge, Eng., 1971), and Michael Bentley, The Liberal

Mind, 1914-1929 (Cambridge, Eng., 1977). The Liberal party leader's ability to adapt to the rigors of postwar politics may be judged from H. H. Asquith, The Paisley Policy (London, 1920), a compilation of speeches during his successful by-election campaign; H. H. A.: Letters of the Earl of Oxford and Asquith to a Friend [Mrs. Hilda Harrison], 1915-1927, ed. Desmond MacCarthy, 2 vols. (London, 1933-4); and Robert Kelley, "Asquith at Paisley: The Content of British Liberalism at the End of Its Era," Journal of British Studies, IV, no. 1 (1964), 133-59. Michael Bentley exposed the fragmentation and indecision within the Asquithian Liberal group in "The Liberal Response to Socialism," Essays in Anti-Labour History: Responses to the Rise of Labour in Britain, ed. Kenneth D. Brown (London, 1974), and "Liberal Politics and the Grey Conspiracy of 1921," Historical Journal, XX (1977), 461-78.

Torpor and confusion among the Asquithian elite, and unceasing gamesmanship on Lloyd George's part, misled observers into regarding the Liberal party of the early twenties as moribund. That such was not true is indicated by the rich literature of ideological Liberalism that poured from the presses as younger party members--and some old-timers--sought their bearings and experimented with fresh ideas. The place of these lucubrations in contemporary thought was identified by P. J. Philip in his 1951 dissertation for the London School of Economics, "English Political Ideas from 1918 to 1939." A sampling of the literature of the "new New Liberalism" might include Elliott Dodd, Is Liberalism Dead? and Liberalism in Action: A Record and a Policy (London, 1920, 1922); Ramsay Muir, Liberalism and Industry: Toward a Better Social Order, The New Liberalism, and Politics and Progress: A Survey of the Problems of To-day (London, 1920, 1920, 1923); Christopher Addison, The Betrayal of the Slums (London, 1922); H. E. Crawford, Liberalism Yesterday and To-day (London, 1922); C. F. G. Masterman, England after the War (London, 1922); the "New Way" series, including pamphlets by Muir, Walter T. Layton, Ernest D. Simon, and Sir William Beveridge among others, published in 1923-4 by the London Daily News; Sir Alfred Mond, Liberalism and Modern Industrial Problems (Llanelly, Wales, 1925); J. M Keynes, The End of Laissez Faire (London, 1926); and T. J. Macnamara, If Only We Would (London, 1926). Numerous articles by Ramsay Muir and Ernest D. Simon, the foremost Liberal ideologues of the twenties, appeared in the Nation and the Contemporary Review. Essays in Liberalism: Lectures and Papers Delivered at the Liberal Summer School at Oxford (London, 1922), is a valuable guide to postwar Liberal thought; so is John Campbell's monograph, "The Renewal of Liberalism," The Politics of Reappraisal.

The Summer School Movement, which allied with Lloyd George constructed a Liberal socioeconomic policy in many ways more progressive and realistic than Labour's, has not been scrutinized in a full-length monograph. In addition to the brief study in this book, there are older articles by James K. Pollock, "Auxiliary and Non-Party Organizations in Great Britain," Southwestern Political and Social Science Quarterly, XI (1931), 393-407; and Joseph R. Starr, "The Summer Schools and Other Educational Activities of the British Liberal Party," American Political Science Review, XXXI (1937), 703-19, and "Research Activities of British Political Parties," Public Opinion Quarterly, I (1937), 99-107. There is also quite a lot about the Summer Schools in John Campbell, Lloyd George: The Goat in the Wilderness, cited below. Biographies of the movement's luminaries include R. F. Harrod, The Life of John Maynard Keynes (New York, 1951); Stuart Hodgson, ed., Ramsay Muir: An Autobiography and Some Essays (London, 1943); Asa Briggs, Social Thought and Social Action: A Study of the Work of Seebohm Rowntree, 1871-1954 (London, 1961); and Mary Stocks, Ernest Simon of Manchester (Manchester, 1963). A wealth of material about Liberal economic and fiscal projects in the 1920s will be found in the Collected Writings of John Maynard Keynes, 24 vols. projected (London, 1971-   ). Lloyd George's contribution, ideological as well as financial, to the "new New Liberalism" is surveyed in the present work and in Campbell's Goat in the Wilderness. There is a good check list in the latter of policy reports and campaign documents subsidized by the Welshman during the twenties.

John Campbell, Lloyd George: The Goat in the Wilderness, 1922-1931 (London, 1977), is the most complete examination of the Welsh Wizard's tergiversations between the fall of the Coalition and the formation of the National Government. His private life during these years was irreverently divulged by his secretary, A. J. Sylvester, in The Real Lloyd George (London, 1947), and by his elder son in My Father, Lloyd George, previously cited. There is much of interest in his letters to his mistress-helpmate, Frances Stevenson, published as My Darling Pussy, and some acute observations about him by another political buccaneer, Sir Oswald Mosley, in My Life (London, 1968). The Lloyd George Fund is discussed objectively in the present work; it is eyed malevolently in The Lloyd George Millions, a pamphlet published in 1927 by the London Morning Post. The best contemporary reports of the negotiations to salvage "Lloyd George's lucre" for the party's war chest are in the Liberal Magazine, vols. XXXIV and XXXV (1926-7).

The clammy reunion of the Asquith and Lloyd George factions for the "protection election" of 1923 is effectively dealt with in several of the books already cited, especially those by Wilson (1966), Douglas (1971), and Campbell (1977). To these should be added the early chapters of Richard W. Lyman, The First Labour Government (London, 1957), also important for its information on Liberal parliamentary behavior during the 1924 session. Chris Cook made some trenchant points about the bad luck of the Liberals at the polls in "A Stranger Death of Liberal England," Lloyd George: Twelve Essays. Alan H. Taylor wrote about "The Effect of Electoral Pacts on the Decline of the Liberal Party" during the twenties in the British Journal of Political Science, III (1973), 243-8. Chris Cook, The Age of Alignment: Electoral Politics in Britain, 1922-1929 (London, 1975), a collection of diverse essays rather than an integrated study, utilizes this author's customary psephological approach. 1920s Liberal politics at the often mucky grass roots level has been examined antiseptically by Cook and much more animatedly in Frank Gray, Confessions of a Candidate (London, 1925), and Charles Fenby, The Other Oxford: The Life and Times of Frank Gray and His Father (London, 1970). Other lively recollections of '20s Liberalism, by an eventual defector to Labour, are in Joseph M. Kenworthy (Lord Strabolgi), Sailors, Statesmen and Others (London, 1933). Kenworthy was a prolific and usually perceptive contributor to the Fortnightly Review, Nineteenth Century and After, Outlook, Saturday Review, Spectator, and other political journals between about 1924 and 1930.

"Asquith versus Lloyd George: The Last Phase and Beyond," an essay by Stephen E. Koss in Crisis and Controversy, is not only a reinterpretation of the breakdown of their fragile entente but a review of recent historiography and hagiography concerning these statesmen. Koss referred to the second act of George Bernard Shaw's Back to Methuselah (1921), an early farcical caricature of their feud; shorter and perhaps funnier are Peter Ibbetson's lampoons in the Nation: "Lord Ox and Brer Goat" (June 12, 1926), and "The Shadow Cabinet" (January 8, 1927). Asquith's side of the terminal quarrel is given in Vivian Phillipps, My Days and Ways (privately published about 1943), an autobiography by his private secretary and chief whip;* Lloyd George's version is in his letters to Frances Stevenson (My Darling Pussy) and her published diary. There is much about the petty and ridiculous bickering between the Liberal factions in such biographies as J. A. Spender, Weetman Pearson, First Lord Cowdray (London, 1930); Sir Charles Mallet, Herbert Gladstone (London, 1932); and Sir Robert Hudson (London, 1930), also by Spender. These unashamedly Asquithian memoirs by and about several of the Welshman's most splenetic foes include useful--though slanted--accounts of the anti-Lloyd George Liberal Council of the late 1920s. The fecund correspondence between the four keepers of the Asquithian grail--Gladstone, Hudson, Phillipps, and Sir Donald Maclean--about Lloyd George, his fund, and his shady friends is buried in their papers in various archives; there are a few extracts from these almost apoplectic and often comic letters in Morgan's Age of Lloyd George and Campbell's Goat in the Wilderness, but more ought to be published.

VII

Two dissertations examine the politics of Liberalism and radicalism in the late twenties and early thirties: James Allen Braden, "The Liberals as a Third Party in British Politics, 1926-1931: A Study in Political Communication" (Ohio State University, 1971), and Jerry M. Calton, "The Party That Never Was: A Study of the Failure of the Campaign for Political Integration among Left-Wing and Radical Groups in Britain, 1929-1939" (Washington University, 1970). This latter theme was ventilated much earlier by Joseph Burgess, in Will Lloyd George Supplant Ramsay MacDonald? Past, Present and Prospective Controversies over Liberal-Labour Alliances (Ilford, Eng., 1926). Bernard Norling

---

*I have not seen this book, but several scholars have cited it.

analyzed the Liberal journalism of the interwar period in "Mirror of Illusion: Political Opinions in the English Liberal Press, 1919-1939," a 1955 dissertation for Notre Dame Univeristy. Yet another thesis by E. A. Rowe (Oxford University, 1959) is the most thorough study of "The British General Election of 1929," in which the Liberals made their last hopeful effort to win a majority or a solid minority of House of Commons seats. Gordon West, Lloyd George's Last Fight (London, 1930), is a sound journalistic report of this Liberal campaign. Party propaganda for this do-or-die election included J. M. Keynes and H. D. Henderson, Can Lloyd George Do It? An Examination of the Liberal Pledge (London, 1929), and Hubert Phillips, The Liberal Outlook (London, 1929). The latter author's Handbook of Liberal Industrial Policy (London, 1928), a guide for candidates and campaign workers, is a compendium of the program that emerged from the Summer Schools and Lloyd George's policy studies.

Robert Skidelsky, Politicians and the Slump: The Labour Government of 1929-1931 (London, 1967), is the standard work on the subject and has much information on Lloyd George's frustrated efforts to prop up this minority administration until it had enacted an elec- toral reform bill beneficial to the Liberals. Also instructive are John Campbell's Goat in the Wilderness and pp. 133-9 of L. G. (London, 1932), Basil Murray's biography of the Liberal leader. The Liberal case for electoral reform—proportional representation or trans- ferable votes—was laid before the public in numerous books and pamphlets, including Harold Storey, Electoral Reform: An Examination of the Four Possible Systems (London, 1929), and a heavy-handed fictional satire by Ramsay Muir (pseud., "An Impenitent Politician"), Robinson the Great (London, 1929). The eventual fall of the MacDonald Labour government, while Lloyd George was hospitalized and hors de combat, is discussed in Skidelsky's book and in exhaustive detail in Reginald Bassett, Nineteen Thirty-One: Political Crisis (London, 1958).

A day-by-day record of the Welshman's political activities, during the 1931 crisis and until his death, is contained in Life with Lloyd George: The Diary of A. J. Sylvester, 1931-45, ed. Colin Cross (London, 1975). The often acerbic entries in the long-suffering secretary's journal, although probably well-founded, should be tempered by less disparaging comments about Lloyd George in such chronicles and reminiscences as

Tom Clarke, My Lloyd George Diary (London, 1939);
W. J. Brown, Brown Studies (London, 1949); Harold
Macmillan, Winds of Change (London, 1966); Sir Harold
Nicolson, Letters and Diaries, 1930-1945, 2 vols., ed.
Nigel Nicolson (London, 1966-7); and Thelma Cazalet
Keir, From the Wings (London, 1967). The three way
split in the Liberal ranks between Samuelites, Simon-
ites, and the Lloyd George Family Party, and other
details about these Dark Ages of Liberalism, are
adequately described in Douglas's History of the
Liberal Party, which should be supplemented by the
following biographical works: Viscount Samuel, Memoirs;
Sir Percy Harris, Forty Years In and Out of Parliament
(London, 1947); Sir Geoffrey Shakespeare, Let Candles
Be Brought In; Viscount Simon, Retrospect (London,
1952); Sir Henry Morris-Jones, Doctor in the Whips'
Room (London, 1955); R. J. Minney, The Private Papers
of Hore-Belisha (London, 1960); and H. Montgomery Hyde,
Strong for Service: The Life of Lord Nathan of Churt
(London, 1968). An analytical study of the Liberal
party during the thirties remains to be published.

Lloyd George's last major political fling--the
"new deal" and the Council of Action--is canvassed in
this book and--as a phase in his lifelong alliance with
the Free Churches--in Stephen E. Koss, "Lloyd George
and Nonconformity; The Last Rally," English Historical
Review, LXXXIX (1974), 77-108. Some of the Council of
Action's publications, and cognate documents, are
listed in the bibliography of Maccoby's English Radi-
calism: The End? Perhaps the most important of them
was Mr. Lloyd George's New Deal (London, 1935), by the
Labour party and National Government defector Lord
Snowden. There are additional references to the "new
deal" episode in Plough My Own Furrow: The Story of
Lord Allen of Hurtwood as Told Through His Writings and
Correspondence, ed. Martin Gilbert (London, 1965);
Harold Macmillan, Winds of Change; Jerry M. Calton,
"The Party That Never Was"; William P. Crozier, Off the
Record: Political Interviews, 1933-43, ed. A. J. P.
Taylor (London, 1973); and Thomas C. Kennedy, "The Next
Five Years Group and the Failure of the Politics of
Agreement in Britain," Canadian Journal of History, IX
(1974), 45-68.

The Welsh Wizard's interventions in foreign policy
debates within and outside Parliament during the late
1930s are worthy of a monograph, but none has yet been
published. There are details about his activities and
opinions--and his occasionally outrageous behavior--

during these years in the various biographies previously cited and in Sylvester's Life with Lloyd George.
C. P. Snow, "Lloyd George: Britain's Great Radical,"
Atlantic Monthly, CCXIX (1967), 68-79, is a sympathetic
character sketch of the old statesman. (This article
is essentially the same as an essay on Lloyd George in
Snow's Varieties of Men [New York, 1967]). Much less
complimentary is the treatment of the Welshman as a
Pétain manqué in E. Tangye Lean, The Napoleonists: A
Study in Political Disaffection, 1760-1960 (London,
1970).

VIII

    Jorgen Scott Rasmussen, The Liberal Party: A Study
of Retrenchment and Revival (London, 1965), is the most
searching study of the party during the war years, the
forties, and the pre-Grimond fifties.   Arthur Cyr
carried on proficiently into the Grimond and Thorpe
eras in Liberal Party Politics in Britain (New Brunswick, N.J., 1977).   In The Liberal Dilemma (London,
1966), Alan Watkins--an experienced political corres-
pondent--saw little hope of the party's revival as a
major force. Jo Grimond, the trendy heir to Liberalism's Asquithian tradition, enthusiastically justified
his 1956-67 party leadership in his Memoirs (London,
1979). The raffish element that has complemented and
embarrassed the earnest and principled acolytes of
British Liberalism--since long before Lloyd George--is
examined in its latest phase in Jeremy Thorpe: A Secret
Life (London, 1979), by three Sunday Times "Insight-
ers," Lewis Chester, Magnus Linklater, and David May.

Croft, Sir Henry Page, later Lord, 120
Curtis, Lionel, 181
Curzon, Lord, 78, 94
Cyr, Arthur, xii, 211-7 _passim_

Harcourt, Lewis, later Lord, 114
Harcourt, Sir William, 4
Hardie, Keir, 4
Harris, Sir Percy, 146
Harrison, William, 127
Hartshorn, Vernon, 178
Hastings, Sir Patrick, 38
Hazlehurst, Cameron, 78
Heath, Edward, 198
Henderson, Hubert: and the Liberal Summer School, 149,
    159, 161; and the Liberal Industrial Inquiry, 173;
    and Lloyd George's unemployment schemes, 177, 187
Herzog, General J.B.M., 203
Hill, L. Raven, 18-23 passim
Hitler, Adolf, 103, 185
Hobhouse, Sir Charles, 135-8 passim, 142, 171
Hobson, J.A., 175
Hogge, James M., 26
Honors issue, 12, 99, 114, 115, 117-20 passim, 140
Howard, Geoffrey, 130, 131
How to Tackle Unemployment (1930), 178, 179, 180
Hudson, Sir Robert: as secretary, Liberal Central
    Association, 4, 131; as Liberal fund raiser, 116,
    132, 133, 134; is critical of Lloyd George, 130,
    134; dismissed by Lloyd George, 14, 136, 137, 138
Hughes, H. Stuart, 214
Hugo, Victor, 105

Imperial (tariff) preference, 34, 170
Import Duties Bill (1931), 15
Inchcape, Lord, 124
Independent Labour party, 4, 5, 152
Independent Radical Group (1924), 13
Inveresk Paper Company, 127, 144
Inverforth, Lord (Andrew Weir), 124
Ireland, 7, 9, 28, 69, 103
Irish home rule, 3, 4, 6, 7, 8, 66, 115
Irish Nationalist party, 6, 9, 191

"Jack the Ripper," 105
Jenkins, Roy, 79, 80, 215
Johnstone, Harcourt, 143-6 passim
Jones, Thomas, 92, 97, 107, 108, 110, 147, 166

Kellaway, F.G., 126
Kerr, Charles, 143
Kerr, Philip. See Lothian, Lord

Keynes, John Maynard, later Lord: and the Liberal
    Summer School, 149, 159-61, 172, 173; and Lloyd
    George's unemployment schemes, 176-7, 187;
    mentioned, 76, 179
Kinnear, Michael, 92

"Labour and the Nation" (1928), 175
Labour party (Australia), 197, 198
Labour party (Great Britain); Liberal defections to, 8,
    10, 30, 115; 150; its advance aided by electoral
    system, 193-5; as a "collectivist" party, 211-3;
    mentioned, 6, 8, 10, 11, 12, 24, 26, 30, 36, 48,
    52, 58, 60, 67, 101, 102, 109, 110, 122, 127, 130,
    140, 141, 142, 145, 150, 153, 155, 157, 160, 162,
    163, 165, 168, 170, 175, 176, 179, 181, 182, 183,
    190, 201, 206, 207, 208, 213, 215, 216
Labour party (New Zealand), 199, 200
Labour party (South Africa), 202-5 passim
Labour Representation Committee, 5, 192
Laissez-faire, 150, 160, 174, 188, 212
Land and Nation League (1925-7), 42, 133, 134, 136,
    138, 172
Land and the Nation. See "Green Book."
Land Inquiry (1912-4), 165-8, 170
Land Inquiry Committee (1923-5), 13, 132, 158, 170-2,
    174
Land reform, 7, 166
Land taxes, 6
Lansbury, George, 179
Lansdowne, Lord, 9, 120
Laski, Harold: criticizes traffic in honors, 118-9
Law, Andrew Bonar, 71, 78, 116, 119, 129
Lawson, Sir Wilfrid, 114, 117
Layton, Walter T., later Lord: and the Liberal Summer
    School, 149, 153, 155, 159, 162; and the Liberal
    Industrial Inquiry, 173, 177, 186
League of Nations, 155, 185
Leamington Conference (1920), 11, 28
Les Miserables, 105
Lever, Sir William, later Lord Leverhulme, 123
Liberal Administrative Committee, 136, 137, 138
Liberal Central Association, 4, 34, 113, 130, 133-40
    passim, 143, 144, 146, 157, 168, 172, 174, 181
Liberal Council (1927-39), 14, 44, 48, 50, 138, 139,
    140, 143
Liberal Imperialist Council (1900-02), 4, 5
Liberal Industrial Conference (1928), 14, 157, 159, 175
Liberal Industrial Inquiry (1926-8), 14, 48, 136, 138,
    157, 158, 172-5, 177, 181, 186

Marconi scandal (1912-3), 7, 69, 71, 167
Marriott, Sir John, 77
Martell, Edward, 214
Marx, Karl, 105
Massingham, H.W., 115
Masterman, Charles F.G., 105, 155, 166, 207
Masterman, Lucy, 155
Maurice, Sir Frederick, 123,124
"Maurice debate" (May 9, 1918), 10, 22, 123
May Committee (1931), 179
Menken, Jules, 174
Milner, Lord, 71, 78, 109
Mond, Sir Alfred, later Lord Melchett, 42-3, 77, 99, 171
Montagu, Edwin, 80
Montagu, Venetia Stanley, 80
Morant, Sir Robert, 166
Morgan, Kenneth O., 102
Morley, John, later Lord, 4, 78
Morning Post, 140
Mosley, Sir Oswald, 89, 90
Mowat, C.L., 108, 109
Muir, Ramsay: and the Liberal Summer School, 149, 151, 153, 155, 157, 159-63 passim, 172, 173; publishes Liberalism and Industry, 152; and the "three party" system, 207; mentioned, 135, 143, 181

Nation, The, 115, 134, 137, 160-1
"National development council." See "Economic general staff"
National Development Program (Lloyd George proposal), 174, 176
National Insurance Act (1911), 18, 166, 189
Nationalist party (South Africa), 202, 203, 204
National Liberal Federation, 3, 4, 11, 28, 34, 113, 114, 130, 133, 151, 157, 159, 171, 179
National Liberal party. See Coalition Liberals
National Liberal Political Fund. See Lloyd George Fund
National party (Australia), 197, 198
"National party" (Great Britain). See "Center party"
National party (New Zealand), 201
National Review, 119, 121, 122, 140, 141
Newcastle Program (1891), 4
New Deal (American), 180, 188, 189
"New Deal" (British). See Lloyd George, David
New Democratic party (Canada), 195, 196, 204
"New Liberalism." See Liberal Summer School
News Chronicle, 186
New Statesman, 161, 183

New Way Series, 155
New Zealand: operation of its political system, 199-202, 204-5, 208, 209
Next Five Years, The (1935), 183, 186
Nonconformity, 4, 5, 6, 75, 151, 185, 212, 213, 214
Noonan, Lowell G., 209
Northcliffe, Lord, 70, 84, 98, 119, 123-8 passim
Northumberland, Duke of: attacks traffic in honors, 119, 120, 122

Observer, The, 180
"Orange Book" (1929), 14, 50, 58, 176-7, 178, 181
Order of the British Empire, 118
Organising Prosperity (1935), 185, 187
Ostrogorski, Moisei Y., 213
Ottawa Agreements (1932), 15
Oxford and Asquith, Lord. See Asquith, Herbert Henry

Paisley campaign (1920), 11, 26
Parliament Act (1911), 6-7, 28
Partridge, Bernard, 24-47 passim, 50-61 passim
"People's Budget" (1909), 6, 165
Percy of Newcastle, Lord, 87
Perris, Ernest, 124, 126
Phillipps, Vivian: and the Lloyd George Fund, 132, 133; is criticized by Lloyd George's friends, 133; quarrels with Lloyd George, 133-8 passim; and the Liberal Council, 139
Phillips, Hubert, 174
Pirrie, Lord, 115
Plender, Sir William, 139
Ponsonby, Arthur, later Lord, 115
Preferential voting, 197, 198, 208
Primrose, Neil, 116, 123
Pringle, W.M.R.: attacks Lloyd George's interest in the Daily Chronicle, 124; is critical of the Lloyd George Fund, 129-30, 131, 134; attacks the "Green Book," 171
"Pro-Boers," 4
Progressive Conservative party (Canada), 195, 196
Progressive party (Canada), 196
Proportional representation, 196, 205-6, 208
Protection issue, 5, 11, 12, 15, 34, 56, 144, 189
Purified Nationalist party (South Africa), 203

Radical Group (1913), 115
Radical Reform Group (1956), 215

Radical Socialist party (France), 206, 207
Rae, Douglas W., 197
Rasmussen, Jorgen, 214
"Red Guard" (1960s), 216
Reading, Lord, 121, 122, 125, 126, 128, 142, 143
Reform Acts: 1832, 3; 1867, 3, 191, 192, 199; 1884-5,
    3, 192
Reform party (New Zealand), 199, 200, 201
Rent Restrictions Act (1915), 167
Representation of the People Act (1918), 10, 151, 193
Reynolds's News, 123
Rhodes, Cecil, 114
Riddell, Sir George, later Lord, 100, 119, 167
Robertson, Sir William, 123
Robinson, Sir Joseph B., 114, 120
Roosevelt, Franklin D., 58, 180, 182, 183, 188
Roosevelt, Theodore, 78
Rosebery, Lord, 4, 5, 44, 115, 140
Rothermere, Lord, 119, 123, 141
Rowntree, Seebohm, 173, 178, 180
Rowntree family, 160
Runciman, Walter, later Lord, 24, 50, 134, 138, 171,
    177, 188

St. Davids, Lord: and the Lloyd George Fund, 127, 141,
    142, 143, 145
Salisbury, Lord, 117, 120
Samuel, Sir Herbert, later Lord: as Liberal party
    chairman, 14, 46, 138, 140, 142; and the National
    government, 15, 56, 144; mentioned, 16, 24, 50,
    60, 84, 105, 143, 169, 174
Schnadhorst, Francis, 114
Scott, C.P., 77, 87, 152
Scott, Edward T.: and the Liberal Summer School, 149,
    152, 153
Seely, Sir Hugh, 145
Selborne, Lord, 117, 120
Shakespeare, Sir Geoffrey, 89, 90, 92, 94, 95, 99
Shaw, George Bernard,   2
Shepard, Ernest Howard, 48-9
Simon, Ernest D., later Lord: and the Liberal Summer
    School, 149-55 passim, 159, 162, 163, 172, 173
Simon, Sir John, later Lord, 14-5, 24, 26, 56, 99, 177
"Simonites." See Liberal National party
Sinclair, Sir Archibald, later Lord Thurso, 16, 143
Smith, F.E. See Birkenhead, Lord
Smuts, J.C., 203
Snowden, Philip, later Lord, 60, 105, 178, 179

Vansittart, Lord, 79
Vincent, John, 213

Wallace, Edgar, 93
Ward, Sir Joseph, 200, 201
"Ware formula," 197
Webb, Sidney and Beatrice, later Lord and Lady
    Passfield, 105, 160, 162, 177
We Can Conquer Unemployment. See "Orange Book"
"Wee Frees" (Liberal faction), 26, 28
Weekly Westminster, 160
Weir, Andrew. See Inverforth, Lord
Wells, H.G., 162
Welsh Church, disestablishment of, 151
Whigs, 3, 95
White, James, 124
Wilson, Harold, 215
Wilson, Trevor, 212
World War, First, 7, 18, 22, 82, 111, 150, 151, 167,
    193, 197, 199, 200, 202, 207, 213
World War. Second, 163, 187, 188, 190, 203, 204, 211,
    214

"Yellow Book" (1928), 14, 58, 149, 159, 163, 174-5,
    176, 180, 181, 183, 186, 187
Yorkshire Evening News, 124
Young, Edward Hilton, later Lord Kennet, 171
Young, Kathleen Scott, later Lady Kennet, 86
Young Conservatives (1930s), 181, 183, 186, 189
Younger, Lord, 119, 129
Yule, Sir David, 126

"Zinoviev letter" (1924), 170

ABOUT THE AUTHOR

Don M. Cregier is professor of British history at the University of Prince Edward Island, Charlottetown, Canada. His previous works include The Decline of the British Liberal Party: Why and How? (1966); Bounder from Wales: Lloyd George's Career Before the First World War (1976); and Novel Exposures: Victorian Studies Featuring Contemporary Novels (1979). Professor Cregier has also contributed articles and reviews to professional journals, and several essays on modern British history to the Academic American Encyclopedia. He is currently preparing a study of Lloyd George's activities during the First World War, and a revisionist interpretation of the political role of the Irish Nationalist party. The present book has been aided by grants from the Canada Council, the Social Sciences and Humanities Research Council of Canada, and the University of Prince Edward Island.